CASS SERIES: STUDIES IN INTELLIGENCE
ISSN: 1368-9916

INTELLIGENCE SERVICES
IN THE
INFORMATION AGE

Also in the Intelligence Series

INTELLIGENCE SERVICES IN THE INFORMATION AGE

Theory and Practice

MICHAEL HERMAN

FRANK CASS
LONDON • PORTLAND, OR

First published in 2001 in Great Britain by
FRANK CASS PUBLISHERS
Crown House, 47 Chase Side
Southgate, London N14 5BP

and in the United States of America by
FRANK CASS PUBLISHERS
c/o ISBS, 5824 N. E. Hassalo Street
Portland, Oregon 97213-3644

Website: http://www.frankcass.com

British Library Cataloguing in Publication Data

Herman, Michael, 1929–
    Intelligence services in the information age: theory and
    practice. – (Cass series. Studies in intelligence)
    1. Intelligence service – Great Britain 2. Great Britain –
    Foreign relations – 1945 –
    I. Title
    327.1'241

ISBN 0-7146-5199-0 (cloth)
ISBN 0-7146-8196-2 (paper)

Library of Congress Cataloging-in-Publication Data

Herman, Michael, 1929–
    Intelligence services in the information age: theory and practice/
Michael Herman.
        p. cm. – (Cass series – studies in intelligence)
    Includes bibliographical references and index.
    ISBN 0-7146-5199-0 (cloth) – ISBN 0-7146-8196-2 (pbk.)
    1. Intelligence service. 2. Information warfare. I. Title II.
Series.
    UB250 H47 2002
    327.12–dc21

2001047012

Typeset in 11 on 13.25pt Ehrhardt by FiSH Books
Printed in Great Britain by MPG Books Ltd, Bodmin, Cornwall

Contents

For John Prestwich,
Queen's College Oxford and Bletchley Park

Foreword

Michael Herman is such a rarity that he verges on being a collector's item! A former intelligence insider who eschews the traditional British practitioner's disdain for theory, he loves to tread another jagged and difficult boundary – that between the historical and the current.

The great and perhaps least predictable of global shifts since 1945 – the moment in October 1989 when Mikhail Gorbachev told Erich Honecker he could not expect the Soviet garrisons in East Germany to save his regime – changed the world of intelligence profoundly. Michael Herman has been persuasive and eloquent, not least within these pages, about the degree to which the East–West confrontation *was* an intelligence and counter-intelligence war.

It was very fortunate that he came on the scholarly market in time to write not just about the greatest geopolitical contest of the decades since 1945, but also to think aloud about the post-1989 scene in terms of the ambiguities and the ethics of the unanticipated and often baffling new world in which intelligence and security services now found themselves operating.

This collection will be a must in both the university seminar room and in those clandestine conclaves where the secret servants of state ponder the defence of their respective realms.

Peter Hennessy
Attlee Professor of Contemporary History,
Queen Mary, University of London
August 2001

Preface

'Intelligence' – usually interpreted as 'secret intelligence' – was a central element of the Cold War, on both sides; never before was intelligence so extensive, institutionalized and prized in peacetime. After the end of the Berlin Wall it was initially expected to fall back into a more modest place, as part of the 'peace dividend'; and there was indeed some retrenchment. But it became increasingly clear in the course of the 1990s that intelligence was a major element in the new, turbulent, globalized world of diverse and swiftly changing threats, challenges and responses: a world increasingly conscious that (as put in a British intelligence recruitment brochure) 'government cannot make the right decisions unless it has the full picture'. Hence the combination of new requirements with advances in technical collection has recently caused intelligence budgets to start increasing again. Coverage is extending in its areas and subjects; yet part of the effort is still in the long-standing targeting and methods associated with big power tension – as dramatically illustrated in the early months of 2001 in the extensive tit-for-tat diplomatic expulsions from the Washington and Moscow embassies after the discovery of Russian espionage in the FBI, followed immediately by the Sino–American crisis over the Chinese collision with the US reconnaissance aircraft off Hainan. In such matters it is as if the Cold War film is being re-run; perhaps its intelligence aspects never really went into abeyance. We have an information-rich world, with data available in unprecedented volumes and at unprecedented speeds; yet the special and concealed activity of intelligence remains part of it, and here to stay.

This book is made up of published and unpublished papers bearing on this situation, written, with one exception, over the last five years. Three main questions run through them, particularly the substantial chapters at the beginning and end. One is what actually distinguishes this 'intelligence' from the rest of government knowledge. Governments have many other sources of information. Political leaders have access to the reports of diplomats and all their other international contacts, plus the massive output of worldwide news services and other media. They rely on intelligence over only relatively limited fields. Military forces now have their own increasingly sophisticated observation, reconnaissance and surveillance efforts, many of which are labelled and handled as 'operational information' (or 'action information') and not 'intelligence'. Intelligence itself is sometimes seen as a special kind of secret knowledge, sometimes as government's expert on particular subjects, and its role balances uneasily between the two. In Chapter 1 I therefore consider what gives it its distinctive identity, and go on to discuss the extent to which, in an increasingly international world, there are worldwide standards of intelligence objectivity – or should be.

The second question – really a group of questions – relates to intelligence strategy and management at a national level. What resources does a country need? How should the effort be effectively organized and managed? How does it fit into the context of other international relationships, particularly with the US superpower? Chapters 4 and 5 discuss these questions as they apply to the British effort. Chapter 4 considers the UK's unique 'upper second class' status, derived from its intelligence's scale and quality combined with the value of its transatlantic alliance. It goes on to make recommendations on three aspects of its effectiveness: the balance between collection and analysis; the growing importance of intelligence satellites in space; and the role of central management. Chapter 5 complements this discussion with a study of the Joint Intelligence Committee as it was at the heart of this system in the mid-1950s, and comments on its subsequent development. Chapter 6 compares this British community with its American analogue and sketches the differences and similarities.

The third question focuses on intelligence's international effects in the context of ethical foreign policies. What does intelligence do for international security and the quality of international society? Does it make for a better world or a worse one? Chapter 13 attempts a judgement. It distinguishes between the effects of intelligence as knowledge and the effects of the covert methods used to produce it. The result is an ethical balance-sheet, and a number of suggestions for some changes in emphasis in the future.

Other chapters also bear on these questions. Chapter 2 discusses intelligence's long-standing association with diplomacy, and what differentiates the two. Chapter 3 expands on the relationship between intelligence and the plethora of other military information now available in the so-called Revolution in Military Affairs. On relationships with the United States and other larger powers, Chapter 7 describes the Norwegian policy of 'robust dependence' in the Cold War, and Chapter 8 comments on New Zealand's position as the smallest member of the UK–US–Old Commonwealth alliance.

Chapters 9–12 are historical recollections of the Cold War and reflections on it, but also touch on aspects of intelligence's nature. Chapter 9 is a preliminary assessment of the value of the Western effort throughout those years: was it worthwhile, and was it a winner or loser in the long-running conflict with the quite different Soviet system? Chapter 10 records personal impressions of intelligence in the British Cabinet Office in the early 1970s, and of the old 'public service' values of those working there as part of central government. Chapter 11 is a paper published in 1993 on the long-running controversy over the government decision in 1984 to ban national trades unions at the British Sigint centre, plus a current comment on the subsequent re-unionization in 1997. Despite the satisfactory ending the question still remains: whether an intelligence agency can fit into the normal pattern of government service, or whether it needs separate rules to cater for its special position. Chapter 12 reflects on intelligence's single-source/all-source duality, with particular reference to the effects on its work on Soviet targets. The distinction has to be made between the single-source covert intelligence collectors and the all-source analysts, but can obscure the intellectual continuum between the two. The two stages need equal talent and professionalism, and this has not always been the case.

These shorter chapters therefore provide cross-bearings on the main themes of intelligence's identity, value and place in the world. Much intelligence is necessarily based on secrecy, yet there are penalties if it remains too far behind the wire. It is in some ways 'special', 'different' and 'vital'; in other ways it is just another of government's knowledge producers, with its own specialist field abutting on others, and sometimes overlapping them. Its proper position is a mixture of the two. A strand running through the book is the need for both its critics and supporters to keep a sensible balance between them, amid all the shocks and changes of the Information Age.

On the greatest of these modern shocks, a brief Afterword has been added (as Chapter 14) on the intelligence implications of the World Trade Center–Washington catastrophe of 11 September 2001.

Acknowledgements

I am grateful to those who encouraged me at seminars and conferences to develop themes originally appearing in my *Intelligence Power in Peace and War* (Cambridge: Cambridge University Press, 1996). In the chapters here that have appeared in print elsewhere I have made some corrections and additions, but in the main kept to the original forms. On the unpublished material I am grateful to those who commented upon drafts, particularly Raymond Cohen, Alan Budd, Leslie Houlden, Andrew Linklater and Per Ilsaas. Thanks are also due to Byron Shafer and other members of Nuffield College Oxford for their long-standing hospitality; to the Warden and Fellows of St Antony's College for their current support; and to Richard Aldrich for encouraging this production and commenting helpfully on the whole manuscript. Former official colleagues have given security clearance to the texts, without of course bearing any responsibility for their contents. My wife Ann has as usual been tolerant of the time and energy devoted to this retirement hobby.

Part I

Intelligence and Information

1

Intelligence's Essence

The official intelligence discussed in this book has no distinguishing adjective; it tends to be just called 'intelligence', both in general usage and in formal descriptions.[1] Other kinds of intelligence are usually expanded, for example into 'business intelligence' in the private sector and 'criminal intelligence' in law enforcement.[2] Occasionally the intelligence discussed here becomes 'national intelligence', as in the recent official British booklet on 'National Intelligence Machinery',[3] but for most purposes it stands alone. Yet as Sherman Kent explained in his classical description of it, it denotes a *particular* kind of knowledge, the type of organization producing this knowledge, and the activity pursued by the organization.[4] This chapter considers the particularity that distinguishes it from other information activities, and speculates on its future in the Information Age.

Some things about it are obvious enough. As an institution it serves central and not local government. It deals with information, but in ways that differ from the information-gathering and information-handling that take place as integral parts of government and military command-and-control. It is a specialist activity; in military terms it is 'staff,' not 'line'. As such it developed over the same period as the state's other information specialists. Thus Britain's naval and military Intelligence Departments developed in almost exactly the same period in the nineteenth century as official statistics, and its Joint Intelligence Committee (JIC) was established in the twentieth century in parallel with its Central Statistical Office, and for much the same reasons.[5] Intelligence and statistics resemble each other as specialized information collectors and interpreters, each providing its own distinctive window on to reality.

But intelligence does not have the professional status of other specialists.[6] Institutionally its boundaries are sometimes arbitrary or fuzzy; thus although the JIC has nominal oversight of 'British intelligence activity as a whole', by no means all of it comes in practice within its purview.[7] The use of the intelligence label also varies from country to country; the US State

Department's Bureau of Intelligence and Research is a member of the American intelligence community, while the comparable British Foreign and Commonwealth Office's Research and Analysis Department is emphatically not classified as 'intelligence'.[8]

Just as confusing is the variety within intelligence itself. More than other information services, it is torn between its twin skills of collecting information and evaluating it. It is partly government's specialist on certain collection and exploitation methods, but partly also the expert on certain subjects, using both intelligence and non-intelligence material for its all-source analysis. The Humint, Sigint and imagery agencies are specialists in their own single-source collection/exploitation techniques; by contrast the expertise of CIA's Directorate of Intelligence and the British Defence Intelligence Staff and Assessments Staff is on a range of subjects, not on the means of gathering information about them. Another internal dichotomy is between 'foreign intelligence' with overseas targets, and its rather different, more inward-looking 'security intelligence', with its domestic components or implications. There are other notable differences in intelligence cultures, particularly between the military and civilians.

Yet despite these diversities intelligence has a distinctive status, and all states of any substance recognize it as a permanent part of their apparatus. This chapter therefore examines its common factors from four viewpoints, as *activity*, *subjects*, *product* and *functions*. None of these presents a uniform aspect, and indeed as much time has to be spent in qualifying conclusions as making them. Nevertheless a picture emerges of intelligence's character.

This picture is not a universal one. What is examined here is mainly the current system in the UK, US and Old Commonwealth, with a bias towards the British example. I therefore go on to consider whether this English-speaking intelligence can be regarded as part of a wider 'Western' model, and to what extent it is – or should be – a worldwide standard.

ACTIVITY

Intelligence's main activity is information-gathering and exploitation; all-source analysis is a smaller component, and covert action (to be touched on later) is smaller still. The main common feature is the sensitivity of its collection/exploitation (and covert action), for reasons that include questions of propriety and legality but are mainly based on the vulnera-bility of its sources and methods to countermeasures.[9] From this comes intelligence's special secrecy, extending from collection/exploitation to cover most aspects of analysis. Secrecy is intelligence's trademark: the basis of its relationship with government and its own self-image.

Yet, here as elsewhere, not all intelligence corresponds completely with the generalization. There are in fact wide variations in the source protection needed. Not all its collection/exploitation is in the mainstream activities of Humint, Sigint and imagery, and the other intelligence sources – special surveillance of various kinds, Masint (the American acronym for Measurement and Signature Intelligence, such as underwater and atmospheric Acoustint), POW interrogation, and the procurement and study of foreign military equipment – are generically less sensitive than the main ones. Even the mainstream sources have varied sensitivity within them. Humint sources range from secret agents in place to the routine interviewing of refugees and travellers; British interviews of Kosovo refugees by its Defence Debriefing Teams on behalf of the Hague Tribunal were a form of Humint, but hardly a deep secret. Sigint has codebreaking at one extreme of its sensitivity, but also includes far less sensitive activities such as the monitoring of foreign radars for order-of-battle purposes. Satellite imagery was once regarded as a deep secret but its existence is now commonly acknowledged, and in the handling of its product the Director of America's National Reconnaissance Office (NRO) claimed in 1999 that 'classification and compartmentation barriers continue to fall' and that 'a large percentage of NRO products is now being released at the collateral SECRET classification level'.[10] Additionally, whatever the sensitivity of particular operations and output, these main sources are themselves not unique to intelligence. Some satellite photography is now available commercially. Law enforcement has always used human sources as informers and has long experience of telephone-tapping; now it even has some codebreaking under its control.[11]

The actual picture is therefore of gradations of fragility. Specially sensitive and important sources are surrounded by a wider glacis of secrecy that provides protection in depth. Within this glacis there are gradations of sensitivity, rather than black-and-white distinctions between sensitive sources and robust ones. Intelligence's special protection in each case should be a balance of the risks and penalties of disclosure against the need for it to be usable. Secrecy is relative, not absolute.

This receives some recognition. Intelligence organizations are no longer covert, and over recent years there has been greater flexibility over the release of historical material, as in the American declassification of satellite imagery up to the middle of the Cold War. But intelligence as a whole is still held to be uniquely secret, rivalled in government only by details of nuclear deployments and procedures.[12] In Britain this secrecy has long antecedents; the Secret Service Fund goes back to the Restoration and its Vote to 1797, and intelligence inherits a traditional respect for Secret Service. Intelligence's culture is based on secrecy and a sense of embattlement, not without reason; its penetration was the other side's highest priority target in the Cold War, and the media's urge to tease out its secrets perpetuates its sense of being under siege.[13] Its position with government rests on its special sources; the authority of 'if you knew what I know'. The thrill of secret knowledge makes Ministers read intelligence in their evening boxes, even if they leave more mundane items to the next morning. If intelligence has any single, defining characteristic in the eyes of governments and publics it is this secrecy and the mystique it attracts.

SUBJECTS

The subject-matter reinforces this idea of 'specialness'. It excludes the normal run of home affairs; Britain had its 'Home Intelligence' in the Second World War, but this investigation of public attitudes and morale subsequently evolved into opinion polling.[14] Intelligence is targeted on 'them' not 'us', with espionage, subversion, sabotage, terrorism and covert foreign influence as part of 'them'. In formal terms the scope of foreign coverage appears unlimited. The JIC's terms of reference charge it not only with warning on 'direct or indirect foreign threats to British political, military or economic interests', but also with assessing 'events and situations relating to external affairs, defence, terrorism, major international criminal activity, scientific, technical and international economic matters'.[15] The US effort exists similarly to provide information for national decisions on 'foreign, defense and economic policy, and the protection of United States national interests from foreign security threats'.[16] The CIA has a wealth of expertise that reflects this broad remit. 'The greatest concentration of analytical experts on international economic issues resides not in any of the executive departments but in the Central Intelligence Agency ... [where] about one-third of its analytic talent concerns itself with economic issues of one kind or another.'[17] There is also an official market for its studies on new subjects. A CIA study of the international incidence of Aids was reported in early 2000 to have led to the designation of Aids as a threat to American security.[18] There are no official guides to the foreign subjects intelligence should *not* tackle.

Yet in its role of government's all-source expert there are real limitations to the subjects on which it carries authority. In writing about the American system, Jack Davis has pointed to the areas where intelligence has 'comparative advantage' over other sources of knowledge,[19] and these tend to be those of the fungible but recognizable idea of 'national security'. Actual or potential violence everywhere – along with weapons and explosives, their use or intended use, the capabilities they provide, their scope for development and the threats they constitute – is intelligence's biggest subject. Linked with it are warning of attack and the study of foreign military forces, international arms supplies, the proliferation of weapons of mass destruction, and terrorism. Intelligence is the expert on violent change, threats of it, and instability and situations in which these figure. Such subjects tend to produce difficult and opaque targets. Hence intelligence is also the expert on secretive regimes and indeed clandestinity of all kinds, one of the factors linking foreign intelligence with security intelligence.

In practice its all-source product extends to much wider areas, including foreign affairs generally; the JIC's prime fields are officially stated to be 'security, defence and foreign affairs'.[20] Agreed intelligence estimates can be useful in reducing policy disagreement on almost any subject; intelligence's relatively broad role in Washington perhaps springs partly from the special problems of policy coordination there. Nevertheless there are still limits on its authority. Despite the importance of the warnings it gives of foreign political developments with economic consequences, and economic changes with political effects, it is rarely government's pundit on economics *qua* economics. The same applies to the international financial market. The British experiment in the late 1960s and 1970s of a separate economic JIC, of equal standing to the older non-economic body, did not survive. Similarly intelligence is not normally regarded as the authority on close allies, even though governments' constant problem is forecasting their behaviour. British intelligence is not tasked with providing warnings of US military action; being surprised by the American invasion of Grenada in 1983 was not counted as a failure on its part. Neither was it expected to monitor the international spread of the virus that produced Britain's crippling foot-and-mouth epidemic in early 2001.

National security has thus provided a focus for intelligence's expert position. Sir Percy Cradock described the JIC under his chairmanship in the 1980s and early 1990s as working in

the hard world of shocks and accidents, threats and crises.... Here the
news was usually bad, more about the errors, less about the achievements. It was the dark side of the moon, history pre-eminently as the
record of the crimes and follies of mankind.[21]

Some developments over the last decade have tended to underline this
character. One is the increased coverage of non-state targets, such as
foreign movements, companies and individuals, many of them associated
with insurrection, terrorism, arms transfers and other security-like
subjects. Another is the increasing scale of international movement and
communication, widening the scope of security intelligence and the threats
with which it is concerned, overseas as well as at home. Thus the US has
relatively few domestic terrorist threats but extensive ones abroad, while
polyglot London by contrast has become a setting for conflicts between
foreign governments and their opponents. Most important of all has been
the increased use of Western armed forces in varied roles over the last ten
years, all of which need virtually a wartime level of intelligence support.
One side-effect has been an unexpected revival of the topographical and
similar physical and environmental components of military intelligence,
not only for land operations but also for planning and targeting aircraft and
cruise-missile strikes. All this emphasizes the need for authoritative intelligence on 'security' matters (including support to military forces), to a far
greater extent than was expected in the immediate post-Cold War years.

   But this describes intelligence's position as government's expert on
subjects, and not when it passes the product of its single-source collection/
exploitation direct to its policy-making and decision-taking customers.
Here covert intelligence in supplementing government's other knowledge
has always ranged over a much broader spectrum of subjects. Being well
informed in this way was a factor in Britain's successful policy of 'punch-
ing above its weight' internationally despite economic decline after 1945;
good intelligence of this kind improved effectiveness and contributed to
national influence. Intelligence may not be the expert on friends, but in
negotiating with them, or some of them, government values its ability to
give it a peep at the hands held around the table. In these and other
contexts, then, intelligence's service of single-source collection/exploita-
tion adds missing pieces to government's picture; as such its contribution
is broad but relatively shallow, compared with the narrower range of
subjects on which it is the all-source authority. The fit between these two
kinds of intelligence is not complete.

This disjunction should not be overemphasized. Despite the diverse subjects it illuminates, collecting foreign secrets has tended to be most important on the security-related subjects, including terrorism, that coincide with intelligence's expert authority. If plotted on a scale from completely non-security matters at one end to unequivocal security threats at the other, intelligence as a whole would still be weighted towards the security end.

This situation is not static. In recent years economic espionage and the covert collection of scientific, technical and financial secrets have had worldwide publicity as growth areas – probably not for the UK and US, but as a priority activity elsewhere, perhaps by France as well as Russia. In the English-speaking community there is a comparable growth area in assistance to law enforcement on the drugs trade, money laundering and other organized crime. Combating drugs is now a major CIA commitment and a JIC First Priority requirement. Assistance to law enforcement may be expanding. Britain's Security Service is reported to have been tasked with searching for police corruption, and its Secret Intelligence Service (SIS) with tracking down the gangs who organize the entry of illegal immigrants to the UK.[22] Illegal immigration is even said to have been a matter for JIC assessment.[23] Distinctions between law enforcement and security may themselves be increasingly blurred, for example when armed forces' peace support operations in Bosnia and Kosovo need intelligence on the local or international mafia.[24] And security has vastly expanded in other directions in the minds of governments and publics over the last ten years to embrace considerations of international order, justice and humanitarianism. Like armed forces, intelligence is increasingly concerned with other peoples' security, not only with its own state's.

Nevertheless it still retains a core (if latent) role as part of the protection mechanism against the ultimate threats to national integrity: military defeat and loss of sovereignty, overthrow by revolution or insurrection, and combinations of the two. It is a warning system against the graver kinds of surprise. Its constant preoccupation is evaluating serious risk. To revert to Sir Percy Cradock on the JIC: 'Trouble, or the prospect of trouble, from China to Peru, provided that it had implications for Britain, demanded and received its mention and its judgement.'[25] From this comes intelligence's image of a special seriousness, a marked difference in degree from information in the normal run of government business. The compellance of 'national security' – however interpreted and reinterpreted – still contributes to intelligence's distinctive character and influence. If it is read in the Ministerial box partly for the thrill of secrecy, the attraction is also the possibility of unusual importance. As Peter Hennessy described Prime Ministers' relationships with intelligence, 'most premiers love this side of their work – so much more exciting than dealing with local government finance'.[26] Secrecy and subjects combine to make it in some way 'special'.

PRODUCT

The nature of the product provides another part of the identity. Whether single-source or all-source, most intelligence output has a significant element of 'processing', as is reflected in the military distinction between 'unprocessed data of every description' (information) and 'the product resulting from the processing of information' (intelligence).[27] Intelligence is like archaeology; a matter of interpreting evidence as well as finding it. It is not 'raw news' or a simple recording of information. In establishing its current 'Situation Centre' the UN has only gone part-way towards an international intelligence capability.

The degrees of processing vary. Many covertly acquired documents and intercepted messages need careful exegesis, but others are relatively transparent, even though translation is usually needed even for these. The Soviet intelligence triumphs against Western nuclear weapons programmes lay in acquiring original documents and scientists' explanations of them, not in expert interpretation of the material obtained. Another category of relatively unprocessed intelligence is held in what the Americans neatly describe as 'data warehousing', typically the topographical and similar intelligence on out-of-the-way places that is drawn on only if military deployments make it needed.

But most intelligence product incorporates more intensive processing, often of a fairly complex kind, especially of the relatively 'soft' evidence available amid concealment and deception. Part of this processing involves specific intelligence skills such as Sigint analysis and imagery interpretation, but these merge into more general canons for handling evidence and drawing conclusions. Intelligence has to persuade its users through what American literature has called the 'analytic tradecraft' of a demonstrated trail of evidence, assumptions and conclusions. A key point about modern intelligence is that these canons reach back into the large single-source producers and infuse the intelligence process as a whole. Any idea that the collectors produce 'facts' for all-source analysts to 'interpret' is far too simplistic.[28] All intelligence incorporates 'cleverness' in the sense of its underlying Latin original, *intelligere*. Some of the modern surprise at 'intelligence failure' stems from the semantic implication that it is in some way more irrational than other kinds of misjudgement.

The emphasis on processing in this general sense is reinforced by the forecasting role. Intelligence's greatest value is as a guide to the future. Recent comment has questioned this, following Robert Gates's use of the dictum that intelligence deals with secrets rather than mysteries: 'secrets are things that are potentially knowable', while in mysteries 'there are no clear-cut answers, often because the other leaders themselves do not know what they are going to do or have not worked out their problems'.[29] But all the future is a mystery; even if actors have precise plans they may be changed or not realized. Governments have to make assumptions about future possibilities and uncertainties, and where else but to intelligence should they turn on the subjects on which it is the expert? To quote Sir Percy Cradock again: 'We were members of an older and shadier fraternity, all those who over the centuries have claimed to read the future for their masters: the shamans and soothsayers, sybils and readers of entrails, Macaulay's "pale augurs muttering low".'[30] This is an inherent part of intelligence's role, though using evidence, argument and judgement rather than divination. Its ancient roots are partly in secrecy and concern for security, but partly also in rulers' search for preternatural wisdom.

Other aspects of processing come from intelligence's need to present its product to be useful to its varied customers; US writers refer to 'tailored output' to meet specific user needs. In short, the relationship with decision-takers is an active and not a passive one, and the accent on analysis, presentation and persuasion distinguishes intelligence from information sources that produce what is more like 'data', for example the radar plots available for immediate operational use, or real-time warnings of missile launches. Despite its 'warehoused' material, intelligence is similarly distinguished from much 'information on demand'; in the modern jargon, it works more by 'push' than 'pull'. Its processing gives 'added value' to its collected evidence. A corollary is that it tends to deal with difficult questions in which there are elements of concealment or deception.

These are broad generalizations, with plenty of exceptions and borderline cases. As one example: surveillance of the USSR for warning purposes in the Cold War developed to include massive flows of relatively simple, single-source intelligence reports signalled between warning centres. Much other product is equally ephemeral or mundane. Nevertheless cleverness in a wide sense distinguishes intelligence from data.

How far this will continue to apply in the modern digitized world can be debated. A specialist literature has developed about the power of Open Source Intelligence (Osint), from the Internet and elsewhere, and the scope for 'data mining' within it.[31] A typical claim is that many of the expanding military requirements for improved maps can be met from commercial imagery and similar open data.[32] Though intelligence has developed its specialist Osint units, it is not clear whether this 'data mining' will develop intrinsically as an intelligence skill or as a new branch of expert librarianship; perhaps in practice a mixture of both.[33] Similarly in military matters modern technology's ability to produce a real-time Virtual Battlefield by computer has blurred distinctions between sophisticated operational (non-intelligence) sources and the traditionally 'cleverer' intelligence ones.[34] Thus in 2000 an American Department of Defense study envisaged handling the hitherto separate activities of intelligence, surveillance and reconnaissance on a much more holistic basis.[35] Clearly intelligence can no longer be equated simply with any kind of clever processing.

What can be suggested here is however that, whatever the implications of the new advances, intelligence will continue to be distinguished not only by unusual secrecy but also by a particular kind of judgement. It will exploit the digitized revolution and contribute to real-time battlefield information, but its product as a whole will retain its characteristic of relative depth – perhaps, at least in military contexts, depth rather than real-time speed. An aim will continue to be providing insights on targets' minds, rather than just the observation, location and measurement of 'things' such as ships, aircraft and all kinds of military equipment.[36] It will remain geared to 'understanding', seeing situations from its targets' points of view, and assessing implications; one of its qualities will continue to be a kind of specialized insight. For the all-source stage the characteristic is best captured by the label 'assessment'.

FUNCTION

Cleverness therefore adds to intelligence's flavour of secrecy and importance. For its most important feature, however, we must return to its position as 'staff' rather than 'line'; its role as an information specialist in its relationship with power. This seems self-evident in the way described at the beginning of this chapter. As put at the military operational level: 'The role of Operational Intelligence is to provide commanders and their staffs with the fullest possible understanding of the adversary and of the operational environment... in order that they can plan and conduct operations successfully.'[37] Intelligence does not propose decisions, take them or execute them. Diplomacy resembles intelligence as an information system, as in a retired British diplomat's description of the Foreign Office as 'a huge assessment machine... a capacious and versatile digestive system fed by a massive intake of information';[38] but with the difference that this is not separated from the world of policy-making and action. From this comes the idea of policy-free intelligence, its ethic of truth-seeking and objectivity, and its self-image of telling truth to power, or (as a British Director General of Intelligence put it) as telling 'all those who won't listen to all the things they don't want to know'.[39]

This sounds idealized, and like intelligence's other features needs qualifications. In the first place the picture of it as an information specialist is not strictly complete, even in formal terms. It has its complementary role of defensive security. The British SIS, Government Communications Headquarters and Security Service are officially the intelligence and security services, and the security role includes the protection of national information, including electronic security and the protection of what British government calls the 'National Information Infrastructure'. In this increasingly important area it is an actor in standard-setting, policy formation and government's decision-taking. It is even in the market for providing advice and services to the private sector.

Even outside this defensive role, governments look to intelligence for a variety of activities unrelated to information. Covert action is normally carried out as an intelligence function, as by the CIA's Directorate of Operations. This does not positively have to be the case; Churchill's wartime mandate to 'set Europe ablaze' was issued to the Special Operations Executive, not SIS, but intelligence's secrecy makes it a natural home for covert activities. It is also close to deception and the burgeoning subject of information warfare. It additionally provides an alternative to diplomacy – sometimes a rival to it – for dealings with foreign governments as well as unavowed contacts with oppositions, terrorist movements (as in British governments' exchanges with the IRA before the cease-fire) or disreputable individuals. Intelligence liaisons are themselves of political significance, as in their influence on Britain's Atlanticist stance. Security intelligence is closely involved in governments' internal security and counter-terrorist operations, though usually with some separation from legal processes and executive responsibility. In all these respects intelligence is directly or indirectly one of government's actors.

Even if these qualifications are set aside, the separation from executive government and command can be debated. Intelligence cannot always limit itself to its targets; its own government's present policy may be part of the situations it analyses and the outcomes it forecasts, and discussion of it comes close to policy assessment. The same applies even more to forecasting foreign reactions to what its own government is thinking of doing. Peter Hennessy argues that JIC assessments after Egypt's nationalization of the Suez canal in 1956 amounted to a policy warning that UK military action would be very risky.[40] In 1999 intelligence may well have been required – indeed should have been required – to assess how Milosevic would react to various projected forms of NATO bombardment: in effect, to recommend how to achieve the desired effect and assess how long it would take. Professional net assessments of this kind also drag intelligence into evaluating its own side: one of the unsolved problems of the Cold War was objectively comparing the USSR's military effectiveness with NATO's.

Underlying these problems is the balance between the ethic of truth-seeking and the need to be useful. Effective intelligence has to show the relevance of what it produces. It is part of government, part of the team, not an academic observer or a licensed Cassandra. Its professionals crave access to their customers, and influence for their product. Rightly so: they need both physical and metaphorical proximity to government. In his catalogue of Anglo–French intelligence failures in 1940 Ernest May mentions the Deuxième Bureau's view of itself as a priesthood, enjoined to 'a kind of scholastic exactitude', remote from the operational planners.[41] Similarly a former DCI and CIA Director, Admiral Stansfield Turner, was rude about his analysts as 'tweedy, pipe-smoking intellectuals who work much as if they were doing research back in the universities whence many of them came'.[42] In reaction a considerable American literature developed on the need for closer links between intelligence and decision-takers. One of Turner's successors exhorted the analysts to be 'down in the trenches with the policy-makers', to understand the users, their issues and their policy.[43] 'Opportunity analysis' was advocated, 'identifying opportunities or vulnerabilities the United States can exploit to advance a policy'.[44] Empathy with the users was the key.

Britain's compact 'Whitehall village' generates this closeness, as does the unusual degree of policy-makers' participation in the intelligence process. The JIC has always been chaired by a professional diplomat, and other Foreign Office members carry considerable weight in it. From 1985 to 1992 the JIC Chairman quoted earlier was also the Prime Minister's

Foreign Policy Adviser and, in his own words, 'intelligence and policy were as closely linked as they have ever been in British government'.[45] These may be marks of effectiveness, but modify any impression of a separation from policy, or staffing by a priesthood.

Nevertheless a certain distance between intelligence and policy still remains, in Britain and elsewhere. Though fascinated by government, intelligence officers stay on the right side of the thin line separating them from explicit policy advocacy; except by invitation they are voyeurs, sometimes interlocutors, rather than participants by right. They have their own quasi-professional assumptions about their distinctive role and standards. The American literature on making intelligence more useful took these professional norms for granted. Intelligence may be in the policy trenches but it still wears a different uniform.

It can of course be argued that objectivity is an unrealizable ideal anyway; that in any case personal risks and rewards colour individual judgements. 'It is more satisfying, safer professionally, and easier to live with oneself and one's colleagues as a military hawk than as a wimp.'[46] Even if intelligence is not in government's pocket it has its own mindsets and interests. Its concern with warnings and threats disposes it to pessimistic views. Cold War history is littered by 'worst case' intelligence estimates of the adversary. It may seem that there are no objective approaches, only particular viewpoints.

Fortunately intelligence's usefulness does not depend on achieving objectivity in any absolute sense; merely that it strives for it, and from a position different from its users', with a different cast of mind and different skills and more knowledge. Politicians, diplomats and generals believe in their own objectivity, but forget their psychological investment in the decisions they have previously taken. 'Men who have participated in a decision develop a stake in that decision. As they participate in further, related decisions, their stake increases.'[47] Policy analysis and planning units also claim objectivity, but they too must see situations in terms of what should be done about them. Intelligence with its degree of policy freedom can have different preconceptions. If it is sometimes accused of stressing dangers it can point out that Cassandra was right after all. In any case it does not habitually demonize its targets; for much of the Cold War the CIA's Directorate of Intelligence was a voice of moderation amid more extreme views of the Soviet threat.[48]

There is indeed a worrying conflict between these aspects of intelligence and its role in covert action, but the scale there is quite small. The

Baconian dictum that knowledge itself is power does not actually fit the intelligence communities to which it has been so indiscriminately applied. Without the responsibilities and distractions of power, intelligence has at least a chance of understanding its targets better than those it serves. It has to be on its user's side; but with the stance expected of a professional adviser towards his client. The Senate's confirmation hearings in 1991 over Gates's appointment as Director of Central Intelligence, discussing the alleged politicization of assessments of the Soviet Union, deserve attention as an articulation of democratic assumptions about intelligence's professional ideals.

But this is only half the system; the other half is government's recognition of this intelligence role and its willingness to listen. Whether this is to an interdepartmental system like the JIC or a central agency like the CIA is not the point. Whatever institutions intelligence has, and despite all the philosophic questions about the idea of objectivity, governments' recognition of its role and importance is the key feature. It is conveyed partly in the rubric 'our job is to bring you unwelcome news'[49], but also in the fact that it is not required to recommend action. The modern addition of all-source assessment on these terms to the ancient art of acquiring others' secrets makes for a better quality of decision.

'ENGLISH-SPEAKING' AND OTHER CONCEPTS

The picture of English-speaking intelligence therefore combines these features of secrecy, subjects and intellectual content with this wafer-thin but genuine separation between all-source assessment and recommendation. The picture is of course impressionistic, not a complete landscape. Nevertheless it is the nature of the English-speaking entity. Its distinctiveness internationally does not lie in covert collection/exploitation – all states have that – but in the idea of objectivity. The question arises of its wider validity, for Western countries and worldwide.

The idea of military intelligence as all-source, expert, objective study of enemies and potential enemies is part of military culture in all Western countries; indeed the nineteenth-century development of military intelligence staffs was not an English-speaking innovation but imitated the Continental model first developed in Prussia. Most of the West, too, has the idea of internally focused security intelligence distinct from normal law enforcement; the US is the odd man out in retaining this activity as a function of the

FBI and not a separate intelligence organization. Continental intelligence was rebuilt after the Second World War with an eye on the British and American models. The West German system developed under particular US influence; the Norwegian drew at the same time on British examples; and collaboration in the Cold War, NATO and the European Union has produced a general interplay of Western intelligence ideas. British intelligence feels particularly at home in Scandinavia. Israel has drawn similarly on Second World War models and subsequent Western liaisons, particularly with the US. Japan and Taiwan have been under similar US influence.

There are still many institutional variations. The English-speaking countries' primacy of foreign intelligence over security intelligence reflects the position of long-established and relatively secure regimes with world interests; intelligence in insecure regimes is more inward-looking. The main Latvian intelligence institution for example is the Office for the Protection of the Constitution, a title conveying the priority: though even there the problems over the ethnic Russian minority are bound up with assessing Moscow's intentions. Even in more secure environments the British and American devices of top-level JIC assessments and National Intelligence Estimates have met with interest but not much imitation. The English-speaking idea of an 'intelligence community' has had a lukewarm reception. Intelligence's input to policy is still seen quite widely as secret knowledge competing with diplomatic and other inputs.

Nevertheless there is some convergence with English-speaking countries' ideas. Most Western countries now recognize intelligence as a national activity of some kind, rather than a set of disparate ones. Terrorism has exacerbated rivalries between foreign and security intelligence agencies, but has also pointed to intelligence as a whole as the main weapon against it. Events in the former Yugoslavia have given other intelligence a similar salience. Extensive Western contacts have an effect on professional standards through peer pressure. Covert action has confused public attitudes, particularly in the US, France and Israel (and also over British anti-terrorist action against Irish terrorism), but there are general assumptions that intelligence's proper role is advisory and not executive. There have been many seedy intelligence organizations, but criticism of them incorporates some common standards. Governments and élites in Continental Europe resent the UK–US relationship, but mainly in envy. The French-led move to develop intelligence in the European Security and Defence Identity aims at imitating the transatlantic alliance, not at setting new standards. There is a liberal 'Western' concept even if it still needs the inverted commas around it.

What really gives it some credence is to compare it with the totally different system of its former Soviet rival. Intelligence there was in one sense completely subservient to power, in another a major part of repressive power itself. Intelligence leaders were part of the ruling élite, with control of intelligence as their power base. Intelligence was one of the highest national priorities, but was seen as inseparable from covert action abroad and internal repression at home; information-gathering, covert action and repression were linked as weapons in the struggle with the USSR's enemies, with no doctrinal distinctions between them. The only prized information was intelligence covertly acquired, and policy-free all-source assessment for the leadership was an impossibility; intelligence could not compete with the regime's deeply ideological world view.[50] Stalin's remarkable attempt to imitate the US in coordinated assessment was bound to fail, though it lingered on for some years.[51] John Gaddis has commented on this period that 'it was no longer permitted there [Moscow] to distinguish between state interests, party interests, and those of Stalin himself'.[52] The same applied to the subordinate intelligence systems like the East German Stasi. Soviet successes in covert intelligence-gathering did not displace major misperceptions about the West, and indeed material was selected and interpreted to reinforce them. Arguably the Western victory in the Cold War included a victory for the Western concept of intelligence; or at least a defeat for the Soviet system.

Similarities can be found in other authoritarian regimes. Despite the internal power of the Gestapo and the multiplicity of intelligence organizations, Nazi Germany was not an intelligence state on Soviet lines, yet Hitler resembled Stalin in the dislike of unwelcome information and objective analysis. Sir Michael Howard has described Fascism as a movement with roots in 'will and action as against reasoned discussion and peaceful cooperation'.[53] Gaddis has argued similarly on Hitler and Stalin that 'there seems to have been something about authoritarians that caused them to lose touch with reality... autocratic systems reinforce, while discouraging attempts to puncture, whatever quixotic illusions may exist at the top'.[54] Intelligence is prized for facilitating internal control and acquiring foreign secrets, but not for objective judgement.

So few comparative studies have been published that it would be hazardous to categorize all national intelligence systems as either 'Western' or 'authoritarian'. Classifying intelligence is like classifying forms of government, but with less public data. Nevertheless a basic difference can be suggested between systems in which intelligence assesses in the way described here, with a status and ethic, and those where it does not. This second category includes systems in which intelligence is subservient to the leadership, part of the leadership itself, or struggling to become it; those in which information-gathering and covert action are inseparable; and those where it is totally absorbed in keeping leaders in power. But it also includes those states which are not necessarily authoritarian but where intelligence is still seen as a matter of procuring 'secrets', not necessarily put into context and assessed objectively as a regular input to policy. To return to the analogy with government statistics, the differences in intelligence's position can be likened to the contrast between states where professional statisticians' inputs really drive decisions, and those where they cut no ice if conflicting with policy or ideology.

How big is this 'non-Western' element compared with the 'Western' model? The Russian SVR, the successor of the Humint 'foreign intelligence' element of the KGB, is now under formal restraints through the legislation of the 1990s, including a ban on covert action;[55] but there is little Western knowledge on how far these are observed. The FSB, the successor of the internally focused part of the KGB, makes frequent claims of the extent of Western espionage and covert action, and encourages a spy mania. Ex-KGB cronyism seems a feature of the Putin regime, and it would be surprising if the Soviet model of 'special services' as major power players has been overtaken there or in the Russian 'near abroad'. Chris Donnelly has commented on Russia's new National Security Concept that in the list of threats

> There is no prioritisation and no analysis of risk versus probability.... In many central and East European countries, the intelligence services still reflect the heritage of closed societies. Open information, a system to evaluate it, and politicians and civil servants educated to understand it, are essential today to enable intelligence to be used properly. It is not clear how long it will take many of the new democracies to develop this particular attribute of modern society.[56]

Elsewhere the character of Chinese intelligence remains enigmatic, but the nature of the regime makes its encouragement of unwelcome advice seem unlikely. More obviously autocratic-style intelligence still continues in Iraq and presumably in North Korea, and perhaps also in some of the Arab world. Pakistan's inter-service intelligence organization has been a major player in Pakistani politics over the last twenty years, and it would be

surprising if its intelligence assessments on India have remained unpoliti-
cized.[57] There is a general impression of politicized intelligence in Africa,
though the direction taken by the South African system will be an important regional influence for the future. But what generalizations can be made
about intelligence in South America? Academic analysis of the systems
there is still at a fairly early stage.

Much more comparative work is needed. But I suggest nevertheless
that the idea of intelligence assessment with some policy-neutral freedom
and quasi-professional standards ranks as a 'Western' one, and has a place,
even if an inconspicuous one, in the Western ideas now competing for
global support.

A GLOBAL IDEAL?

Intelligence has attracted little attention in discussion of Westernization
and 'conflicts of civilizations'. The media image of the CIA has given intelligence a bad reputation, and governments have preferred its international
contacts to have a low profile. But two official British statements merit
consideration. The first was in 1994 when the Director-General of the
British Security Service 'went public' over her Service's role as the
defender of democracy against politically directed violence; 'a security
service such as MI5 is compatible with personal liberty within our democracy. It does not conflict with it but enhances it.'[58] She went on to refer to
the links that the UK had established after the end of the Cold War with
the successor security services in the former Warsaw Pact countries,
'particularly to help them establish a democratic framework for their
work'.[59] The idea of intelligence's democratic accountability, legal control
and objective of sustaining democracy and the rule of law should have this
part in Western advice elsewhere.

The second was in 1999, and is perhaps of even greater interest here.
As part of the programme for eliminating world poverty, the British
Secretary of State for International Development unexpectedly announced
assistance to the underdeveloped world for 'the security sector' including
'training to improve the objectivity of threat analysis, especially on the
civilian side of government' and 'strengthening the capacity of [local]
intelligence services to assess genuine outside threats'.[60] Presumably the
aim was to reduce the incidence of Third World conflicts and excessive
arms purchases preceding them.

It therefore provides some endorsement for the view that proper intelligence assessment is a means of reducing governments' recklessness; that it encourages leaders to value information, reason and argument rather than conviction, emotion and impulse.[61] Objective assessment is part of good governance and 'soft' national security; it is good for international society. If this is true for the Third World it applies with even more force to large non-Western powers – to Russia and China, and probably also to the Middle East and Indian subcontinent. Britain commends it to the Third World as part of liberal democracy, but it is really the eighteenth-century Enlightenment's respect for knowledge and reason. Of course completely rational government is an unachievable ideal, and even the best of intelligence does not guarantee wisdom.[62] But it helps, and tends to produce better international behaviour. The significance of the 1999 British announcement was in the way it took intelligence out of its normal context of covert activities and secrecy and pointed to its threat analysis as its legitimate and commendable aspect.

The same view of it is even more relevant to international action for security and humanitarian motives, under UN mandates and otherwise. All those writing about peace-making, peace-enforcement and the other varieties of international intervention over the last decade have emphasized the need for better intelligence, including improved services to UN officials and better sharing between international participants. Collective action by coalitions of the willing depends on common assessments of the situations they are dealing with. In the Second World War it became axiomatic that the UK–US Combined Chiefs of Staff meetings to determine Allied Grand Strategy should be based on mutually agreed estimates of Axis intentions and capabilities. The same principle is equally applicable to modern international operations.

Yet there is considerable difficultly in applying it. There is no 'international intelligence' to call upon as an institution. There are some precedents for intelligence collection and analysis operating under UN control – tactical Sigint and photo-reconnaissance units in the Congo in the early 1960s;[63] the American U2 aircraft put under UNSCOM control over Iraq, and the substantial analysis staff which UNSCOM created to exploit this and other evidence[64] – but these are isolated examples and special cases. International intelligence will develop as an entity, but it will be a long haul. International action still depends on national intelligence inputs, and will continue to do so in the foreseeable future.

To some extent these are already provided. Two former American DCIs argued some years ago that American intelligence should become an international good,[65] and the US subsequently committed itself to intelligence support for international organizations.[66] At a pragmatic and *ad hoc* level the US and its partners are doing what they can, especially where NATO practices for intelligence inputs can be applied. But one limitation remains the need to protect national sources in largely transparent international operations with intense media coverage. Another lies in the practical problems of using national intelligence collectively, even when it is passed to selected international participants. Governments need confidence that English–speaking countries' inputs are not being rigged to support particular national positions, but there are no intelligence staffs of international civil servants to assess them. As put by an eminent UN Task Force, 'the Security Council has a growing need for high–quality and timely strategic analysis'.[67] There and elsewhere there is no machinery akin to the British Joint Intelligence Committee through which international participants can discuss policy-free assessments drafted for them by professional staffs without international allegiances.

Improvements up to a point can be made at technical and procedural levels, by more discriminating national secrecy classifications, better provision for sanitization to eliminate precise source information, and international standards for protecting intelligence, as in the way NATO security rules are now part of the concept of European Union operations. Secrecy is so deeply ingrained in national and international views of intelligence that sustained efforts are needed on these fronts to make it more useful internationally.

But the problems are not only technical and procedural; they involve basic attitudes to intelligence. The UN insists on regarding it as 'information', losing sight of its functions of understanding and forecasting. Nations still identify intelligence with covert collection and covert action, something best not talked about, and incompatible with the ethics of UN and other principled intervention. Intelligence support for international operations is still seen as a matter of secrets shared bilaterally behind closed doors. The idea of international assessment staffs and JIC-type machinery produces reactions of shock-horror; even in the European Union the idea is making snail-like progress. There is much talk about the need for UN 'analysis',[68] but the distinction is not yet recognized between policy-free intelligence assessment and policy analysis of what should be done. Intelligence conclusions and policy advocacy are still muddled up in international forums, as they were in the British government in the First World War. Britain is right to advocate objective threat analysis in the Third

World, but it is even more important as a *desideratum* for collective international action. Yet in getting this accepted there is the problem of intelligence's duality, between covert methods and secrecy on the one hand, and objective and usable all-source assessment on the other. The first colours proper consideration of the need for the second.

Intelligence will continue to be a mixture of secrets and non-secrets. At a purely semantic level, 'assessment' instead of 'intelligence' has crept in slowly over the last thirty years;[69] and perhaps it could go further. For most of its functions the JIC is actually a Joint Assessment Committee; and CIA's Directorate of Intelligence is a Directorate of Assessment (or analysis and assessment). There would be some cosmetic value if international arrangements were given the label of assessment rather than intelligence. But intelligence as a whole will continue to be feared as long as it is assumed that all nations automatically spy on each other.

Chapter 13 discusses the ethical issues that arise. It notes the current trend towards the coverage of more non-state targets and international 'baddies', much of it related to requirements of international security, justice and humanitarianism rather than national interests in any narrow sense. The requirement to supply the Hague Tribunal with imagery pointing to execution and burial sites in Kosovo exemplified the new kind of target. The chapter suggests worldwide standards of conduct whereby the more intrusive kinds of intelligence collection were expected to concentrate on matters of genuine national security or international concern; more support of international action, and less use of covert means to steal other countries' technology. The effect would be to swing the emphasis some way from the predominance of national covert collection/exploitation towards intelligence as the all-source expert. Rather less secrecy would be needed, consistent with the revolution in the amount of information available from open sources. Intelligence would continue to have its duality, but with a more even balance between its single-source and all-source roles, and perhaps more separation between them in international contexts.

Is any of this likely to happen? Intelligence is deeply wedded to its secret components, yet the interpretation of secrecy changes over time. There was a remarkable official blueprint for post-war British intelligence in 1945 which envisaged a single institution divided into two, one part dealing with secret intelligence, the other with open sources, even with some public access to it.[70] Was this pie-in-the-sky or an idea ahead of its time? It is worth recalling that government statistics in Continental countries were originally regarded as state secrets.[71] The confidentiality of the personal details collected is still as heavily protected as if they were intelligence sources, but statistics as the processed results are now taken for granted everywhere as essential but quite unspectacular inputs to government.

Intelligence may move some way down a similar road towards less pervasive secrecy. Its assessment role may become a recognized government profession with national and international standards and status, and less mystique about it. Assessment staffs may become as normal as other national and international experts. Intelligence as a whole may be rather less exciting, but more useful to international society.

A shift of this kind would be a long process even in the West, and even longer elsewhere. Intelligence standards everywhere are bound up with a complex of other governmental values, and Western ones are not always suitable for export. Regimes everywhere have the kind of intelligence that fits their nature. Nevertheless the 'Western' idea of intelligence as objective judgement and forecasting deserves recognition, and a place in any concept of liberal international order.

NOTES

1. See the US National Security Act and Presidential Executive Orders, and the British Intelligence Services Act 1994.
2. As for example in the British National Criminal Intelligence Service (NCIS) created in the early 1990s. Its mission statement quoted in early reports was 'to provide leadership and excellence in criminal intelligence'. Its role was restated in Section 2 of the Police Act 1997 in terms of 'criminal intelligence'. Interpol similarly set up an Analytical Criminal Intelligence Unit in 1993.
3. *National Intelligence Machinery* (Norwich: The Stationery Office, 2000). Some US official publications also distinguish between 'foreign intelligence' and 'counter-intelligence'.
4. S. Kent, *Strategic Intelligence for US World Policy* (Hamden, CT: Archon Books, 1965 edition), introduction p. xxiii. Compare Loch K. Johnson's conclusion in *Secret Agencies: U.S. Intelligence in a Hostile World* (New Haven, CT: Yale University Press, 1996) that although intelligence comprises information, process, mission and organizations (pp. 2–4), the most useful way of considering it is as 'a cluster of government agencies that conduct secret activities' (p. 13).
5. For the early history of British government statistics see R. Ward and Ted Doggett, *Keeping Score: The First Fifty Years of the Central Statistical Office* (London: HMSO, 1991), pp. 1–39. Churchill directed in January 1941 that 'the figures so collected [by the new Central Statistical Office] should form an agreed corpus which will be accepted and used without question' (p. 30). Its role in UK–US exchanges of statistics using common forms and definitions is described on pp. 36–9; the Allies' Grand Strategy depended not only on agreed

intelligence estimates about the enemy but also on agreed statistics about their own resources.

6. Such as statisticians, economists, accountants and legal advisers, and other experts in agencies like the British Food Standards Agency, recently established so that 'consumers are able to make an informed choice about the health consequences of the food they buy' (*Oxford Today*, 12, 3 (Trinity Term 2000), p. 4).

7. From *National Intelligence Machinery*, p. 19. Peripheral and part-time intelligence activities are discussed here in Chapter 4.

8. Though still separate from policy. According to its head, 'It is critically important that their output, with only rare exceptions, should be policy-neutral' (R. Lavers, 'My Job: Challenging Received Wisdom', *RUSI Journal*, 145, 6 (December 2000)).

9. The reasons for secrecy are discussed in M.E. Herman, *Intelligence Power in Peace and War* (Cambridge: Cambridge University Press, 1996), pp. 88–91.

10. K.R. Hall, 'The National Reconnaissance Office: Revolutionizing Global Reconnaissance,' *Defence Intelligence Journal*, 8, 1 (summer 1999), pp. 8–9.

11. Press reports announced the establishment of Britain's Government Technical Assistance Centre for law enforcement, with functions including codebreaking; it is said to be subordinate to the NCIS though located within Security Service premises (*The Times*, 12 June 2000).

12. And perhaps in modern Britain by the relationship between the Crown and Prime Minister; see P. Hennessy, *The Prime Minister: The Office and Its Holders Since 1945* (London: Allen Lane Penguin Press, 2000), pp. 60–1.

13. The relationship between secrecy and morale is discussed in Herman, *Intelligence Power in Peace and War*, Chapter 18.

14. For 'Home Intelligence' see T. Harrison, *Living through the Blitz* (London: Penguin, 1978).

15. *National Intelligence Machinery*, p. 19.

16. Executive Order 12333 (December 1981), paragraph 1.1.

17. Johnson, *Secret Agencies*, p. 149.

18. *The Times*, 1 May 2000.

19. 'Comparative advantage' is illustrated as existing through such factors as 'research, special sources, extensive data bases, advanced methodologies' (J. Davis, *The Challenge of Opportunity Analysis*, published by the CIA's Center for Study of Intelligence, July 1992, p. 2). The phrase was picked up in the CIA's Strategic Plan issued in August 1996 (*Directorate of Intelligence in the 21st Century: Strategic Plan*, p. 10).

20. *National Intelligence Machinery*, p. 15.

21. P. Cradock, *In Pursuit of British Interests: Reflections on Foreign Policy under Margaret Thatcher and John Major* (London: Murray, 1997), p. 37.

22. *Sunday Times*, 9 April 2000; *The Times*, 28 June 2000.

23. *Intelligence and Security Committee Annual Report 1999–2000* (London: The Stationery Office, 2000), paras. 89–90.

24. Discussed in A. Hills, *Doctrine, Criminality, and Future British Army Operations: A Half-Completed Understanding* (UK Strategic and Combat Studies Institute, Occasional Paper No.39, April 2000).

25. Cradock, *In Pursuit of British Interests*, p. 40.

26. Hennessy, *The Prime Minister*, p. 83.

27. British *Joint Operational Intelligence* (Joint Warfare Publication 2–00, 2000), Annex 1A, p. 1.

28. The intellectual interplay of single-source and all-source analysis is discussed in Chapter 12.

29. Remarks by R. Gates, as CIA's Deputy Director for Intelligence, on 'Analysis' in R. Godson (ed.), *Intelligence Requirements for the 1990s* (Lexington, MA: Lexington Books, 1989), p. 115. The same analogy is used in B. Berkowitz and A. Goodman, *Strategic Intelligence for US National Security* (Princeton: Princeton University Press, 1989), Chapter 4.

30. Cradock, *In Pursuit of British Interests*, p. 42.

31. Most recently R.D. Steele, *On Intelligence: Spies and Secrecy in an Open World*, (Oakton, VA: OSS Academy, 2000).

32. Steele, *On Intelligence*, p. 102.

33. Tapping the 'virtual' world of Internet service providers and networks may resemble the reception of radio signals from the ionosphere; some of these are identified public radio broadcasts available to anyone, while others are undeclared military and other communications that need specialist Sigint skills to find and identify them. Perhaps there is a similar difference in Osint between normal techniques and the special ones of 'data mining'.

34. For discussion see Chapter 3.

35. Presentation at RUSI conference on 'Information Superiority', July 2000.

36. Access to minds is essentially intelligence; observation or measurement of things may be intelligence, as in imagery interpretation, but also can be non-intelligence 'action information', as in the operational use of radar. Intelligence can embrace the sources and methods of both historiography and archaeology; the 'action information' sources are restricted to those of archaeology (Herman, *Intelligence Power in Peace and War*, pp. 82–7).

37. *Joint Operational Intelligence*, 1-1.

38. R. Hibbert, 'Intelligence and Policy', *Intelligence and National Security*, 5, 1 (January 1990), p. 113.

39. Vice-Admiral Sir Louis Le Bailly, letter to *The Times*, 3 August 1984.

40. P. Hennessy, *The Prime Minister*, pp. 230–6.

41. E.R. May, *Strange Victory: Hitler's Conquest of France* (New York: Hill and Wang, 2000), p. 385.

42. S. Turner, *Secrecy and Democracy: The CIA in Transition* (New York: Harper and Row, 1986), p. 113.

43. Godson, *Intelligence Requirements for the 1990s*, p. 111.

44. Davis, *The Challenge of Opportunity Analysis*, p. 1.

45. Cradock, *In Pursuit of British Interests*, pp. 45–6.

46. Herman, *Intelligence Power in Peace And War*, p. 247.

47. Quoted by Johnson, *Secret Agencies*, p. 28, from J.C. Thomson, 'How Could Vietnam Happen', *Atlantic Monthly*, 221 (April 1968).

48. For a discussion of American intelligence and policy in the Cold War see C. Andrew, *For the President's Eyes Only: Secret Intelligence and the American Presidency from Washington to Bush* (London: Harper Collins, 1995). For the CIA's record in estimating the Soviet Union in the 1980s see D.J. MacEachin, 'CIA Assessments of the Soviet Union', CIA's *Studies in Intelligence* (semi-annual unclassified edition, no.1,

1997), and K. Lundberg, *CIA and the Fall of the Soviet Empire: The Politics of 'Getting It Right'* (Harvard Intelligence and Policy Project, 1994).

49. Sir Maurice Oldfield as chief of SIS to James Callaghan as Foreign Secretary (Hennessy, *The Prime Minister*, p. 71).

50. And yet Soviet military intelligence at a professional level was taught assessment of the enemy of a positivist, statistical kind as a basis for planning; the combat capability of NATO divisions was assessed as a percentage of a Soviet division. It is not clear how far these methods influenced GRU inputs at the top level.

51. V.M. Zubok, *Soviet Intelligence and the Cold War: The 'Small' Committee of Information, 1952–3* (Washington: Woodrow Wilson Center Cold War History Project Working Paper no. 4, 1992).

52. J.L. Gaddis, *We Now Know: Rethinking Cold War History* (Oxford: Oxford University Press, 1997), p. 13.

53. M. Howard, *The Invention of Peace: Reflections on War and International Order* (London: Profile Books, 2000), p. 67.

54. Gaddis, *We Now Know*, p. 291.

55. For the legislation and its interpretation see V. Kirpichenko, 'Foreign Intelligence Service in the New Environment' in H. Shukman (ed.), *Agents for Change: Intelligence Services in the Twenty-First Century* (London: St Ermin's Press, 2001), and G. Bennett, *The SVR: Russia's Intelligence Service* (Camberley: Conflict Studies Research Centre, 2000).

56. C. Donnelly, 'Shaping Soldiers for the 21st Century', *NATO Review* (summer–autumn 2000).

57. Indian intelligence has itself been criticized recently by a former Special Secretary of the Cabinet Secretariat, though more for lack of assessment machinery than obvious politicization (V. Balachadran, *The Times of India*, 21 September 2000).

58. S. Rimington, Richard Dimbleby Lecture, *Security and Democracy* (London: BBC Educational Developments, 1994), p. 15.

59. Rimington, *Security and Democracy*, p. 5.

60. Department for International Development Policy Statement, *Poverty and the Security Sector*, 1999, pp. 4, 6. In the same vein of promoting Third World stability, SIS is reported to have been tasked with providing advance warning of coups against legitimate African heads of state (*Independent on Sunday*, 23 July 2000).

61. See Chapter 13.

62. For a brief but brilliant summary see Z. Bauman, *Times Literary Supplement*, 20 February 1998, reviewing R. Jervis, *System Effects: Complexity in Political and Social Life* (Princeton: Princeton University Press, 1997). The problem is 'not our ignorance, which can be rectified by more homework', nor is it 'the incommensurability of the immense variety of human actors and the capacity of our mental faculties which can handle but a limited number of factors'; it is ultimately 'born of a contradiction born of human action and in principle irredeemable: in order to be effective, action must be well targeted, but being well targeted, it cannot but leave out of sight everything around the target – more often than not, inviting utterly unpleasant repercussions'.

63. A. Walter Dorn, 'The Cloak and the Blue Beret: Limitations on Intelligence in UN Peacekeeping', *Journal of Intelligence and Counterintelligence*, 12, 4 (winter 1999–2000), pp. 422–5.

64. T. Trevan, *Saddam's Secrets: The Hunt for Iraq's Hidden Weapons* (London: HarperCollins, 1999), pp. 89–91, 143.
65. Turner, *Secrecy and Democracy*, pp. 280–5; W.E. Colby, 'Reorganizing Western Intelligence', in C.P. Runde and G. Voss, *Intelligence and the New World Order* (Bustehude: International Freedom Foundation, 1992), pp. 126–7.
66. 'To the extent prudent, US intelligence today is ... being used in dramatically new ways, such as assisting the international organizations like the United Nations .... We will share information and assets that strengthen peaceful relationships and aid in building confidence' (*National Security Strategy of the United States* (Washington: White House, January 1993), p. 18).
67. *Words to Deeds: Strengthening the U.N.'s Enforcement Capabilities, Final Report* (UN Association of the USA, December 1997), p. 20.
68. For example the Brahimi Report (Report of a Panel on UN Peace Operations, August 2000), on the proposed UN Information and Strategic Analysis Secretariat (pp.65–75).
69. The UK created its Assessments Staff in 1968. What was originally the Canadian Joint Intelligence Committee became the Intelligence Assessment Staff. Recently the intelligence-producing part of the British Defence Intelligence Staff became the Defence Intelligence Assessment Staff.
70. Public Record Office CAB 163/6, report dated 10 January 1945.
71. Thus the French statistics developed in the eighteenth century were 'secret and linked to the royal prerogative' (A. Desrosières (tr. C. Naish), *The Politics of Large Numbers: A History of Statistical Reasoning* (Cambridge, MA: Harvard University Press, 1998), p. 28.

2

Intelligence and Diplomacy[1]

Diplomacy gradually became more 'respectable' in the twentieth century, but still retained connections with intelligence. Since this paper was published the succession of spy cases and related diplomatic expulsions has continued. Diplomacy and intelligence are both competitors and collaborators.

Governments inform themselves through intelligence as well as diplomacy. The two interact and sometimes compete; indeed intelligence has been described as a new 'anti-diplomacy'.[2] This paper outlines intelligence's character; describes the boundaries between it and diplomacy; and discusses the relationships between the two. The 'intelligence' considered here is mainly Western-style, though some of its features apply more widely, for example to Soviet intelligence and its Russian successor. 'Diplomacy' is here taken to include both diplomatic representation overseas and the institution of the national Foreign Offices and Foreign Ministries to which diplomats report and which in large measure they staff.

MODERN INTELLIGENCE INSTITUTIONS

Evolution

Intelligence can be regarded loosely as 'information'; diplomats used to speak of reporting 'political intelligence', and newspapers gave 'racing intelligence'. However, it is by no means the whole of governments' knowledge or information-gathering. Government intelligence describes the specialized organizations that have that name, and what they do and produce. This circular definition is unavoidable unless intelligence is equated with all governmental information and its collection and handling.

The evolution of intelligence as a separate institution is a phenomenon of the last century and a half. Of course governments have always collected 'intelligence' as 'information', with diplomacy providing some of it for more than the last four centuries. States have always also had a sub-category of 'secret intelligence'. Walsingham, the Elizabethan Secretary of State, is usually regarded as the first identifiable British intelligence chief, running his agents to penetrate Catholic threats to the monarchy at home and over-seas. In the first half of the eighteenth century Britain had an agent network covering French and Spanish naval bases. In the same century the growth of diplomacy led all European countries to have their so-called 'Black Chambers' for intercepting and deciphering foreign diplomatic correspon-dence. Trying to read each other's mail became a support for diplomacy everywhere, as it has remained ever since.

However, intelligence barely existed over these centuries in the modern sense of permanent, professional institutions, separate from diplomacy and Foreign Offices. Diplomats were expected to run their own secret agents as part of their normal information-gathering and political action; but, except through diplomacy's overt and covert collection, information-gathering was relatively uninstitutionized and *ad hoc*. Armies and navies needed intel-ligence in war, but did not have systematic collection or permanent intelligence departments in peacetime. Kings, ministers and generals ran their own agents and evaluated their reports as a normal part of statecraft. The concept had not yet evolved of specialist intelligence staffs geared to producing information and forecasts.

This pattern changed after the middle of the nineteenth century, mainly for military reasons. The new technologies of the industrial revolution produced new forms of war, in which armies and navies needed pre-planning based on stores of information about potential enemies and their railways and topography. Permanent military and naval intelligence depart-ments were established in Britain in the 1870s and 1880s and in America in the 1880s; rather earlier in Continental countries. At first these did not impinge on diplomacy's position. Embassies provided information on foreign forces through their military and naval attachés. Military intelli-gence in the Victorian age of glasnost operated mainly on a mixture of these reports and public information, plus some gentlemanly travelling and spying by officers on leave.

Nevertheless secret intelligence grew in the late nineteenth and early twentieth centuries. The rate of technical and operational change in mili-tary capabilities increased, and the 'timetable war' of planned mobilization and deployment increased the value of getting 'the plans' of potential opponents; on both counts states became more secretive. Late in the day by

Continental standards, the British Secret Service Bureau was formed in 1909 for espionage and counterespionage. The First World War subsequently magnified the scope for espionage, and the victory of Communism in Russia gave it a long-lasting peacetime importance and link with ideology and subversion.

The First World War also saw two technological developments: radio interception or signals intelligence, following the introduction of radio; and the application of airborne photography. The Second World War was even more an intelligence war, particularly with the scale of Western successes in breaking enemy ciphers. The early years of the Cold War then saw intelligence collection develop on a quite unprecedented peacetime scale, even further increased by the introduction of American and Soviet satellite surveillance in the 1960s. Coincidentally the Cold War also made diplomacy less valuable in antagonists' monitoring of each other. Western embassies in Moscow existed in a kind of quarantine, and reciprocal restrictions were imposed on Soviet Bloc diplomats in the West. The diplomatic right of 'freedom of movement and travel' became increasingly circumscribed by limitations in the interests of the receiving states' 'national security'.[3]

Two features of intelligence analysis also came to the fore over the same period. First, total war (and subsequent policy-making on the Soviet threat) needed total intelligence, not restricted to military matters, on the adversary as a whole and all his national capabilities. Second, national grand strategy in both war and peace needed intelligence presented for efficient top-level decision-making. British assessment by the Joint Intelligence Committee (JIC) and the similar post-war American machinery for producing National Intelligence Estimates (NIEs) developed the concept of bringing all relevant information together in an interdepartmental consensus over its interpretation, and presenting the results as a basis for policy deliberation, so that Cabinets, ideally, would argue about what should be done and not about the underlying intelligence. One of the differences between the Axis and the Western allies in the Second World War was that the Axis had no systems of this kind. Much the same applied to the Soviet Union throughout the Cold War, as is perhaps still the case in Russia.

Thus intelligence became part of the twentieth-century growth of government. Britain now spends rather more on intelligence than on diplomacy, and about a twentieth of the cost of defence. America spends more, both absolutely and proportionately: very much more than on diplomacy, and about a tenth of its defence budget – a high figure which reflects American budgetary conventions over tactical military intelligence, and also the heavy costs of intelligence satellites.[4] France has had a considerably expanded intelligence programme since the Gulf War.[5] The overall effect is that diplomacy's traditional task of knowing foreign countries is now shared by intelligence as a complementary and potentially rival institution, of comparable weight to diplomacy in Western Europe, and greater weight in America. As Sir Reginald Hibbert, a retired British diplomat, described the result: 'secret intelligence, from being a somewhat bohemian servant or associate of the great departments of state, gradually acquired a sort of parity with them.'[6]

Components and Characteristics

This world of intelligence institutions – in English-speaking countries, the 'intelligence community' – has evolved with two interlocking components. The first is *collection* by special means, seeking information not otherwise available. This is 'covert intelligence' or 'secret intelligence' – from spies, radio interception, code-breaking, covert photography and the like. Intelligence collectors include the British Secret Intelligence Service (SIS) and Government Communications Headquarters (GCHQ), and in America the CIA's Directorate of Operations (for human sources) and its Directorate of Science and Technology (for advanced technical collection), the National Security Agency for signals intelligence, and the National Reconnaissance Office and National Imagery and Mapping Agency for imagery satellites. The essence of these single-source organizations is that they are experts on their particular techniques.

The second (much smaller) component is the *evaluation* of reports from different secret sources against each other, and against non-covert ones: press reports, radio broadcasts, diplomatic reporting and all the other information at governments' disposal. Its object is to provide the best available picture and make the best possible forecasts. All this is the activity of all-source analysis, and putting the output to decision-takers as finished intelligence. Secret intelligence is only a part of this totality, and does not necessarily have to be an ingredient. Thus all-source organizations like the British Defence Intelligence Staff and JIC, and the American Defense Intelligence Agency and the CIA's Directorate of Intelligence, are experts on particular subjects, sometimes foreign countries as a whole. In the same way, military commanders' intelligence staffs everywhere are their experts on the foreign forces with which they have to cope.

In the West these two aspects of intelligence have often evolved as separate organizations, and sometimes in tandem, as in the CIA's development as both a single-source collector and an all-source analysis agency. But there is almost always a barrier of some kind between the two; thus even in the CIA its collection and analysis are virtually separate organizations. Hence the English-speaking countries have developed the concept, with some influence on Western intelligence as a whole, of intelligence as a two-stage process of single-source collection followed by all-source analysis, with the implicit principle that intelligence collectors should not have the responsibility for final assessment. This is quite contrary to what was the KGB's view of intelligence, as covert, single-source information fed direct to policy-makers – perhaps still the philosophy of its successor, the SVR.

Intelligence in both its single-source and all-source aspects has also evolved since 1945 as a multinational activity. The USSR depended on its Warsaw Pact subordinates for about 30 per cent of its espionage. Elsewhere the Anglo-American and Commonwealth intelligence alliances and exchanges are well known, but after 1945 the Cold War and international terrorism each produced many other international intelligence connections. In the present decade the increasing volume of international action over Iraq, Bosnia, nuclear proliferation and similar subjects will have extended the scope of such exchanges. Arguably intelligence with its extensive and growing international networks is becoming an inchoate international system in its own right, alongside diplomacy.

INTELLIGENCE–DIPLOMACY BOUNDARIES

Functions and Methods

Like any other governmental activity, intelligence has untidy and sometimes artificial institutional boundaries. But the separation from diplomacy is reasonably clear; clearer for example than between intelligence and military 'combat information' and Electronic Warfare on the battlefield. Diplomacy and its international legitimization go back to the Renaissance and the Treaty of Westphalia, and have always linked the dual activities of information-gathering on the one hand and foreign policy formation and execution on the other. Intelligence as a separate institution is more modern, and has no more than tacit international recognition. Apart from its small and specialized component of covert action, its essence is providing information and forecasts for others to act on. Unlike diplomacy, it is not a decision-taking and executive institution.

In practice there is usually a separation between the intelligence and diplomatic professions. Modern technical intelligence collection – by Sigint and similar methods – is no part of the diplomat's curriculum vitae. Even where embassies contain intelligence officers running human sources under diplomatic cover, no one in the know confuses the two professions. There are exceptions, particularly when intelligence officers become major players in political relationships with their host countries. But on the whole diplomats are the 'front door' people in the international system, while intelligence officers of all kinds go figuratively (and sometimes actually) up the back stairs. Diplomats are insulted if labelled as intelligence collectors; and international intelligence relationships, however important, are usually veiled in a decent obscurity.

This diplomatic–intelligence separation is in fact a relatively recent development. A general assumption from the Renaissance onwards was that diplomats were licensed spies and would recruit their own secret agents, and this lasted until at least the first part of the nineteenth century. Even in the subsequent years of Victorian rectitude the British Foreign Office was not above obtaining Russian documents by bribery; Salisbury wrote in 1875 that 'we receive pretty constantly copies of the most important reports and references that reach the Foreign Office and War Office at St. Petersburg'.[7] No doubt some diplomats, in some countries, still indulge in covert collection of this kind. Even Canada incorporates an 'Interview Division' as part of its Department of External Affairs; though there is no suggestion that this covers anything more than seeking information in Canada (albeit on a confidential basis) from travellers, refugees and similar non-covert sources.

Nevertheless, over the last two centuries the distinction has gradually evolved in diplomatic convention and protocol between acceptable and unacceptable methods of acquiring knowledge, and was encapsulated in the 1961 Vienna Convention's definition of a purpose of diplomacy as including ascertaining conditions in the host country *by all lawful means*.[8] Though these means have never been defined, it is usually fairly clear in practice where diplomacy stops and covert intelligence starts.[9] Diplomats cast their net widely in seeking information, but usually avoid infringing their host countries' laws; or at least think seriously before so doing. Even where questions of legality do not arise directly, potentially useful contacts with oppositions and dissidents may be off-limits to diplomats; so too may developing useful sources among the seamy sides of local life.

Intelligence officers on the other hand are less restricted in their contacts, and can use means denied to diplomacy. Even in Soviet embassies, genuine diplomats left agent-running and recruitment to their KGB and GRU colleagues. From his experience of British diplomacy Hibbert offered the generalization that about 50 per cent of a diplomatic mission's information comes from the public sources of the host country; 10-20 per cent from confidential contacts by virtue of a diplomat's special position; and 20-25 per cent from indiscretions and leaks of one kind and another; but he differentiated this last category from the remaining 10 per cent or so of covert intelligence, characterized by him as information *bought and sold* from local sources, or otherwise obtained though professional intelligence work.[10]

Overlaps between intelligence and diplomacy exist, and will be discussed later. Nevertheless an essential difference between the two types of information-gathering is conveyed in Hibbert's description. Diplomatic sources may be confidential, but are not clandestine, and the same applies to the methods used to develop them. Unlike intelligence, diplomacy's acquisition of knowledge is an overt activity, notionally open to permanent surveillance, and employs methods which its government is prepared to defend publicly. In the present British government's terms, it is consistent with an 'ethical' foreign policy.

Subjects

If the difference in functions and methods between single-source intelligence and diplomatic information-gathering is reasonably clear, the distinction between intelligence's and diplomacy's subject matter is more clouded. Intelligence collection adds to the sum of government knowledge from other sources, including diplomacy. But for authoritative, all-source appraisals governments look to diplomats and Foreign Offices on some things, and to all-source, finished intelligence on others. Whom do they rely on for what?

Often the answer is clear. Diplomats are not experts on foreign armed forces, insurrections or mixtures of regular and irregular fighting as in Bosnia. Intelligence carries special weight wherever violence, military power and secrecy are involved, as on current subjects such as armed conflicts, terrorism, international arms exports, nuclear proliferation, clandestine operations by foreign governments, and other inputs to 'security policy'. But the position is more open when governments need political or politico-economic assessments. Intelligence studies Ruritania; but so also does the Foreign Office, the State Department and their equivalents elsewhere. Diplomats and Foreign

Ministries are the natural foreign experts, and in the daily decisions in foreign policy they make their own interpretations of all the information to hand; international affairs could not be conducted otherwise. But on some matters, and for some decisions, governments seek more authoritative assessments and look to all-source intelligence for them. Especially if secret material is involved, intelligence assessment has then an authority that overrides departmental interpretations linked with policy commitments. If the assessment is interdepartmentally produced and agreed, it also helps to keep different Ministers and their departments in step.

The general effect of this duality is for intelligence to be one of the modern specialist institutions that limit Foreign Offices' hegemony. Where all-source intelligence assessment is influential, intelligence ceases to be seen as just an input to diplomacy; on the contrary, diplomatic reporting becomes valued as an intelligence ingredient. Things have changed from the time before the Second World War when the British Foreign Office could object to the formation of the JIC on the grounds that it (the FO) was the only authority for assessing foreign countries. As Hibbert, commenting on the present position of the Foreign Office and Treasury, put it:

> There is now an invisible force exercising a certain pull on these great bodies [the FCO and Treasury], in much the same way as stars and planets invisible to the naked eye or even through telescopes can be deduced by astronomers to be influencing the courses of visible heavenly bodies, bending them from the trajectories that might be expected on the basis of visible data. The invisible force is exerted by the joint intelligence and assessment machinery in the Cabinet Office.[11]

The same can be said even more forcibly of the influence of the CIA *vis-à-vis* the State Department.

Thus intelligence and diplomacy are to some extent competing. Certainly they compete for national resources, though perhaps not very actively; Congress does not seem to compare the value of the State Department's information-gathering with the CIA's, and Britain has no established machinery for weighing the annual intelligence and diplomatic budgets against each other. But in the main their information-gathering is complementary, and the basic intelligence/diplomacy relationship is not competitive, but is that of producer and customer. Intelligence produces foreign knowledge for which, at least in peacetime, diplomacy is one of its major customers and users.

There are also other, less straightforward links between the two institutions. Diplomacy makes use of intelligence's international relationships, but at the same time it reflects them; intelligence and diplomacy influence each other. Diplomacy also provides intelligence facilities, but at the same time constitutes a target for foreign intelligence attacks. Additionally, despite the general separation of intelligence and diplomatic functions and methods, there are institutional and operational overlaps of various kinds. These various connections are examined in the following survey.

INTELLIGENCE–DIPLOMACY RELATIONSHIPS

Diplomacy as an Intelligence Customer

Little needs to be said here of intelligence as an input to foreign policy-making at the grade of top-level strategy, where national and international security are involved.[12] Throughout the Cold War, Western policies were driven (though to varying extents) by intelligence assessments of Soviet objectives and policies and East–West military balances, and by specific intelligence on Soviet activities. Policy-makers look to intelligence for objective and accurate evaluations and forecasts, free of policy preconceptions. Intelligence may fail through reinforcing policy-makers' received wisdom, through its own preconceptions or through one of the many other causes of intelligence failure; or policy-makers may just ignore it.[13] But in failure as in success it is one of the major elements on which foreign policy draws.

However – rather less obviously – intelligence also assists diplomacy at a more tactical level. Hibbert suggested that secret intelligence's addition to diplomatic information is mainly of confirmatory value:

> It is very rare for it to contradict what has already been deduced from non-secret information. Its great virtue is often that it gives immediacy, practicality and focus to general conclusions which have already been reached. Secret and top secret intelligence mostly has value only for very short periods. It tells you what is intended tomorrow or next week, not in the longer term. It gives you the negotiating ploy at the next meeting or the initiative which is to be launched next month. Its value is usually tactical: strategy depends more on the picture put together from the broader, non-secret, general intelligence material.[14]

Elsewhere this contribution of single-source material has been valued in terms of 'calibrating' policy-makers' judgements reached by other means. If intelligence has helped Britain to 'punch above its weight' in the second half of the twentieth century, this contribution has been tactical as well as strategic; perhaps even more so.

Diplomacy is also an intelligence customer in a quite different way: as the recipient of threat assessments and technical advice for diplomacy's defensive security measures. Diplomatic people, premises and communications have long featured as intelligence targets. Eighteenth-century ambassadors could be suborned by their receiving governments.[15] Embassy ciphers are traditional intelligence targets; thus Christopher Andrew has recounted how a British ambassador in St Petersburg between 1904 and 1906 complained of the way his staff were being bribed by the Russian Okhrana to hand over diplomatic ciphers, to the extent that 'emissaries of the police are constantly waiting in the evening outside the Embassy in order to take charge of the papers procured'.[16] Intelligence attacks on embassies and their staff, using agent penetration, entrapment or other means of recruitment, and electronic attacks and other bugging, became a well-publicized part of the Cold War.

Modern nations worry about having their ciphers broken, their embassies bugged or otherwise penetrated, and their diplomatic staff recruited as hostile agents; no government wants a public scandal over its diplomacy's defensive arrangements. Intelligence collection therefore also serves its own nation's diplomacy as the offensive poacher turned defensive gamekeeper, assessing threats, setting diplomatic security standards and bringing counterespionage and counterintelligence to bear on foreign penetration.[17] In this, again, diplomacy is an intelligence customer.

Intelligence as a Diplomatic Factor

Diplomacy mobilizes or exploits national assets in the formation and execution of policy; intelligence is one of them. National reputations for good intelligence carry international weight. The United States' possession of unrivalled intelligence, particularly from satellites, is accepted as an element in American hegemony and the influence that springs from it. British diplomacy similarly gains from being thought to be well informed on a worldwide basis. A nation's record of good or bad security, reflecting the quality of its defensive intelligence, has a similar influence; West Germany's penetration by East German espionage throughout the Cold

War was always a factor in limiting its admission to the most sensitive Anglo–American counsels within NATO.

In more specific ways, intelligence may be a national requirement – a second-order 'national interest' – of sufficient importance to influence foreign policy, or at least need handling at a diplomatic level. America's need for interception sites around the periphery of the USSR was one factor in the bargains struck with host countries for the creation of its worldwide system of Cold War alliances and bases. One element of the post-1945 UK–US 'special relationship' (though only one of many) was the UK's position as convenient 'real estate' for intelligence facilities within range of the Soviet Bloc and its activities. Surveillance facilities of value to the US as well as the UK were also a significant factor in the British decision to retain the Sovereign Base Areas in Cyprus when the island was granted its independence in 1960.

Similarly the provision of intelligence support and intelligence facilities can be cards in the diplomatic hand: part of a bargain, or a political signal, or a means of influence on its own account. US supplies of real-time satellite imagery are said to have been part of the price of keeping Israel from entering the Gulf War. America has provided intelligence reports as a security and confidence-building measure as part of Middle East peace settlements.[18] Similarly it disclosed intelligence to both India and Pakistan in 1990 as a means of dissuading them from drifting into war; the former Deputy Director of Central Intelligence (and future DCI) of the day, sent by the US President to see the leaders of both countries, recalls that 'the card I played heavily was that I was not a diplomat but an intelligence officer by training and that the reason I was there was that the American government, watching the two sides, had become convinced that they were blundering towards a war and that they [might] not even know it'.[19] Britain moved quickly after the collapse of the USSR to establish liaison on security intelligence matters with the new Central and East European governments, partly for professional intelligence reasons (particularly exchanges on terrorism) but also for political influence, *inter alia* through advice 'to help them establish a democratic framework for their [intelligence] work'.[20] In the same way withdrawing supplies of intelligence can be a means of punishment, as in the American withdrawal from some intelligence services to New Zealand after its banning of port calls by US warships carrying nuclear weapons.

There is also a more subtle interaction between intelligence's own overseas relationships and the wider political–diplomatic ones in which these are set. Like other professional exchanges, intelligence's liaisons have some insulation from international politics. The transatlantic exchanges of intelligence survived the Anglo–American breach over the Suez invasion of 1956; intelligence relationships between Britain and the Old Commonwealth were barely affected by the British entry to the EEC and the subsequent move towards the European Union. On a wider canvas, Soviet espionage in the Cold War was sufficiently widespread to encourage counterespionage cooperation between unlikely allies.

Yet intelligence rarely operates as a completely free agent; political alignments set the general context of its liaisons. In their scope and intimacy these relationships reflect foreign policy; contrary to liberal mythology, British intelligence collaboration with South Africa under apartheid was severely inhibited by political considerations. Intelligence relationships reflect foreign policy in this way, but also influence it. The UK–US intelligence alliance is seen as one of the benefits flowing from the Atlantic pillar of British policy, but is at the same time one of its powerful supports. At one level the intelligence relationship brings a variety of professional and political benefits to both parties. At a different level, its intelligence-sharing reinforces the general similarity of world views that in turn underpins the political alliance. An open question about the Cold War is who was the transatlantic persuader, and who the persuaded. Arguably the same question can be applied to intelligence-sharing throughout NATO.

It should be added that intelligence can also be an agent of foreign policy in more specific ways, reinforcing diplomacy or sometimes as an alternative to it. Covert action is usually a small, specialized aspect of Western intelligence activities; but it is one of the mechanisms at government's disposal, over the wide spectrum from undeclared political influence to the clandestine use of force, and colours worldwide perceptions of the CIA, as well as the KGB. Similarly intelligence can be a back-channel for inter-government communication and negotiation, as when Jim Callaghan as Prime Minister asked SIS to ensure that the Argentine government were aware of his undeclared naval movements to protect the Falklands in 1977.[21]

Embassies as Intelligence Bases

The position of diplomats and their premises as targets for foreign intelligence services has already been noted. Its counterpoint is the role of embassies as professional intelligence bases. After diplomats ceased to recruit and run their own human sources, specialist agent-runners and recruiters began to use diplomatic cover for the purpose. After the First World War the British Secret Intelligence Service (SIS) operated under the cover of Passport Control Officers at diplomatic and consular posts, and other countries operated in similar ways. In the Cold War the extensive Soviet deployment of KGB and GRU officers under diplomatic cover was well attested; Britain expelled 105 such officers from London in 1971, and of the 20 Soviet civilian diplomats in Copenhagen in 1966, 14 were intelligence officers.[22] The Cold War also saw embassies used as electronic collection bases; the Soviet Union was said to have such operations in some 60 diplomatic premises in the 1980s, and comparable American operations in Moscow and elsewhere have received some publicity.[23] One way and another, embassies in the Cold War came to resemble medieval castles – under a kind of intelligence siege, but with their sallyports manned for operations in the midst of the besiegers. From the incidence of diplomatic expulsions in recent years it would seem that embassies' associations with intelligence have not ceased.

Overlaps in Intelligence Assessment

Intelligence and diplomacy are institutionally separate, yet there are overlaps of various kinds. Though diplomats – or at least genuine diplomats representing well-behaved regimes – do not participate in covert collection or covert action, a feature of the British system is the considerable part played by diplomats in all-source intelligence assessment. The Foreign Office chaired the JIC for many years, and has tended to dominate it. After the Falklands War the chairmanship was made a non-departmental Prime Ministerial appointment to encourage independent judgement, but those appointed in this way were ex-diplomats – a former Permanent Under Secretary remarked that 'Mrs Thatcher removed one Foreign Office chairman only to replace him by another from the same source'[24] – and in recent years there has been a reversion to the main feature of the previous practice.[25] Apart from the JIC chairmanship, the Chief of the Assessments Staff has almost always been a Foreign Office secondee, with a powerful Foreign Office element among his staff; and Foreign Office representatives attend all levels of the JIC's interdepartmental process. Commonwealth countries vary in the extent to which they follow these practices, but an active or seconded diplomatic presence of some kind is a feature of most of their assessment arrangements.

Those who interpret government in terms of bureaucratic politics can see the British arrangement as the Foreign Office's means of containing the threat posed by the JIC – by capturing it. Be that as it may, the influence of the (non-intelligence) Foreign Office in the (intelligence) JIC process helps to ensure that its output is accepted as a genuine interdepartmental product. More important, by tapping diplomacy's professional foreign knowledge it increases assessment's chances of being right. It contrasts in these ways with the small part that the Foreign Service professionals in the State Department seem to play in the American intelligence assessment process.

It is true that the British practice introduces problems of balance. Though they are trained observers of many things, diplomats do not have good track records in perceiving threats of surprise attack. (Military men on the other hand are given the stereotype of producing 'worst case' assessments of foreign capabilities, for the good reason that they have to bear the brunt if situations go wrong; it has been said that the British system works because the military overestimate threats and the diplomats underestimate them, though reality is more complex.) Too much diplomatic influence may also overemphasize the 'policy-relevance' of intelligence assessments, perhaps discouraging 'inconvenient' papers which do not fit policy-making assumptions and timetables. Nevertheless the intelligence/diplomatic linkage is a fact in the British system and less formally in some others; surely it is a strength.

Overlaps and Dual Roles in Embassies

Intelligence's 'diplomatic cover' in embassies conceals operations quite separate from diplomacy. Yet in the nature of things there is some overlap between covert intelligence collected in this way and normal embassy information-gathering. Covert sources developed by intelligence using this diplomatic cover may overlap with diplomats' own more confidential ones; it may sometimes be accidental whether a line of information gets handled as sensitive diplomatic reporting or covert intelligence. Even where this does not apply, intelligence officers may contribute to normal embassy coverage through perfectly overt contacts and discussions while acting out their diplomatic cover.

There are also the situations in which the local intelligence and security authorities are a key part of the host country's governing regime. The intelligence liaison with them – if there is one – then becomes a key part of the political relationship, indispensable for accurate embassy assessment and reporting. Understanding the regime and influencing it may then depend on the intelligence relationship rather than orthodox diplomacy.

These are however overlaps between institutionally separate activities. Military and other defence attachés on the other hand are genuinely of two worlds, combining their diplomatic status and representational functions with potentially important intelligence roles and allegiances. Military and naval attachés were appointed in the course of the nineteenth century essentially as information-gatherers; the first of them was appointed by Prussia in 1817, and British attachés' appointments began after the Crimean War.[26] In the relatively open conditions of that century their information-gathering was largely by non-covert means, though they ran agents when necessary. With the increased military secrecy of the early twentieth century they made more use of covert methods. In the special conditions of the Cold War, attachés indeed operated in the Eastern and Western blocs virtually as full-time licensed spies, and unscheduled observation of the host countries' forces was their highest priority. The long-standing connection of military attachés with intelligence is indeed recognized in the Vienna Convention's stipulation that nominations for them are subject to the agreement of the receiving country, a provision that applies to ambassadors but not to other diplomats or other specialist attachés.[27]

Yet the connection with intelligence is very variable; in many overseas posts the requirement to report on local forces is unimportant compared with military liaison and export promotion. Even in the extreme conditions of the Cold War, attachés steered clear of recruiting spies; their intelligence collection consisted primarily of observations. These often entailed defying local regulations and surveillance intended to prevent them, with attachés pushing their luck against the risk of being declared *persona non grata* (PNG); but the threat of being declared PNG exercised some curb upon the risks taken and methods used. Though sometimes an embarrassment to diplomats (and sometimes restrained by them), the attachés retained their position as part of institutionalized diplomacy.

In the far more open post-Cold War world their observation has fewer connotations of covert intelligence-gathering (though the activity or suspicions of it remain, as when US officers were declared PNG by China in 1995 for observing military installations),[28] but attachés' value as licensed observers remains, as contributors not only to intelligence analysis but also to international openness and confidence-building. Indeed at a time in which the British Defence Secretary has cited 'defence diplomacy' as a growing armed forces' commitment, the scale of military liaison with diplomatic status may increase. It may be a pointer to the future that the national military inspection teams created through the arms control and confidence-building treaties of the 1980s and 1990s are protected by the Vienna Convention.[29]

CONCLUSIONS AND REFLECTIONS

Intelligence and diplomacy share an objective: seeking knowledge and understanding of foreign countries. But they have evolved as separate institutions, with rather different perceptual lenses; only the defence attachés retain institutional links with both of them. For intelligence, information and understanding (plus the presentation of the results to users) are sought as ends in themselves; for diplomacy they are adjuncts to policy and action. Intelligence and diplomatic information-gathering differ in most of their methods, and even in the use of human sources they operate under different conditions and constraints.

The information outputs of intelligence and diplomacy are often complementary, though intelligence includes coverage and expertise on matters such as warning, military forces, war, limited conflict and terrorism, in which diplomacy is not geared to specialize. In general terms, top-level foreign policy formation leans on intelligence, rather than purely diplomatic assessment, when the subjects have a 'national security' content.

Despite their common functions of information-gathering and building up knowledge, the principal relationship between intelligence and diplomacy is of producer and customer. Diplomacy uses intelligence not only for strategy but also for tactics, as well as in the specialized area of its defensive security. But this primary producer-customer relationship is accompanied by a variety of subsidiary interactions, influences and overlaps. Intelligence as a national institution and international system has some weight in its own right, but is by no means insulated. Diplomacy uses national intelligence capabilities as an element in power and influence, a card in the negotiating hand; sometimes on the other hand it needs to negotiate to meet intelligence needs. Diplomatic and intelligence relationships with foreign countries interact, usually reinforcing but sometimes modifying each other.

Given the expansion of intelligence in the last half-century relative to diplomacy, two questions arise over the alignment of the two institutions. One is whether there should be greater separation between them. Diplomacy provides intelligence cover and facilities, and is an intelligence target, hence needing defensive intelligence support. Arguably some distancing between intelligence and diplomacy is desirable, at least to the extent that the association between them (and the targeting of foreign diplomats and premises) should be kept within reasonable limits, and not expanded to a renewed Cold War scale.[30]

The other question is how far intelligence should be seen as diplomacy's rival: the 'anti-diplomacy' cited at the beginning of this paper. It is part of the regimes and government systems it serves, and gets its character from them. With its role of defending the Soviet system against enemies at home as well as overseas, the KGB was active as a foreign policy-maker, as in its influence in the final decision to invade Czechoslovakia in August 1968.[31] Soviet diplomacy overseas was always in competition with Soviet intelligence's use of diplomatic accreditation and premises, with the KGB's and GRU's presentation of material their officers had routinely gathered, through their diplomatic cover and local press, reading as if it were the specially authoritative product of secret agents and 'confidential contacts'. Intelligence was in effect a powerful rival to diplomatic reporting. In this as in other things the Soviet regime got what it wanted.

By contrast the record of English-speaking intelligence, and indeed Western intelligence as a whole, is of only limited competition with diplomacy. It is true, especially in Washington, that intelligence attracts resources and attention that diplomacy might otherwise have commanded; and that some of those making American foreign policy have chosen to work through CIA's Directorate of Operations and not through the State Department. It is also true that some DCI's have had full Cabinet status; that one (Casey) pursued policies of covert action with a very personal imprint; and that the position of the CIA has been one factor in the decline of the State Department. CIA Heads of Station overseas have sometimes operated virtually as alternative Heads of Mission. The competitive nature of American foreign policy-making has no doubt encouraged these roles at times. Yet considering intelligence's strength and status, the attractiveness of covert action and the fluidity of American policy-making and execution, the overall record of the CIA is of considerable restraint. One of the most unjust verdicts on it is that it was a 'rogue elephant'; as the critic in the 1970s who coined the phrase (Senator Church) admitted shortly afterwards, the real rogue elephant had been in the White House.[32] It has not consistently sought to become either a policy-maker or a diplomatic system in its own right.

The restraint has applied even more in the different conditions of the UK. There has never been a 'Minister of Intelligence' who could become a rival in foreign policy, and two historical accidents have caused intelligence to remain under Foreign Office influence to an extent not found elsewhere – in the USA, France, Germany or Israel, for example. The first was the post-1918 reorganization whereby the SIS (and, with it, GCHQ's predecessor organization) became vested under Foreign Office control.[33] The second was the Foreign Office's assumption of the chairmanship of the JIC in 1939, even though the committee was (and remained) basically an armed forces' sub-committee of the Chiefs of Staff. Intelligence has never been regularly represented in Whitehall's interdepartmental executive machinery at an official level, and has never sought to develop as a alternative to diplomacy.[34]

Of course it has not been devoid of policy influence. The Head of SIS had some weight with the Prime Minister as a policy adviser in the years just before the Second World War, and at the time of the Munich crisis his service produced an important policy paper with the title 'What should we do?' as the 'views of SIS', advocating ceding the Sudetenland to Hitler.[35] Heads of Agencies still have a ritual 'right of access' to the Prime Minister, though it is doubtful whether they use it to influence foreign policy. At all levels a close producer/customer relationship can and should involve discussion of policy and policy options. Additionally, covert action and back-channels are available to Ministers as complements to diplomacy or alternatives to it. But there is no evidence that British intelligence has sought to make foreign policy, even in the 1980s when the Prime Minister was at loggerheads with the Foreign Office.

British readers take this for granted; yet it is surprising in the light of modern intelligence's budgets and status. However often it is quoted, the dictum that 'knowledge is itself power' has not actually guided intelligence's institutional development. Its professionals have developed and maintained a professional ethic akin to that of statisticians and other information experts, not that of diplomats or others who exercise power or advise on its use. This is one of Britain's important intelligence legacies, to some extent to the West as a whole, certainly to the Commonwealth, and – most crucially, and with occasional reservations – to the United States.

NOTES

1. Published as 'Diplomacy and Intelligence', *Diplomacy and Statecraft*, 9, 2 (July 1998).

2. J. Der Derian, *Antidiplomacy: Spies, Terror, Speed, and War* (Oxford: Blackwell, 1992).

3. For the basis of these rights and restrictions see Vienna Convention on Diplomatic Relations (1961), Article 26.

4. For British figures see Chapter 4.

5. Ibid.

6. R. Hibbert, 'Intelligence and Policy', *Intelligence and National Security*, 5, 1 (January 1990), p. 115.

7. J. Ferris, 'Lord Salisbury, Secret Intelligence, and British Policy toward Russia and Central Asia, 1874–1878', in K. Neilson and B.J.C. McKercher (eds), *Go Spy the Land: Military Intelligence in History* (London: Praeger, 1992), p. 129.

8. Vienna Convention on Diplomatic Relations (1961), Article 3, part 1.

9 It is interesting that the 1963 Vienna Convention on Consular Relations reproduces the reference to ascertaining conditions and developments 'by all lawful means', but qualifies these conditions and developments as in the 'commercial, economic, cultural and scientific life of the receiving state' (Article 5). There is no reference to military matters, though the convention authorizes 'any other functions entrusted to a consular post' provided that they are 'not prohibited by the laws and regulations of the receiving State or to which no objection is taken by the receiving State'.

10. Hibbert, 'Intelligence and Policy', p. 112.

11. Ibid., p. 117.

12. Discussed in M.E. Herman, *Intelligence Power in Peace and War* (Cambridge: Cambridge University Press, 1996), Parts III and IV.

13. For intelligence failure see Herman, *Intelligence Power*, Chapters 13 and 14.

14. Hibbert, 'Intelligence and Policy', p. 113.

15. For an example see J. Black, 'British Intelligence and the Mid-Eighteenth Century Crisis', *Intelligence and National Security*, 2, 2 (April 1987), p. 216.

16. C. Andrew and O. Gordievsky, *KGB: The Inside Story of its Foreign Operations from Lenin to Gorbachev* (London: Hodder and Stoughton, 1990), p. 11.

17. Discussed in Herman, *Intelligence Power*, Chapter 10.

18. Details in Herman, *Intelligence Power*, Chapter 9.

19. C. Andrew, *For the President's Eyes Only* (London: Harper Collins, 1995), pp. 516–17.

20. S. Rimington, *Security and Democracy – Is There a Conflict?* (Richard Dimbleby Lecture 1994) (London: BBC Educational Developments, 1994), p. 5.

21. For this episode (still not fully explained) see A. Danchev (ed.), *International Perspectives on the Falklands Conflict* (London: Macmillan, 1992), pp. 138–9; and J. Callaghan, *Time and Chance* (London: Collins, 1987), p. 375.

22. O. Gordievsky, *Next Stop Execution* (London: Macmillan, 1995), p. 152.

23. D. Ball and R. Windrew, 'Soviet Signals Intelligence (Sigint): Organization and Management', *Intelligence and National Security* 4, 4 (October 1989), p. 621. For press and other claims about American operations see J.T. Richelson, *The US Intelligence Community* (Third edition. Boulder: Westview, 1995), pp. 191–2.

24. D. Greenhill, *More by Accident* (York, England: Wilton 65, 1992), p. 126.

25. The last few chairmen had been Foreign Office officials on temporary secondment to the Cabinet Office's Overseas Secretariat, doubling until 2000 responsibilities

for policy coordination in the Cabinet Office with JIC chairmanship. For criticism, see Sir Percy Cradock, *In Pursuit of British Interests* (London: Murray, 1997), pp. 46–7. Cradock himself, and his immediate successor, combined the chairmanship with acting as the Prime Minister's Foreign Policy Adviser, but this interesting arrangement has not been continued. For a change in 2000 see Chapter 5.

26. P. Towle (ed.), Introduction, *Estimating Foreign Military Power* (London: Croom Helm, 1987), p. 86.

27. 1961 Vienna Convention, Article 7, discussed in M. Hardy, *Modern Diplomatic Law* (Manchester: Manchester University Press, 1968), p. 28.

28. *The Times*, 24 February 1995.

29. Stockholm Document (September 1986), repeated in subsequent CFE documents. Note however that in the Cold War the British Military Mission (BRIXMIS) to the Soviet forces in East Germany operated with no reference to diplomatic immunities (except for its couriers and dispatch riders). The Robertson–Malinin agreement of 1946 under which it operated provided the missions with reciprocal rights of 'freedom of travel' (with qualifications) and immunity for their buildings, but not with the range of other diplomatic immunities.

30. Herman, *Intelligence Power*, pp. 370–5.

31. See *Cold War International History Bulletin*, Issue 3 (Washington: Woodrow Wilson International Center, fall 1993), pp. 6–8. KGB influence in the Soviet invasion of Afghanistan in 1979 is discussed in Issues 8–9 (winter 1996–97), pp. 128–32.

32. Andrew, *For the President's Eyes Only*, p. 421.

33. F.H. Hinsley with E.E. Thomas, C.F.G. Ransom and R.C. Knight, *British Intelligence in the Second World War*, Vol.I (London: HMSO, 1979), p. 17.

34. Though see Note 25 about the position of recent JIC chairmen.

35. C. Andrew, *Secret Service: The Making of the British Intelligence Community* (London: Sceptre edition, 1986), pp. 561–2.

3

Intelligence and the Revolution in Military Affairs[1]

The lessons of the subsequent Serbia/Kosovo air campaign have not outdated the issues discussed in this paper: the challenges of new technology to traditional military divisions between 'int' and 'ops'; the limitations posed by concentrating on the provision of real–time situational pictures; and the need to maintain the objective of getting inside the mind of the enemy.

There is an extensive literature on the so–called Revolution in Military Affairs, the RMA. The revolution is held to rest partly on the new capabilities for the use of precision weaponry and control of one's own forces (in military terms, 'Blue'), but also – and perhaps more significantly – on a technological transformation in the gathering, processing and exploitation of information on 'Red': the enemy and his environment.[2] Commanders have always complained of intelligence's inadequacies, echoing Shakespeare's 'Oh where hath our intelligence been drunk; where hath it slept?'[3] The extreme RMA enthusiasts now envisage a new 'system of systems'[4] providing world surveillance, which 'should enable those with the appropriate tools and organizations to know everything all the time and, when necessary, take appropriate action with precision–guided weapons'.[5] According to *The Times*, 'the battlefield has given way to "battlespace", dominated by air power and intelligence'.[6]

Yet the practical implications remain unclear. Will RMA simply make military intelligence more effective, or does it posit some new, twenty-first century institution to replace it? What actually is the nature of the Red knowledge assumed in the concept of an RMA; does it embrace all intelligence or just a part of it? This is an attempt to examine these related questions.

INTELLIGENCE AND INFORMATION

RMA writings refer variously to 'information' on the enemy and 'intelligence', and do not seek to distinguish consistently between the two. They recognize that intelligence is not the totality. The literature cites different information sources – intelligence, surveillance and reconnaissance (ISR,[7] or ISTAR in British official documents where target acquisition is included) – but does not differentiate between them; sensibly so. Military doctrine sometimes portrays intelligence as a distinctive kind of knowledge:

> Collected data becomes information when processed into usable forms such as reports or images. This information is transformed into intelligence by purposeful analysis, interpretation and collation with related information and background to meet the specific needs of the user.[8]

But this is crude epistemology, and a distortion of usage; first-line reports from air photo interpreters and Sigint stations are still intelligence reports, even though they are far removed from authoritative assessments. Usage also blurs distinctions between intelligence and the other sources, sometimes with deliberate euphemisms. American satellite intelligence collection is planned and controlled by the National Reconnaissance Office; and in recent years the UN has taken to using 'information' to describe 'intelligence' in all UN-controlled operations. Language is still further confused when (non-intelligence) surveillance, target acquisition and reconnaissance become 'intelligence' if their output is incorporated into intelligence staffs' all-source analysis and output; as indeed it sometimes must be.[9]

In this semantic muddle the starting point is to regard intelligence simply as information, and to see the distinction between it and the other elements of ISR/ISTAR in the first instance simply as an institutional one, a matter of subordination. Surveillance, target acquisition and reconnaissance come under operational control and meet immediate operational needs; feeds to intelligence are a bonus. Intelligence on the other hand is a separate institution, existing to collect information by specialized means and to meet decision-takers' needs for a much wider variety of purposes. As a circular definition: intelligence comprises the organizations with that name, and their activities and product.

Despite this institutional identity there has never been a clear gulf between intelligence and the product of other sources. Intelligence is part of an information-gathering continuum without sharp edges. A description of politicians' relationships with government information officers has some resonance with the actual dividing-lines between intelligence and the rest of ISR/ISTAR: 'The boundaries ... are better compared with the disputed Amazonian frontier between Ecuador and Peru: no map, no agreement where the border runs at all, a no-man's-land of huge proportions, dense undergrowth and millions of trees.'[10] A visitor to a frigate's operations room sees some sources labelled 'intelligence' while others are 'electronic warfare' or 'action information', without obvious differences in output. He may conclude that the demarcation lines mark no more than the results of intelligence's turf battles with other information gatherers, and on some things he would be right.[11]

Yet this is only a partial view. Intelligence has evolved as a specialization with genuine rationales. Thus,

1. in *content*, the operational sources have tended to provide simple, factual, and largely current 'What? Where? When?' information about the enemy. Intelligence collection, although also providing much of this, has usually had some richer content, particularly through putting different sources together;

2. in *immediacy*, intelligence has been characterized in the past by some human processing and analysis, and hence delay compared with the 'action information' provided by operational sources such as radar. Thus Electronic Warfare is officially distinguished from Sigint by providing information directly and immediately for 'threat detection, warning, avoidance, target acquisition and homing' and other use in the electromagnetic battle;[12]

3. in *sources and methods*, those of SR/STAR have usually been well-known and robust; those of intelligence have tended to be esoteric, covert, susceptible to counter-measures, and hence fragile and needing the protection of secrecy;

4. on *location*, long-range technical sources have tended to develop under intelligence control, while battlefield devices have gravitated towards Ops rather than Int, particularly when they directly drive strike assets;

5. in *expertise*, intelligence has evolved with a unique role as the authority on the enemy, seeking to understand him in depth, as the expert assessor, the forecaster, the reader of the entrails.

There are exceptions and overlaps, and intelligence in all its variety is not marked by all these features; thus POW interrogation and the study of captured documents and equipment have no special sensitivity, but are intelligence specializations nevertheless. But the institutional boundaries are not capricious. Intelligence's turf has been most clearly marked historically from others' by fragile (and hence secret) collection methods, human analysis, veins of relatively rich content, and 'enemy' expertise – all contrasting with the other simpler, more automated and immediate sources.

TECHNOLOGICAL BLURRING

Yet technology is now obscuring boundaries. Computers are reducing the human element in intelligence collection, and intelligence satellites can now provide information for immediate operational use, even in automated sensor-to-shooter modes. The writers on RMA draw on satellites and other forms of Comint (communications interception), Elint ('non-communications' interception, typically of radars) and imagery and make no distinction between the three and the multitude of other, non-intelligence collection systems in operation or envisaged. They emphasize multi-sensor steerage and integration: 'The most significant technical improvements are occurring in our ability to cross-cue the different collection mechanisms, integrate the flows of information from various sensors, and process the information they collect.'[13] So removing old boundaries between intelligence and operational sources might seem a natural part of the RMA concept and the technology that drives it.

One writer, Martin Libicki, has indeed argued for the integration of all Red information-gathering, and perhaps also data on Blue, through the formation of a separate Information Corps to 'facilitate effective joint operations, promote the information revolution in warfare, unify the disparate information elements and give them an identity, create a common ethos for information warriors, and provide a unified interface with civilian information infrastructures'.[14] Military intelligence might thus revert to its earlier, nineteenth-century role of military information and planning, before it came to specialize in 'Foreign Armies'.[15] In a similar vein Major General Roberts has argued that 'people currently associated with handling information will need re-skilling', referring to the new professional skills of Information Manager, Cyber-Librarian and Web-Master, though without precisely identifying the effects on intelligence.[16]

The customary objection to this integration is the special protection of intelligence's sources and methods, with all that this has meant for secrecy and ring-fences. The impression that all intelligence needs exceptional treatment has been encouraged by various influences: the special Ultra channels of the Second World War for safeguarding code-breaking successes; Washington's endemic leakiness in the Cold War which led to a proliferation of special intelligence restrictions; the tendency (at least in Britain) for Elint to attract the mystique of Comint; the secrecy associated with all satellite intelligence, even after the original political impetus for it had lapsed.[17] But of course the real choice has never been between special intelligence protection and complete transparency; the bulk of intelligence has been adequately protected by normal secrecy markings plus disguising its sources. Recent moves away from excessive secrecy over satellite collection were summarized by the responsible member of the US Administration in mid-1998: 'The NRO [National Reconnaissance Office] is now nearing completion of a security reengineering, which has significantly reduced the classification of the overhead product. Today, over 99 per cent of this operational data is available at the SECRET level for direct use by the warfighter.'[18] Source protection no longer means that all intelligence has to be kept out of the RMA melting-pot. A more important question for the relationship between intelligence and the rest of ISR/ISTAR is whether the RMA concept implies that they produce the same kinds of knowledge about the enemy, or different and complementary ones.

KNOWLEDGE OF RED AND ITS OPERATING ENVIRONMENT

Here one gets an impression of two different mental models in the RMA writers' minds. The first, dominant one is of RMA as an all-source technological telescope, providing geo-positional displays of current situations, including movement from radar sources, and television from special surveillance devices. (It is not clear how far this model counts on near real-time imagery interpretation; images distributed electronically to commanders still have to be interpreted by someone. 'A single surveillance satellite on a 15 minute pass produces enough material to occupy 100 analysts with conventional tools for a week.'[19] Presumably it is thought that automatic target recognition will speed up processing dramatically.) The emphasis is on seeing and *pictures* (as in the military 'recognized ground picture'), as a geospatial view of the world. Commanders and subordinates will have 'a shared timely *image* of the battle' (emphasis added).[20] RMA at this level has been summed up by Admiral Owens as 'accurate, real-time situational awareness'.[21]

This awareness is to be achieved by automation. Technological improvements provide 'leaps in the ability to transfer information, imagery and other data to operating forces in forms that are immediately usable'.[22] Human judgement is not excluded, but it is perhaps the judgement of Ops rather than Int. 'Computers do some things "better" than humans .... The role of staffs will significantly diminish.'[23] RMA will 'put the commander back in command'.[24] He will once again 'see' the battlefield himself, with a modern equivalent of Napoleon's and Wellington's *coup d'oeil*, or the maritime legend of Drake's Magic Mirror seeing over the horizon.[25]

On the other hand Owens has been at pains elsewhere to present RMA as a means of providing knowledge of a different, deeper kind. He explained in 1998 that 'situational awareness' had been postulated only as a step towards the deliberately chosen aim of 'dominant battlespace knowledge'. 'Awareness means, roughly, being able to locate, identify, and track major items of military equipment and units, while knowledge connotes the ability to relate such activity to each other and to operational schemes.'[26] And in the same article: 'Knowledge comes from combining the awareness of what and where things are with other information indicating the relationships among, and relative significance of, those things.'[27] Battlespace knowledge was still 'largely an issue of intelligence skills, processes, vision, and, ultimately, courage [to adopt changed methods]', including changes from intelligence's 'painting' of data to 'sculpting' it.[28]

Clearly this is something more subtle than the telescope or Magic Mirror. Information is not only displayed; it is interpreted, presumably with a major input from artificial intelligence linked with data-handling. The implication is that it will deepen intelligence's traditional understanding of the enemy and bring it into real time. One RMA writer claims in this vein that 'DBK [Dominant Battlespace Knowledge] moves us into a world where many decisions can be made with something approaching perfect knowledge'.[29]

Yet this more ambitious version of RMA is an indistinct vision and, sadly, one's reaction is to believe it when one sees it. To venture an analogy from the British National Health Service: computers and communications there are indeed promoting 'accurate, real-time situational awareness' by making complete histories of individual cases immediately available, but the use of artificial intelligence to revolutionize medical human diagnosis (the equivalent of 'battlespace knowledge') is still at quite an early stage. It seems realistic for the moment to see RMA as the first model – accurate situational awareness through displays – rather than the deeper version.

This may nevertheless require some re-drawing of boundaries, to integrate real-time or near-real-time intelligence collection with the other means of locating, identifying and tracking major military equipment and units. If not a new and all-embracing Information Corps, RMA as the telescope/mirror would seem to need at least an 'RMA Czar' to coordinate or control all the real-time ISAR/ISTAR feeding into it, including intelligence. His writ would not extend to non-real-time intelligence, though this intelligence would continue to support the non-intelligence components of ISR/ISTAR in the ways it always has: Electronic Warfare (EW) depends on Elint intelligence to define the hostile radar parameters that EW software is programmed to recognize, and the target recognition features used in imagery recognition have to be identified in the first instance by human photo-interpreters. Information Warfare (IW) similarly needs intelligence's assessments of the enemy's C4I (command, control, communications, computers and information systems) vulnerabilities and the IW threats he poses to oneself.

Intelligence's relationship with RMA may therefore consist partly of integration into a new organization for real-time situational awareness, and partly of providing non-timely support for this activity. This is however only part of the picture, since one other different kind of intelligence still needs to be reconciled with the RMA concept.

INTELLIGENCE'S DUALITY

It is striking that RMA's explanations of enhanced collection and processing are all in terms of the identification and location of 'things'; even Owens' deeper vision of dominant battlespace knowledge is based on making inferences from evidence of this kind. Yet this ignores intelligence's duality. Much of it, whether immediate or long-term, is of the category that fits RMA; the observation/measurement intelligence that sees objects or measures aspects of them, like the rest of ISR/ISTAR. But a second, different category focuses on minds rather than things. It seeks access to its targets' thought and meaning, or to their own flows of information about themselves. Its raw evidence is language, not observations. No agreed terminology has yet been developed, but this category can be labelled 'textual' (or 'message-like') intelligence. 'Communication intelligence' might be a better term, but would be equated too comprehensively with electronic Comint to the exclusion of other linguistically based sources.[30]

The differences between these two categories of intelligence resemble those between archaeology and conventional historiography.[31] Archaeologists discover and measure artefacts and physical traces, while historians base themselves on documents and other human recollections. Both contribute to historical truth, but in different ways. A distinguished classical scholar has commented that, despite the inferences that an archaeologist can draw from his material, he suffers from a major drawback if there are no written records: 'His people are dumb... [he] then is in much the same position as the interpreter of aerial photographs: his information is hard fact, but its interpretation is often difficult and conjectural.'

Thus imagery is observation/measurement intelligence *par excellence*, with the strengths and limitations of archaeology. Non-textual Sigint is similarly based on the measurement of radio signals, as in Elint's analysis of the technical characteristics of radars, the location of transmitters by Direction Finding, and some aspects of Traffic Analysis. The same applies to the other material categorized by the Americans as Measurement and Signature Intelligence (Masint). Intelligence of all these kinds stays figuratively 'outside' its targets, collecting and analysing their 'externals'; studying bodies rather than minds.

On the other hand the textual or message-like evidence from intercepted radio messages, line-tapping, bugging, eavesdropping and computer hacking consists of texts, or records of conversations; the evidence is essentially linguistic. Like historical documents, it touches on targets' 'internals'. Some of this textual intelligence conveys thoughts, attitudes, intentions, commands and policies, or provides other insights into minds. Other textual material is more factual, producing 'inside' information from the target's own information stock. Getting into the opponent's C4I can give access not only to his thinking but also to his locations, inventories and the other information he needs to communicate. The breaking of Axis ciphers in the Second World War illuminated enemy capabilities as well as intentions; deciphered daily returns on German tank strengths and fuel stocks were the basis of successful British Desert War generalship.[32] Textual sources can therefore be richer than the observation/measurement ones; access to enemy minds can give situational awareness a third dimension. Precisely for this reason the textual sources have a high priority for targets' countermeasures, and need the protection of secrecy.

TEXTS IN RMA

Textual sources are not mentioned in RMA discussion and seem to play no part in its concepts. The real-time telescope/mirror shows objects; it does not, cannot, display targets' thoughts and other intangibles, and it is unlikely to detect what is deeply concealed or silent. Technology will give the RMA commander excellent observations and measurements, from which he can draw inferences about the future; but he will still have the limitations of an archaeologist without texts to anchor his hypotheses to reality. The commander will be well sighted, but in some degree deaf and illiterate in assessing his enemy. Nothing is allowed in RMA for the prize of textual intelligence straight from the horse's mouth.

To some extent this shows a healthy realism. RMA's proponents probably assume that textual sources cannot be counted upon, certainly not in near real time. They may also value the relative usability of observation/measurement intelligence, compared with the security protection needed for textual successes.

Nevertheless it is strange to ignore the textual sources completely. Dominant battlespace knowledge has existed on occasions in the twentieth century, but it has usually turned on code-breaking successes. Moreover RMA doctrine combines a 'best case' view of technology's ability to observe and measure with a 'worst case' view of the prospects of textual exploitation. It is assumed that observation/measurement attacks will increase their edge over defensive 'stealth':

> The contest between stealth and anti-stealth will be long and drawn-out, but again the betting has to be against stealth for any platform large enough to encompass a human.... Thus even with stealth, everything ultimately can be found. All objects have mass and thus gravity. Every object moving in a medium creates vortices and must expend energy doing so. If nothing else, objects of a certain size have to occupy some space for some time.[33]

Yet the conventional forecast for textual sources is the reverse, with defence outstripping the intelligence offence. Thus,

> The computer and communications technologies on which the system-of-systems are based are becoming less, not more, susceptible to the various forms of information warfare. A race will probably always exist

between those who seek to ensure the security of information-based systems and those who seek to overcome their security measures. Yet, the trend favors effort to increase, not degrade, security.[34]

Similarly,

> The privacy and authenticity of personal communication is likely to improve.... Thanks to digital telephony, public-key cryptography, and free silicon, secure digital communications will need but one cheap phone chip. Encryption will be so easy as to be norm. Such encrypted messages will be unbreakable by any supercomputer. Eavesdropping would have to take place at the source or the destination but not in between. Intercepting signals intelligence as a way of figuring out what the other guy is doing will soon be useless.[35]

In summary, 'Sooner rather than later the use of public-key encryption and digital signatures will limit our ability to exploit (other than detect) such radio-frequency or any other communications'.[36] The assumptions about stealth and anti-stealth are not the subject here, but the forecast about textual sources needs examination.

TEXTUAL PROSPECTS

Despite the secrecy surrounding textual intelligence, five points can be made. First, the balance of advantage between devising codes and ciphers and breaking them has always fluctuated between attack and defence. Outcomes are likened by David Kahn to an organism's biological dichotomy between seeking information about the outside world and minimizing the information available about itself; the two imperatives are incompatible, yet survival depends on a balance between them.[37] From the Renaissance onwards, users' belief in the invulnerability of their security systems has been as often misplaced as justified. The German conviction in the Second World War that the Enigma cipher was unbreakable is only one of a long line of historical examples.

A second historical conclusion is that cryptanalysts tend to do better than initial assessments suggest, perhaps because there are greater incentives to break others' ciphers than detect weaknesses in one's own. Perfect security needs a dictator's ability to enforce rules by terror combined (impossibly) with a free society's ability to question the rules' effectiveness and suggest better ones. Moreover cryptanalysis is not a pure science; it has always 'cheated' where it can, by suborning cipher clerks, capturing foreign cryptographic material, or using any other means to hand. Opportunities of this kind exist in both war and peace. The belief that modern encryption devices are all fool-proof, traitor-proof (or bribery-proof) and selected by rational actors with perfect information, has echoes of Fukuyama's equation of the end of the Cold War with the End of History. Equally relevant are the attempts by Western governments to control the spread of high-quality devices and retain access and influence. None of this guarantees cryptanalytic success. It tends to come less from attrition – though this has its place – than from finding defensive gaps and exploiting them with maximum opportunism. To apply military typology, success is sequential rather than cumulative.[38] As in war, there is an important element of luck.

Third, the cryptanalytic successes of the Second World War have diverted attention from another historical lesson about textual material: the yield to be gained from studying apparently unrewarding clear texts and conversations in depth. Telephone tapping in the trenches in the First World War stimulated the analysis of enemy conversations. British blockade intelligence in the two World Wars drew on the analysis of normal commercial telegrams. Intelligence on the German economy for the Bomber Offensive from 1941 onwards was drawn largely from German newspapers, despite Nazi censorship. R.V. Jones's account of intelligence on the German V-bomb programme illustrates the deductions to be drawn for apparently innocuous documents.[39] Western success in the Cold War in analysing unenciphered telemetry transmitted by Soviet missiles is now a matter of public record in connection with SALT II.[40] Against this background it seems unrealistic to assume that the provision of effective encryption devices will catch up with the needs of an information-hungry world, wedded to speedy communication and maximum use of bandwidth.

Fourth, textual insights are not confined to material from technical intelligence sources. Documents can be acquired from agents, or from the debris of military forces; the British Military Mission to the Soviet Forces in East Germany successfully raided Soviet rubbish dumps for this purpose.[41] Contact with the enemy's mind is also made through defectors, deserters and POW interrogation. Special Forces observe and place observation devices; they could equally well engage in line-tapping, snatching prisoners for interrogation (as in trench raids in the First World War) and seizing cryptographic material (for which special teams were deployed in the Second World War). Other direct action is also sometimes needed to make this material available. Thus cutting the enemy's cables can force him to use radio, as was the effect of some Gulf War bombing and special forces' operations. These methods seem far removed from RMA, yet its technology might have applications. The faxing of snatched documents immediately by Satcom might be a hypothetical illustration.

Finally, there is the question of timeliness. Textual sources (clear or decrypted) will probably not be automated completely. But the Second World War demonstrated that the dream of near-immediate decryption was sometimes realizable, with great effect. Computers have increased the strength of communications security, but still hold out the possibility of real-time decryption successes, and automated translation/transcription aids do something to remove the language barrier in processing foreign texts.

CONCLUSIONS: A BALANCED RMA CONCEPT

Technology may well be providing a revolution in commanders' information about the enemy and the battlespace. If orchestrating and fusing collection as it is now developing needs some re-drawing of boundaries between intelligence and the rest of ISR/ISTAR, then so be it. Whether the new Information Warriors needed for the job would be retreaded intelligence officers or a new breed of specialist is an important matter, but not a crucial one.

But we need to be clear about the kind of knowledge upon which discussion of the RMA is centred. The case for it as 'situational awareness' is convincing, if taken as real-time, all-source displays of the location and sometimes movement of enemy military equipment and units: a major enhancement of commanders' ability to see battlefields and run battles. But claims that the 'system of systems' provides the deeper kind of 'dominant battlespace knowledge' are less impressive – partly because it is not clear exactly what is being claimed, but more particularly since they appear to be based entirely on one kind of information: the observation/measurement of objects, and not the sources that provide access to the target's mind. RMA displays will give the commander the situational awareness that comes from 'seeing', but they will not give him the understanding that comes from hearing or reading the enemy's own data and communications.

In this way US satellite imagery in the Cold War produced excellent intelligence on Soviet military hardware, but remained unilluminating about Soviet motivation. The West had good observations of Iraqi military deployments before the invasion of Kuwait, but remained puzzled about Saddam Hussein's intentions. Even in the Gulf War, the observation/measurement sources were admirable for bombarding static targets but lacked direct 'inside' information to calibrate the battle damage assessments made from imagery. General Horner has described how, elsewhere in the war, the high technology of AWACS radars and moving target indicators could mislead:

> Having the data and understanding what it means are two disparate areas which are often confused.... We inject our own biases into an analysis of intent and our own abilities into measuring the potential adversary's capacity to succeed. The Gulf War is replete with our failures to understand the enemy, to dissect him with the clarity needed to discover his intentions and capabilities.[42]

How much more would this have been the case in mobile land warfare, or at sea and in the air, or if the enemy had had the initiative?

Of course many inferences can be drawn from objects, locations and movements, and technology may well find ways of making these inferences more powerful and reliable. But resting claims of dominant battlespace knowledge solely upon knowledge of this kind seems over-confident and at the same time rather myopic in neglecting intelligence's potential for providing high-grade, direct insights from its message-like sources. Which would have been of greater value to Admiral Jellicoe as night fell during the Battle of Jutland: better sighting reports on the enemy's course and speed (on which he was badly served by his Fleet throughout the confused battle), or a better service from the Admiralty of the German decrypts which provided conclusive evidence of Scheer's intention to escape via the Horns Reef channel?

Two conclusions follow. One is that the collection and exploitation of textual information of all kinds should be given a place in the concepts of RMA, and in the national investments influenced by them. It would be odd if, in a world of burgeoning information and communication everywhere, military doctrine were to solidify around observing and measuring objects, to the exclusion of exploiting targets' own information and communication systems. There is no guarantee of hitting cipher-breaking jackpots. Yet observation and measurement are incomplete without textual inputs of some kind.

Hence the second conclusion: the need for caution about RMA as information dominance and perfect knowledge. Technology promises miracles of ISR/ISTAR collection, processing and presentation, but still at the two-dimensional level dictated by objects. Even with proper attention to the future of textual sources, understanding targets will remain a serendipitous and unpredictable business, with no insurance against error. Despite the reservations here, one applauds the concept of an RMA, but shudders at the aura of infallibility in which it has been presented. It seems a standing invitation to the punishment of hubris.

NOTES

1. Published as 'Where Hath Our Intelligence Been? The Revolution in Military Affairs', *RUSI Journal*, 143, 6 (December 1998), with minor amendments here.
2. In intervention operations the target is now often 'the foreigner' and his area, not necessarily 'the enemy'; but the 'Red' information discussed here covers 'White' and 'Grey' information on foreigners and foreign environments. For a list of the relevant systems involved in the RMA see Admiral Owens' Introduction to S.E. Johnson and M.C. Libicki, *Dominant Battlespace Knowledge* (Washington DC: National Defense University, 1996 edition), p. 3.
3. From *King John*, quoted by R.V. Jones, 'Scientific Intelligence', *RUSI Journal*, 92, 567 (August 1947), p. 352.
4. J.S. Nye Jnr and W.A. Owens, 'America's Information Edge', *Foreign Affairs*, 75, 2 (March/April 1996), p. 28.
5. M. Van Crevald, *A Revolution? What Revolution?* (Paper at the Royal Institute for International Affairs, London, 23 May 1997), p. 2.
6. Leader, 9 July 1998.
7. Nye and Owens, 'America's Information Edge', p. 23.
8. Chairman Joint Chiefs of Staff, *Joint Vision 2010* (Joint Chiefs of Staff, Washington DC, 1997), p. 13. *British Defence Doctrine 1996* refers (3.9, 4.12–14, 6.22) to the need for 'information and intelligence', without distinguishing between the two. In its Glossary (G.7) 'intelligence' is 'the product resulting from the processing of information, both overt and covert, concerning foreign nations, hostile or potentially hostile forces or elements, or areas of actual or potential operations'. Information is defined (G.6) as 'all the knowledge needed by a commander and his force, including intelligence on the enemy, knowledge of own forces, weather, geographic data, etc'.
9. For example, part of improved British intelligence performance in North Africa after mid-1942 was in getting British units' operational 'enemy reports' copied more promptly into intelligence channels (F.H. Hinsley with E.E. Thomas, C.F.G. Ransom and R.C. Knight, *British Intelligence in the Second World War* (London: HMSO, 1979-89), Vol.2, p. 410).
10. Matthew Parris, *The Times*, 24 June 1998.

11. Dating at least from the First World War, when there were intensive cap-badge battles between the British Artillery and Intelligence Corps over who should run 'Artillery Intelligence' for targeting. The artillery won, and was careful that those posted to the job were called 'reconnaissance officers' and not 'intelligence officers'. (B.G.S. Bidwell and D. Graham, *Fire-Power* (London: George Allen and Unwin, 1982), p. 104). Similar issues have arisen in long-running doctrinal disputes since 1945 between Sigint and Electronic Warfare.

12. NATO, *Intelligence Doctrine* 1984, Definitions, p. A-4.

13. Admiral Owens, 'Intelligence in the 21st Century', *Defense Intelligence Journal*, 7 (spring 1998), p. 28.

14. M.C. Libicki, *The Mesh and the Net: Speculations on Armed Conflict in a Time of Free Silicon* (Washington, DC: National Defense University, 1995), p. 69.

15. For the evolution of military intelligence see M.E. Herman, *Intelligence Power in Peace and War* (Cambridge: Cambridge University Press, 1996), pp. 16–19.

16. Major General W.J.P. Roberts, 'Implications of Information Age Operations', *RUSI Journal*, 142, 5 (October 1997), p. 33.

17. For President Kennedy's original reasons for secrecy, to avoid provoking public Soviet protests, see J.L. Gaddis, 'The Evolution of a Reconnaissance Satellite Regime', in A.L. George and others, *US–Soviet Security Cooperation* (Oxford: Oxford University Press, 1988), p. 357.

18. K.R. Hall, 'Leading Intelligence in the 21st Century: The Role of Satellite Reconnaissance', *Defense Intelligence Journal*, 7, 1 (spring 1998), p. 14. Mr Hall was writing as Director of the National Reconnaissance Office and Assistant Secretary of the Air Force for Space.

19. Roberts, 'Information Age Operations', p. 39.

20. J. Cooper, 'DBK and Future Warfare', in *Dominant Battlespace Knowledge*, p. 99.

21. Nye and Owens, 'America's Information Edge', p. 27.

22. Ibid, p. 24.

23. D. Alberts, 'The Future of Command and Control with DBK', in *Dominant Battlespace Knowledge*, p. 85.

24. Owens, Introduction, *Dominant Battlespace Knowledge*, p. 20.

25. 'It was a belief of the old Spaniards that Drake had a magic mirror in which he could see all the movements of his enemies and count their numbers' (quoted from Sir Julian Corbett and applied to Nelson as 'The Admiral's Mirror' by A. Bryant, *Years of Victory* (London: Collins, 1944, p. 113)).

26. Owens, *Defense Intelligence Journal*, 7, 1 (spring 1998), p. 28.

27. Ibid, p. 30.

28. Ibid, p. 40.

29. Alberts, 'The Future of Command and Control with DBK', p. 84.

30. David Kahn has independently suggested 'physical intelligence' and 'verbal intelligence' for the two categories ('Towards a Theory of Intelligence,' *Military History Quarterly*, 7, 2 (winter 1995), pp. 92–7).

31. The analogy with archaeology and historiography is developed in Herman, *Intelligence Power in Peace and War*, Chapter 5. The quotation is from J. Chadwick.

32. R. Bennett, *Ultra and Mediterranean Strategy* (London: Hamish Hamilton, 1989), p. 46.

33. Libicki, *The Mesh and the Net*, p. 30.

34. Owens, *Dominant Battlespace Knowledge*, p. 9.
35. Libicki, *The Mesh and the Net*, pp. 140–1.
36. Libicki, 'DBK and its Consequences', p. 26. For British measures to develop a secure 'Public Key Infrastructure' see Roberts, 'Implications of Information Age Operations', p. 37.
37. D. Kahn, *The Codebreakers* (London: Sphere Books edition, 1973), p. 455.
38. M.C. Libicki, *Defending the Cyperspace and Other Metaphors* (Washington: National Defense University, 1997), p. 70, quoting Admiral J.C. Wylie.
39. R.V. Jones, *Most Secret War: British Scientific Intelligence 1939–1945* (London: Hamish Hamilton, 1978), pp. 332–48.
40. Herman, *Intelligence Power in Peace and War*, pp. 161–2.
41. S. Gibson, *The Last Mission: Behind the Iron Curtain* (Stroud: Sutton, 1997).
42. General C.A. Horner, *Operating in the Emerging Age: The Recent Reality* (paper at the Royal Institute for International Affairs, London, 23 May 1997), p. 2.

Part II

Living with the US:
British and Other Systems

4

British Intelligence in the New Century: Issues and Opportunities[1]

The recommendations here, inter alia, *for a positive attitude towards satellite collection and for more powerful central influence were subsequently echoed by the Parliamentary Intelligence and Security Committee in its Annual Report of November 2000.[2] The recent combination of the posts of JIC Chairman and Coordinator may be a move in that direction.*

British government's 'intelligence' is based on specialized intelligence organizations and their activities.[3] Their main output is 'foreign intelligence' – on a range of foreign affairs, including military and other external threats – plus 'security intelligence' on terrorism, espionage and other threats with covert and domestic components. Intelligence also contributes to the protection of government's information ('information security'), typically through personnel security and the protection of communications and information technology ('ITSEC'). The offensive role of penetrating foreign security defences is combined with acting defensively to protect national secrets; intelligence acts as gamekeeper as well as poacher.

In 1940 Winston Churchill provocatively asked how 'the Intelligence Service' was organized.[4] This 'Service' – or for the last half-century the 'intelligence community' – is based on four organizations.[5] Three of them are officially the 'intelligence and security services', or 'the Agencies', and are:[6]

- Government Communications Headquarters (GCHQ), the national agency for the production of signals intelligence (*Sigint*), from the monitoring of communications and other electronic emissions.
- The Secret Intelligence Service (SIS), producing foreign intelligence from human and technical sources.
- The Security Service which gathers, analyses and assesses security intelligence, as well as advising and acting upon it.

The fourth member is the Defence Intelligence Staff (DIS), which analyses defence-related intelligence for 'the Ministry of Defence (MoD) and the Armed Forces and other Government Departments'.[7] (Strictly speaking its Whitehall element is now the Defence Intelligence *Assessment* Staff – DIAS – but DIS remains the common usage and is retained here.) To weld the community together there is the interdepartmental machinery of the Joint Intelligence Committee (JIC), with the twin roles of coordinating intelligence assessment and community management. It is served by the Cabinet Office Assessments Staff and a Secretariat.

Four features are important for understanding this community. The first is the continuum between security intelligence and foreign intelligence. Terrorism is international, and even when home-based it almost always has international connections; like espionage and the other targets of security intelligence, it manifests itself overseas as well as at home, as threats to British forces, ships, aircraft, embassies and citizens abroad. It can be supported by rogue states or directly practised by them. Security intelligence is increasingly globalized. Nevertheless its responsibilities retain a domestic element of detecting covert 'enemies within' which distinguishes the Security Service's orientation from that of the other agencies.

Second, there is the basic difference between the 'single-source' collectors/exploiters (GCHQ and SIS) who are experts on their own techniques for producing covert intelligence, and the 'all-source' elements (the DIS and the JIC) who are government's experts on the particular *subjects* on which they produce finished intelligence.[8] GCHQ intercepts and exploits foreign communications, and SIS recruits and runs human sources. By contrast, the *raison d'être* of the DIS is the analysis and understanding of foreign military power using all available information. The JIC machinery operates on the same all-source basis, producing interdepartmental assessments and forecasts for the top level of government on 'events and situations relating to external affairs, defence, terrorism, major international criminal activity, scientific, technical and international economic matters'.[9] All-source work of this kind draws not only on covert sources but also on public material and official information such as diplomatic telegrams and military reconnaissance and observation.

The distinction between single- and all-source intelligence is by no means complete; thus the single-source agencies use other material as background in exploiting their own, and the DIS controls some of its own single-source collection and exploitation. Nevertheless there is a key difference between single-source and all-source responsibilities, between collecting/exploiting single-sources and producing finished, authoritative, all-source output. The Security Service in its own specialized area is also an all-source producer in this sense, as well as a collector.

The third feature is the institutional variation in status. The three agencies are self-standing, with Heads personally responsible to Ministers – SIS and GCHQ to the Foreign Secretary; the Security Service to the Home Secretary. Policy on them is kept under collective review by the Ministerial Committee on Intelligence Services (IS) and the Permanent Secretaries' Committee on the Intelligence Services (PSIS), chaired by the Cabinet Secretary, and their combined budgets form the Single Intelligence Vote (SIV). The Parliamentary Intelligence and Security Committee established by the 1994 Intelligence Services Act is also charged with reviewing their 'expenditure, administration and policy'.[10] The DIS on the other hand is one of MoD Central Staffs, managed as part of defence.

The fourth is the inadequacy of describing national intelligence solely in terms of this central community. Within the MoD, the military Chief of Defence Intelligence (CDI) is responsible not only for the DIS but also for 'the overall direction of intelligence within the *defence community*'[11] (emphasis added), including the 'strategic-level' resources of the armed forces. Chief among these is the Joint Air Reconnaissance Intelligence Centre (JARIC), the national centre for producing photographic intelligence (*imagery*). This had some post-war status under JIC supervision, but evolved as an MoD resource, controlled and tasked mainly by the DIS.[12] CDI also oversees the Military Survey Agency, with important intelligence components, and the Defence Intelligence and Security Centre, for training. [Subsequent changes are given in Note 3 on page 138.]

Also under armed forces' control are some expensive airborne assets which are nominally 'tactical' electronic collectors but are really of national significance, and at one time were budgeted as strategic intelligence.[13] There is also the military intelligence staff in Northern Ireland, and the staff at the Permanent Joint Forces Headquarters at Northwood, of growing importance in current arrangements for operations overseas; thus the effective use of intelligence in the Falklands War depended on an improvised Northwood staff of that kind, and not on Whitehall.

Additionally there are the military and civilian elements that have significant part-time or fringe intelligence roles, yet are not categorized as national intelligence resources. Armed forces' ships and aircraft may be engaged on temporary intelligence operations, or regular ones supplementary to their operational roles. The Security Service has close links with police forces'

Special Branches, and the Special Branch of the Royal Ulster Constabulary retains special responsibilities for Irish terrorism in its area, even though like other Special Branches it is also linked with police responsibilities for public order and other law enforcement. The JIC itself still has some subordinate coordinating machinery in British territories overseas. Most important of all, within the central community the Foreign and Commonwealth Office (FCO) plays a major part in the JIC assessment process, and the same applies, though less significantly, to other non-intelligence departments in Whitehall. In short, the central intelligence community is linked with an outer ring of other bodies, of varied degrees of size and central relevance.

There is nothing odd about the imprecision. All organization involves anomalies and imperfect boundaries, and these do not prevent intelligence from being a distinctive activity based on identifiable institutions. But it comprises rather more than just the central community. Hence this paper is concerned with the total *national intelligence capability*: the central community, plus the outer ring of those associated and subordinate activities which have more than merely local or tactical significance.

RESOURCES

This capability suffered considerable reductions at the end of the Cold War, and further contraction continued through the last decade, though more in people than in total costs. The 1996 Estimate for the three civilian agencies showed planned financial reduction by 3.25 per cent over the following four years, with manpower cuts over the same period of 13 per cent, from 9,642 to 8,366.[14] The 1999 Estimate and its forecasts for the next two years suggested that manpower was on a plateau at around 8,350 people. There appeared to be an upward trend in overall spending; £774 million for 1999/2000 was preceded by £730 million and £724 million in 1997/98 and 1998/99.[15] The figure available for 1996/97 for the DIS and other defence intelligence, shown as the CDI slice of the Defence Budget, was £152.6 million. The picture of present strengths used as a basis here is derived from a mixture of public data and working assumptions, and is as follows:

- A Sigint effort of about 4,500 civilians plus a considerable military effort, perhaps now of 2,000, all controlled from GCHQ.
- SIS and Security Service strengths in the region of 1,750 civilians in each.

- MoD (CDI) resources (1996/97) of 4,700 (3,100 uniformed and 1,600 civilian), of which the most important components are probably:
  ◊ the military Sigint manpower controlled by GCHQ.
  ◊ the DIS (or DIAS) with a military and civilian strength now of perhaps 500, mainly for all-source analysis but with some effort devoted to the control and support of the other defence intelligence.
  ◊ JARIC about 500 strong, divided on a 70:30 basis between military and civilians.[16]
  ◊ Military Survey, about 1,150 strong and roughly one-third military.[17]
  ◊ the Defence Intelligence and Security Centre.
- The current Cabinet Office effort (the Joint Intelligence Organization) of 50 in all, divided between the Assessments Staff and JIC Secretariat.

To these figures must be added the other armed forces' resources already referred to, plus the Special Branch officers linked with the Security Service.[18]

In all, the cost of the national intelligence capability to be discussed here can be assumed to be at least £1 billion annually. By comparison with the total intelligence budget, Britain spends significantly less on diplomacy, not quite twice as much on overseas aid, and over twenty times as much on defence.[19]

STATUS

In purely financial terms this effort is commensurate in some respects with intelligence in France and Germany, but there are significantly greater British efforts on Sigint and also, albeit on a much smaller scale, on imagery interpretation. British intelligence as a whole probably has a higher public standing than its opposite numbers in Continental Europe. In its combination of size and quality Britain is, uniquely, an 'upper second class' intelligence power in international terms, still with an unusual degree of world reach.

This work provides HMG with intelligence not only from its own efforts but also foreign liaison sources, and its value is the sum of the two; national investments in intelligence are in some respects subscriptions to a set of international clubs. Britain's high reputation for quality, reliability and source protection underlies its extensive foreign liaisons, but among these the relationship with the United States is paramount and unusually close. Hence the academic 'upper second class' analogy does not quite convey the effect of the UK's large-scale access to the output of the American intelligence superpower. To pursue the academic analogy: Britain enjoys postgraduate status without having paid all the fees. As recipients of national plus American intelligence, as well as the product of other foreign liaisons, British governments receive a quasi-superpower level of intelligence support: perhaps a last vestige of the *Pax Britannica*.

VALUE

Intelligence in an Unstable World

Intelligence as a substantial, permanent feature of Western states was a product of the Cold War, and throughout the 1990s there was substantial discussion of its future. Initially there was a tendency to dwell on requirements outside the traditional security field: not only economic intelligence but also environmental and other new international issues. Terrorism then appeared at centre-stage. For the first half of the decade the British community was also preoccupied with the scope for intelligence assistance to law-enforcement, particularly on drugs and other organized international crime. Over the last few years 'information warfare', including threats to the 'national information infrastructure', has been topical as 'a new form of combat',[20] relevant to terrorism and subversion as well as war between states.[21]

The thread through the 1990s has however been the intelligence challenges placed upon the turbulent post-Cold War world, including a nuclear-tipped, unstable and discontented Russia; all posing 'concerns' rather than threats as previously conceived. American writers have recently distinguished between new policy priorities: List A, threats to national survival (the Soviet Union in the Cold War); List B, threats to national interests but not survival; List C, 'contingencies' indirectly affecting national security without directly threatening national interests.[22] A senior British official some years ago put forward a comparable diagnosis that 'although the big threat has gone, the second order threats are proliferating. The chances of a second order threat turning nasty will be greater... Usually there will be no direct threat to Britain or the West, but not always.... Technology, communications, the media have transformed the world over the last 50 years.'[23]

For purposes of an intelligence strategy these features of the modern world can be taken as read, without translation into precise intelligence requirements and priorities. Some general points will suffice:

- There is a continuing need for covert intelligence on a wide range of issues. The modern world is indeed increasingly open, and covert sources less unique than during the Cold War; but the open sources are often incomplete and misleading. Deeply secretive regimes still exist, such as Saddam Hussein's Iraq, along with the wide and increasing range of opaque, often clandestine non-state targets like terrorist groups and illegal arms traffickers.

- Intelligence's ability to provide useful information continues to increase. Despite the international spread of encryption, the explosion in electronic communications provides ever-increasing intelligence access, and the technology of imagery and other means of surveillance continues to lead the countermeasures of 'stealth' and 'signature reduction'. On technical methods as a whole there is some hyperbole in the American claim of a move to 'a world in which the many kinds of sensors, from satellites to shipborne radar, from unmanned aerial vehicles to remotely planted acoustic devices, will provide information to any user who needs it';[24] but it does reflect something of modern technical intelligence's power. At the same time the world of increasing travel and migration – travel and tourism is said to have become the world's largest single industry[25] – provides increasing scope for developing and exploiting human sources.

- In quantitative terms the biggest intelligence requirement remains military intelligence in support of armed forces. Military forces in the variety of peace support and peace enforcement operations in Bosnia and elsewhere have needed virtually the full range of wartime intelligence support. Targeting intelligence is vital to exploit the power of precision weaponry. Whatever the limitations of the NATO air campaign, Kosovo reinforced the general lesson of the Gulf War that 'what can be seen on the modern battlefield can be hit, and what can be hit will be destroyed'.[26]

- Nevertheless the immediately valuable day-to-day application of good (mainly covert) intelligence is often geared not to military contexts but to 'diplomatic support' to national governments in their international interactions, irrespective of subject. A generalization of some years ago probably still applies, that intelligence sources add perhaps 10 per cent on the subject-matter of diplomatic reporting.[27]

- Despite this direct value of covert single-source reports, the basis of any sound application of intelligence to major decisions remains intelligence's all-source assessment. The relatively small resources engaged in this part of the process remain the main determinant of intelligence's overall cost-effectiveness.

On these foundations it is easy to make the general case for modern intelligence. For military commanders it is an integral part of the so-called Revolution in Military Affairs, but the revolution runs wider. International affairs as a whole are increasingly dominated by information and its speedy use, and intelligence has a firmly established place in this scene. But how much of it is needed by Britain? How important is the remarkable level of intelligence support that HMG receives, and the national effort that sustains it?

Intelligence and the UK's Role

Intelligence's value can sometimes be illustrated quantitatively, in terms such as saving and losing lives, avoiding and incurring physical damage, and financial and economic gains and losses. It was officially claimed before the 'peace process' that security intelligence has prevented four out of five operations planned by Irish terrorists,[28] and annual Defence White Papers gave tallies of terrorist explosives, weapons and ammunition seized. Effects on international negotiations can sometimes (though not often) be expressed quantitatively as the benefits of getting a good deal. Intelligence failures can sometimes be measured similarly. Intelligence warning of Argentine plans to invade the Falklands might have spared HMG the costs of the war and the subsequent capital and running costs of the permanent military garrison and airport; intelligence helped to win the war but failed to prevent it.

Yet the great mass of intelligence does not lend itself to cost-benefit calculation of this kind. Some of it can certainly be related to specific national commitments, threats and interests, as when intelligence requirements are based on British responsibilities for the security of its overseas territories and other specific overseas commitments. The requirements on Irish and international terrorism are clear enough, and these threats largely set the scope of the Security Service and its supporting resources from the other agencies. Something of the same applies to counterespionage and intelligence assistance to law enforcement.

But these are still relatively small demands on the total intelligence capability, and likely to remain so. The main expectations of intelligence are related to much broader aspects of policy. In the late 1980s it was asserted that 'British foreign policy since the war has seen successive governments attempting to maintain international responsibilities without the [material] resources necessary to meet them'.[29] Intelligence had been a constant if unpublicized support. Since the end of the Cold War Britain's improved economic position and heightened military reputation have reinforced the nation's view of itself as an influential world power, an international leader in the Security Council, one of the natural managers in world society.[30] Despite Parliamentary criticism there is effective bi-partisan agreement on the ethical dimension of foreign policy; as put by one of Mr Cook's predecessors, 'it is now, and perhaps has always been, part of the interests of Britain to do what we can with others to achieve a more decent world'.[31] The same consensus underlay the findings of the Strategic Defence Review (SDR) and its concept of expeditionary forces and support for international intervention.

This largely elective, wide-ranging foreign and military policy needs comparable intelligence support – sometimes for specific decisions, but also for more general educational, cumulative and generalized effects. Intelligence reduces the quota of government's mistakes and misperceptions in its chosen world role, and enables it to do better than if it had had to manage without it. Current British defence planning – for intervening for international causes, with surgical precision and mobility and low casualties – requires the 'information superiority' set out in NATO's 1999 Strategic Concept.[32] Having superpower-standard intelligence is an unstated assumption in the British world view and expectations. 'Britain plays with the hand it has been dealt; intelligence is one of the strong cards.'[33] Code-breaking's part in fighting Hitler is part of British folk-memory. Britain sees itself as an intelligence winner, not a loser, and in the last resort cares more about intelligence than trade promotion. In Germany and Japan, by contrast, intelligence successes have no particular place in national history, and intelligence receives lower national expectations. Arguably since 1945 they have needed it less.

Of course it can still be argued that since the early 1980s, perhaps since the Falklands War, successive British governments have had love affairs with intelligence; that it gets too well treated compared with the FCO, BBC external broadcasting and monitoring, the British Council, overseas aid, and the defence budget;[34] that, even with their present foreign policy objectives, Ministers could rely more on reading diplomatic dispatches and *The Economist*, and less on the JIC's weekly intelligence survey. There may be something in this. The highly classified intelligence in Ministerial boxes may sometimes get more attention than it deserves. Yet in general terms the connection between high-profile foreign policy and intelligence support cannot be gainsaid. Proactive British governments without good intelligence would be international loose cannons.

There are also the indirect effects. Britain's international reputation for sound judgement is significantly intelligence-driven, and is a factor in the national influence, inside and outside the transatlantic alliance, the EU and the Commonwealth. Britain's leading part *vis-à-vis* other European countries in the current NATO command structure rests partly on its intelligence superiority. Intelligence is an aspect of British power, both 'soft' and 'hard'. Additionally the defensive security of the 'national information infrastructure' also turns on the quality of the offensive intelligence advice available.

The Transatlantic Factor

Even if the intelligence requirements of Britain's international position are accepted, it can still be argued that the US will meet them anyway. But this is not the normal British view, and for the last half-century Whitehall has assumed that the transatlantic relationship has to be worked at. Intelligence liaisons are ultimately subject to international politics, even though they also shape them. The US was known during the Cold War to withdraw services of intelligence material as a signal or punishment, and not merely to New Zealand. A future Suez crisis would not leave UK–US intelligence relations as unaffected as they were in 1956.

UK policy has therefore been to shore up the relationship by creating as many areas as possible in which Americans can point to substantial British burden-sharing, or at least a British quid pro quo. A grumpy but knowledgeable American has described the British as 'superb intelligence diplomats' in 'making an extraordinarily astute investment buying into the US system, particularly in Sigint'.[35] Britain has sought to make the

British connection indispensable to the US, and this has had a bearing on the size of the present effort. Its quality and modernity have also been influenced by the need to remain America's intelligence ally and keep a foot in the door in expensive, sophisticated, US-led fields. Britain has sought to remain a partner, even if a junior one, rather than be a dependant.

On the whole the resulting quasi-superpower service to HMG has come cheaply. The American intelligence budget is nominally about sixteen times the British total suggested here, though different budgetary conventions for 'tactical' military systems make it difficult to compare like with like; the figure includes American 'tactical' military resources and the comparison overstates the American predominance. But for Britain the transatlantic alliance has been by no means costless. There is no way of computing a precise cost for the future; the many and varied UK–US intelligence relationships are not simple 'on–off' devices. Yet there is no reason to question the conviction that they depend on visible British contributions. Their nature would change drastically if they became seen as an American provision of free goods.

Intelligence and National Stance

These twin features – Britain's chosen role as an active world power, and the importance for it of the American intelligence connection – underlie the broad endorsement of previous intelligence investments by the present government. Intelligence's share of the foreign policy and national security cake can be a matter of detailed argument, but the bottom line is that no British government with its present high-profile foreign and defence policies can afford to run unnecessary risks of intelligence failure, especially if resulting in military casualties. It is illustrative that a complete and updated stock of intelligence on fifty foreign countries is now said to be required to cover the list of contingencies in which new-style British military power may be deployed; and no doubt events will show that even this long list is incomplete.

British intelligence therefore needs to be evaluated in this context, and not in the more traditional terms of threats, interests and commitments. In current military jargon the British army is now capabilities-based and not threat-based, and intelligence has to be seen in the same light.

QUALITY AND CENTRAL MANAGEMENT

Budgets are only one element of Britain's intelligence status; quality is equally important. It is the intelligence multiplier, and needs to be sought for purely national reasons irrespective of its transatlantic and international effects. It costs money but is also a matter of using resources well. It is determined mainly at the single–agency level, but central management also comes into the picture. The remainder of this paper deals with some issues of this kind.

The British community is managed on a basis of agency autonomy, collegial discussion and limited central intervention. There is a surprising degree of inter-agency cooperation. The results command international respect, indeed envy, and compare well with the much more elaborate American arrangements. The Whitehall instinct is therefore not to tamper with what seems to work. In his provocative 1940 question about a single Intelligence Service Churchill was probably renewing his attempt twenty years earlier to be an organizational mover and shaker,[36] but by 1943 he had come to a different view: 'I have a feeling that it would be a mistake at the present time to stir up all these pools.'[37] In not going back to the drawing-board the present government has taken the same view, and rightly so.

Yet British pragmatism carries with it the risk of complacency, of not pursuing improvements from the centre with the energy shown within the individual agencies, of changing things only after post-mortems such as those following the Falklands invasion, the Gulf War and the Scott 'arms to Iraq' Report. Of those three sets of changes, the post-Falklands decision to make the JIC Chairman a non-departmental, Prime Ministerial appointment had been advocated in print by a former Director-General of Intelligence thirteen years earlier;[38] the need demonstrated in the Gulf War for CDI's direction of the overall defence intelligence community had been recognized within the DIS some five years earlier;[39] and Whitehall's short-comings of intelligence-handling seized upon by Scott had been common knowledge for many years. The British are inclined to view American intelligence as the product of an engineering culture, always trying new solutions for insoluble problems, and ignore what this US restlessness achieves. Hence the three central issues to be considered here. All these are relevant to Britain's international intelligence standing, but merit – and need – consideration in their own right.

BALANCE BETWEEN ANALYSIS AND COLLECTION

Detailed Analysis and Institutional Memory

Britain's reputation rests on its covert single-source collection and exploitation on the one hand and on its JIC output on the other. Collection and related exploitation absorb at least 90 per cent of the total budget, and the resources for JIC assessment seem trivial by comparison. Since 1968 the Cabinet Office Assessments Staff, as the kernel of the JIC process, has been staffed by perhaps twenty-five or thirty secondees, including a strong element from the FCO. Talent is what counts there, with a positive advantage in keeping the numbers low.

But between single-source collection and the JIC is the separate stage of detailed all-source analysis, integrating and evaluating all available evidence, monitoring current developments in detail, and acting as the national expert (see diagram). This analysis provides the community's archive and institutional memory. It serves intelligence customers directly on subjects that do not need the top-level JIC imprimatur. Its output ranges from ephemeral situation reports to the results of research and assessment of varying depth, plus the updating of basic information on foreign countries.

THE INTELLIGENCE PROCESS
(from *Intelligence Power in Peace and War*)

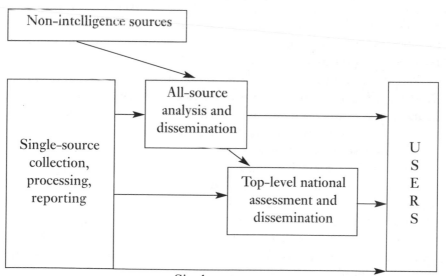

Single-source reports

Throughout the Cold War Britain under-invested in work of this kind and the 'subject' expertise that goes with it. Folk-memories of the Second World War emphasize Bletchley Park and occasionally the JIC; analysis by the wartime army, navy and air force intelligence staffs are less well remembered.[40] All-source desks have a peacetime image of rather mundane military 'collation', and have not had first claim on the community's numbers and quality. Observers have assumed that the Assessments Staff and JIC do everything needed after the single-source agencies have done their own analysis and selection and distributed the results.

Yet the Assessments Staff was never set up for detailed analysis. It was introduced in 1968 when 'think tanks' were in vogue. The Central Policy Review Staff, created two years later and located just above it in the Cabinet Office building, typified the faith of the time (in the words of a Cabinet Secretary many years later) in assembling 'a team of outstandingly talented people who have the capability of coming up with original perspectives and original questions which departments, with all their back-up and resources, haven't found'.[41] The Assessments Staff was conceived in the same spirit, to draw on others for detailed analysis and research, but to bring clear and uncommitted minds to the difficult assessment task, described by a former head of its Australian equivalent as being 'to illuminate what is otherwise unknown, pull together the overall picture, examine choices and possibilities, put this all on one page and get it to policy principals at the opening of business'.[42] The Assessment Staff has remained in this mould. It has occasionally recruited or developed its own gurus, but in most cases its members' knowledge of their subjects has been gained *in situ* during their two-year secondments.

Part of its strength is indeed that it is not self-contained. It draws upon the whole JIC community and provides 'guided collectivism' for the assessment process. Some argue that assessment as an activity needs detachment rather than subject expertise, but sometimes it can be no better than the detailed analysis and institutional memory on which it leans. Hence all-source analysis is needed to support it, as well as to meet the daily and weekly needs of Whitehall's lower- and medium-level policy desk officers on subjects that do not cross the JIC's thresholds of top-level relevance. There are also the threat assessments which contribute to expensive decisions on defence procurement that do not normally go through the JIC route. In short, the success of the Rolls-Royce JIC assessment system can obscure the need for all-source analysis of kinds not possible within the Cabinet Office.

The account given in Sir Richard Scott's report illustrated this need for analysis to pull things together. A succession of different desk officers in policy departments failed to recognize the accumulated significance of a succession of individual, single-source reports which arrived at their desks where they had no machinery for recall and collation. The problems of intelligence's security regulations were compounded by backwardness in information technology; an FCO official had written in 1991 on his department's management that 'the main blot is IT. Our approach appears antediluvian. We are being left behind.'[43] But the situation described by Scott also reflected the underlying shortage of all-source resources for the integration of all available evidence on the Iraqi arms industry. As Scott put it:

> individual items of intelligence taken in isolation might have been passed off as inconclusive.... The cumulative volume of intelligence could not be so passed off... [without an equivalent to] the Nelsonian use of the blind eye. But this, of course, assumes that the user of the telescope had been made aware of all the relevant intelligence. It is probably true that no one person was familiar with all the accumulated intelligence until, in June 1990, the JIC made the assessment required for the Iraq Note [on the Iraqi arms industry].[44]

There was a dearth of the consolidated reports from multiple sources that would have rung alarm bells earlier.

Government reactions to the Scott Report list some shutting of stable doors, mainly in policy departments and over their relationships with single-source collectors.[45] But they did not identify the key difference between single-source production and all-source analysis, or consider the balance between the two. A former Chief of the Assessments Staff is reported to have described the British emphasis on single-source reports as delivering 'farm gate intelligence – you picked it up from the end of the drive at Cheltenham in a completely raw form/...there wasn't a proper mechanism for digesting it'.[46] Scott's account illustrates the need for better all-source digestion. The best test of an intelligence system is the all-source memory it builds up, whether in old-fashioned index cards or through modern information technology.

What has been termed the 'Open Source Revolution' has made it all the more important to get a better balance between collection and analysis. It is now said that there are a hundred million Internet sites worldwide, and a million new Internet users each month. The ability to search what the American Presidential Commission on US Intelligence (the Brown Commission) described in 1996 as 'the vast universe of information now available from open sources'[47] is now a necessity. DIS experts were said to have calculated some years ago that there were 8,000 relevant databases then available worldwide.[48] There is also the volume of 'grey' intelligence, defined as 'information which is not published or widely diffused but to which access can be gained, provided that one knows it exists and has adequate channels of communication'. It was argued in the 1980s in connection with US–Japanese economic competition that 90 per cent of the relevant information was openly accessible, 9 per cent from grey sources such as conference reports, trade association reports and unpublished doctoral theses, and less than 1 per cent from secret sources.[49]

This does not mean that intelligence analysis should become government's universal expert. There are many other specialists and forecasters, particularly on economic, commercial and financial matters. Intelligence cannot be the expert on all the factors which shape international relations. But analysis needs to be able to draw on other specialisms and integrate their material with political, defence and other elements in the matters it is required to understand. Even where this work can be let out to the private sector, intelligence will still need to control it and integrate it with covert material. Its all-source analysis should be led by high-quality staff, with good information technology and funds for subscription to international data bases.

Compared with covert collection this is cheap. The modern world needs marginally less emphasis on covert collection and rather more on analysing its results, often in conjunction with non-intelligence sources. Measures for implementation can now be considered.

Contribution of the Defence Intelligence Staff

Excluding the special contribution of the Security Service, the DIS is the only intelligence agency charged with the detailed all-source analysis just discussed. Defence intelligence organizations have problems in all countries: the difficulty of developing intelligence as a specialist career for uniformed officers; problems of civilian careers; constant turnover of senior uniformed officers; vulnerability to the pressures of military interests. The DIS has compared well with its foreign counterparts, including those of the

United States. In the Cold War its main preoccupation was with the USSR, but then and subsequently it has also provided London with detailed analysis and community memory on all overseas targets and situations in which foreign military and paramilitary forces have been involved. It has been Whitehall's main intelligence centre in British military operations. Subjects like the proliferation of Weapons of Mass Destruction have helped to keep its work at the top of post-Cold War priorities. Additionally it has habitually taken on wider, non-defence tasks such as the monitoring of economic sanctions which no one else could do. It has upheld in intelligence the military tradition of pulling governments' chestnuts out of the fire.

Despite all this, it has never been the jewel in intelligence's crown. Its performance in the Cold War has been criticized by the present author for accepting and reinforcing an uncritical and convenient view of the Soviet threat.[50] Successive generations of intelligence professionals combined respect for the DIS's individuals with criticism of it as an institution. It has not normally had potential three- and four-star service officers posted to it as part of their career development, and it was not noted for recruiting and keeping high-class civilians. For many years it deployed its graduate intake in one specialist area, with few wider opportunities. The main analyst areas were staffed by retired officers, reporting to serving officers on short intelligence tours. Some distinguished intelligence practitioners emerged, but in spite of the system rather than because of it. Its military component lacked stability, and criticism of it had some resonance with the future Bomber Harris's protest (in 1938) – about the lack of continuity in the Bomber Group he then commanded – in which he stated that 'we cannot run a highly technical and complicated business on the floating population of a casual ward'.[51]

Some welcome changes have been made in recent years, but the DIS is still not seen as a centre of excellence. It still needs to develop a handful of first-class people (military as well as civilian); more continuity in its uniformed and civilian scientific elements; and the institutional *esprit de corps* and independence that develop more easily in the intelligence agencies than in the DIS's position as part of the central MoD staff. People should be keen to join it. It should be more formally recognized and tasked as an intelligence producer serving a variety of Whitehall recipients as well as its primary MoD and military customers and the JIC. Materially and psychologically it needs parity of esteem within the intelligence community.

The DIS and National All-Source Analysis

This would not resolve the question whether its analytic remit should be widened. For some decades after 1945 there was a British vision of a 'total' all-source intelligence institution, studying and understanding foreign countries and overseas situations as a whole. In America the CIA Directorate of Intelligence – quite distinct from the Agency's covert collection activities – emerged with this role, with a remit for detailed study of foreign countries and situations in a holistic way, free of any departmental tie. Australia has developed its Office of National Analysis along something of the same lines. Canada some years ago re-subordinated its small External Affairs research group to the Privy Council Office, to work for its equivalent to the JIC in a non-departmental way.

Britain has never created an analogue with this part of the CIA, and has emphasized departmental analysis, with political and defence analysis separated between the FCO and DIS, and foreign economic research shuffling uneasily between various parts of Whitehall. The Joint Intelligence Bureau (JIB) formed after the Second World War had only limited responsibilities, but the 1945 vision did not die completely. When the DIS was formed in 1964 through the amalgamation of the JIB with the three services' intelligence departments, some visualized it as the basis of a central, national institution. Thus its successive heads were civilians, just retired from the services, Deputy Chairmen of the JIC, and held the title 'Director General of Intelligence' (DGI) – not 'Chief of Defence Intelligence', as the post became when converted to three-star serving level in the early 1980s.

The Cold War's emphasis on the Soviet target indeed made the DIS the nearest thing to a British analysis centre on the USSR. It studied the Soviet economy, its science and technology and its Third World aid, trade and penetration, besides Soviet military power and the many things connected with it (though not its internal and external politics and policies). It produced first drafts of JIC papers on these subjects, and on the Soviet target it had a major input at the JIC's Current Intelligence Groups and the JIC itself.

Some of this analysis continues, accompanied by a continued service on the rest of the word. Defence intelligence is a broad subject. Most of the assessments of the unstable world draw on it in some way, and studying foreign military power is itself incomplete without regard to the non-military factors that bear on it. DIS analysts are touchy if accused of knowing about the Ruritanian army but not about its politics and economics, and are usually familiar with this background.

Yet the fact remains that the DIS's job is defence intelligence, and it is not a multi-subject agency like the CIA's Intelligence Directorate. By contrast the responsibilities for economic intelligence outside the old USSR have always been uncertain, and there have been successive attempts to establish it elsewhere. An inquiry in 1969 found against the establishment of a separate Central Overseas Research Department with an economic slant, but recommended that the DIS effort on the Soviet economy should be incorporated in a new Sino–Soviet research unit in the FCO. An economic assessment effort was established in the Cabinet Office in 1968 as part of the new Assessments Staff, but subsequently was run down before being partly re-established. Since the end of the Cold War successive MoD economies have forced the DIS to cut back on what appear to be the non-military frills. There has been a recurrent pattern of the DIS accepting cuts in this way, then having to take on urgent new topics which no one else was equipped to study. There is ambiguity about where the limits of the DIS's responsibility for defence intelligence actually lie.

Hence it is tempting to reorient it towards the pattern of the CIA or the Central Overseas Research Department discussed in 1969. It is a seductive idea, but one to be resisted. Military forces need something like the DIS committed to meeting their military needs and supporting command intelligence staffs. A central agency without military affiliations would never be satisfactory; an American lesson of the Gulf War was the inadequacy of the CIA's direct support of deployed forces.[52] Incorporating the Research and Analysis Department (RAD) of the FCO into a central agency would meet the same objection, that the FCO as an operational department needs its intelligence analysis in-house. Central analysis of terrorism would similarly cut across the Security Service's close relationship with the Special Branches and with the operational arms of police forces and other counter-terrorist actors.

Thus the advantages of central analysis are offset by the loss of close relationships between intelligence customers and 'their' intelligence staffs. The corollary in the US of the CIA's Intelligence Directorate is its widespread duplication by departmental analysis units: the Defense Intelligence Agency and the many other armed forces' organizations; the Intelligence and Research Bureau in the State Department; and so on. The American system thrives on duplication and rivalry, and can afford them. They would not suit the British scale of resources, and the dislike of interdepartmental competition.

In practice the present situation works tolerably well in a pragmatic British way. The DIS works closely with the rest of the intelligence community, and provides a service to London departments outside the MoD when it can. Whitehall is not given to black-and-white terms of reference. Yet in times of stringency the DIS's fortunes are determined by the MoD's view of it as a departmental defence asset, and not by wider needs.

This suggests that others in addition to the MoD and the armed forces should have a say in determining what the DIS does, and what it needs. Its study of foreign subjects on the periphery of defence intelligence should be formally recognized, as should its services of intelligence to non-MoD departments. As a key part of the national capability, it should be subject to (and involved in) nationally supported priorities, resource allocation and community planning. In the military term, it should become formally 'double-hatted' in its analytical role, with responsibilities to the MoD and armed forces on the one hand, and national intelligence management on the other. Its role in the control of national imagery and other sources points in the same direction, and is discussed later in this paper, along with the budgetary and other implications of double-hatted status.

Complementary Approaches

Nevertheless the DIS must remain largely defence-oriented, and formalizing its wider role would not completely meet the challenge of understanding foreign countries holistically. The Western inability to forecast the collapse of the Soviet Union reflected a preoccupation with studying it as a rival and threat, rather than as a society; and the lesson must have some relevance for the post-Cold War world. Understanding Islamic fundamentalism might be a parallel. Understanding 'difficult' foreign areas/countries needs some insight into national character, the Gestalt, 'the functional whole whose properties are not derivable from the sum of its parts'. Hence there is the question whether Britain's posture of 'world reach' is supported by enough provision for area experts, with relevant language and other competence.

The question goes beyond intelligence boundaries. On one view there is no problem. The FCO has an amassed and living knowledge of foreign countries. To quote a working diplomat: 'the Foreign Office is the custodian of information about countries throughout the world...[It] must be prepared when the next crisis in the world arises.'[53] Diplomats are in touch with journalists, bankers and businessmen, and with non-governmental studies of international affairs; Chatham House was established precisely for this purpose. Defence attachés link the diplomats with military developments abroad. Backing up all the working contacts is the overseas expertise of the FCO's 80-strong RAD and its dozen Economic Advisers; the Bank of England on financial matters; and experts in the other Whitehall Departments dealing with overseas matters. Policy officials everywhere digest the open literature. The accumulated knowledge of the DIS and the civilian agencies is on tap to the JIC. What with the high calibre of the Assessments Staff, the non-stop circulation of drafts around Whitehall, the wide range of CIGs, extensive departmental pre-JIC briefings and discussion at the JIC itself, is anything lacking?

Yet manifestly things go wrong, and reality can be different. Many senior diplomats have become area experts, but the mid-career pattern is of expertise in dealing with successions of foreign countries rather than understanding particular ones deeply. An FCO team itself recognized the difference between its diplomatic 'generalists' and its more knowledgeable Research Officers:

> Policy towards a country should not be formulated solely by a political department only one of whose members has ever served in the region, and none of whose members is capable of uttering more than courtesies in the vernacular of the country concerned.[54]

At one period covered in the Scott Report, FCO's Middle East Department had three heads in a year; out of 20 desk officers only three had had experience of the countries they were dealing with, and their average time in post was six months.[55] In Whitehall as a whole everyone is always taking over or moving on, and even when policy-makers are genuine experts they lack what the FCO team cited as the 'intellectual and operational independence that comes from freedom from policy commitment'.

Hence the need for area specialists. But the staff of RAD have borne their share of FCO cuts, beginning with a 17 per cent reduction conceded in 1978 in response to the CPRS survey. There has been repeated heart-searching about their position, and the in-house scrutiny in 1993 sought to make better use of their expertise through a controversial reorganization.[56] The DIS has never systematically encouraged the learning of foreign languages, though it has benefited from the presence within it of former defence attachés. The FCO's and DIS's research classes are separate from each other, small, and with career prospects that do not rival those of the policy-makers, or those offered by the intelligence agencies. In the post-imperial era Britain cultivates specialist overseas expertise in a rather casual way.

There is no clear correlation between area expertise and intelligence performance. The CIA is full of experts with academic backgrounds, but this does not guarantee success. It failed to forecast the Shah's fall, despite having an Iranian expert of great experience on its staff.

Yet in reviewing the record of intelligence failure it is difficult not to conclude that area knowledge has a place in reading foreign leaders' minds. The misinterpretation of the evidence on preparations for the Yom Kippur attack on Israel turned on a failure to believe that Sadat could choose to attack for reasons other than clear-cut military victory. It is still not clear to what extent NATO's expectation of a speedy Serbian collapse over Kosovo drew on incomplete understanding of Serbian politics or of Yugoslav military doctrine of camouflage and concealment. The same applies to the need to understand foreign terrorists' mindsets, and those of the IRA.

The DIS has already been discussed. Other inexpensive ways of developing and using a bigger pool of area expertise can be suggested as follows. First, as the author has advocated elsewhere, there should be some tinkering with the composition of the Assessments Staff to build up a rather greater proportion of intelligence professionals within it, complementing but not replacing the diplomatic secondees from the FCO.[57] Second, continued efforts should be made to tap expertise outside government, not just by cultivating contacts but also by developing consultancies with Chatham House, Oxford Analytica and similar institutions, perhaps with some central, JIC funding of 'Team B' assessments to complement official ones. The present 'Foreign Office Fellowships' scheme of temporary expert appointments in RAD might also be extended to the Assessments Staff and DIS. The practical problems over securing senior, well-qualified academics should not be underrated. But 'area studies' developed as a recognized academic discipline through American academics' experience of intelligence in the Second World War, and academia might be able to do something to return the compliment.[58]

Third, there should be some interdepartmental planning of overseas analysis. The JIC has its programme for finished reports and papers, and RAD and the DIS have their equivalent lists of work-in-progress to meet department requirements. There is ample contact and discussion of drafts, but no national system for coordinating research and study. The JIC could usefully develop a strategic, annual, interdepartmental analytic programme. The fact that Whitehall departments are increasingly driven by immediate, short-term needs makes it all the more important to have a strategy of some kind for research, whether in-house or by contract. It is odd that the JIC produces priorities for single-source collection, but not for the all-source work that exploits it.

Alongside these practical suggestions, there is also the more tantalizing vision of a Central Overseas Research Department, on the lines of the Government Statistical Service and Office of National Statistics. British government statistics grew up on a departmental basis in almost exactly the same period as organized intelligence developed in the second half of the nineteenth century in the Admiralty and War Office Intelligence Departments. A.J.P. Taylor's description of government statistics in the 1930s – 'four separate departments collected industrial statistics; five classified employers of labour; two produced rival and conflicting figures concerning overseas investment'[59] – could have been applied to intelligence of that period. The JIC subsequently evolved to produce coordinated assessments on the enemy, and the Central Economic Intelligence Service (renamed the Central Statistical Office (CSO) in 1941) to do the same on Britain's war effort. The CSO cooperated with Washington to produce joint wartime statistical statements, much as the JIC cooperated to produce agreed UK–US intelligence estimates for the Combined Chiefs of Staff. The similarity continued after 1945, when the Government Statistical Service developed as a statistical community with a matrix of central and departmental control. Specialist statistical divisions have for many years been integral parts of government departments, yet owe a parallel professional allegiance to the Head of their Service.

Can a lesson be drawn from this for establishing a Whitehall-wide foreign research profession? The problems of area expertise spring largely from the small size and limited opportunities of the departmental graduate research pools. Government statisticians, economists and others have an interdepartmental identity in government-wide specialist classes. Perhaps the overseas specialists need a similar identity, as a Foreign Research Officer class spanning the present FCO Research Cadre, the DIS, some posts in the Assessments Staff, and perhaps other parts of government – even, just conceivably, some presence in the civilian intelligence agencies. Wizardry in interception and code-breaking and other single-source skills will still be important. But they will increasingly have to be matched by developing all-source area expertise in assessment and interpretation. It is difficult to see how this challenge will be met without something beyond purely departmental responses. For its chosen world role Britain invests in high-quality diplomacy, armed forces and intelligence collection. Is there the right national investment in understanding the foreign areas and situations in which we are prepared to act?

COVERT COLLECTION: THE CHALLENGE OF SATELLITES

The Intelligence Revolution

These proposals for all-source analysis have minimal financial implications. If cuts are needed in the future – contrary to the present indications of intelligence expenditure on a plateau – they should be directed at collection, not analysis. Some adjustments between different collection agencies might be needed from time to time. The human sources of SIS and the Security Service may have some degree of insulation through their targeting on Irish and other terrorism, international trade involving the proliferation of weapons of mass destruction, and links with organized crime. Sigint as the biggest collector is a target for economies, though there (and elsewhere) technology provides scope for savings in running costs in return for capital investments. However the dominant issue of future resource allocation concerns satellite imagery, on which Britain has no collection of its own.

Satellite collection, embracing both Sigint and imagery, has indeed been the main area where British policy over the UK–US relationships has been tested.[60] American and Soviet collection of this kind first developed in the early 1960s and subsequently became the most important intelligence development since the introduction of radio interception and aerial photography in the First World War. It revolutionized imagery by providing guaranteed and uncontested observation of foreign territory, initially by traditional photography and latterly with the addition of all-weather radar imagery and other refinements. The imagery results are of particular military importance and are the greatest intelligence contribution to the Revolution in Military Affairs. The effect on the interception of foreign radars and similar electronic emissions (Elint) is almost as great, with similar consequentials for Electronic Warfare. Media comment suggests that the significance for communications intelligence (Comint) is less all-embracing, but is still very great.

In all, the impact of satellites on intelligence can be likened to the effects of radar on war. Their effects have not completely dominated Western operations over Iraq and the former Yugoslavia, since aerial reconnaissance and drones have been able to share the load. But satellites have been major contributors, and remain unmatched where conventional air reconnaissance cannot be guaranteed.[61] The Falklands campaign would have been very different had modern satellite surveillance been available to focus upon it. States with collectors in space have a quite different reach from those without them.

Yet the cost and variety of these systems pose major problems. By and large, intelligence satellites are not multi-purpose and are designed for one kind of collection, and the only safe generalization on costings is that they are more expensive by several orders of magnitude than any comparable ground-based collection. Unofficial estimates have put the cost of American Keyhole (imagery) satellites as two billion dollars each, but the complete accountancy for satellites, launch costs and ground segments is not available.[62] Any conceivable non-US system can match only a small proportion of these American systems; 'the disparity between the United States and other nations is quite marked. US investment in ISR (intelligence collection, surveillance and reconnaissance) – particularly the high-leverage space-based aspects of this set of systems – exceeds that of all other nations combined.'[63] Costs may now be coming down, and there is talk of lightweight, low-orbit satellites, each costing about 30 to 50 million dollars. Additionally there is the growth of commercially available imagery satellite material which may enable some national requirements to be met by this open source; though questions remain about this material's quality, reliability and speed of response, for example for the targeting of precision weapons.

In fact a process of specialized intelligence satellite proliferation already involves an increasing group of second-class powers. This collection in the Cold War was the two superpowers' prerogative, perhaps accompanied by some Chinese developments, but subsequently the French Helios system was launched in 1995 (costing the equivalent of 1.5 billion pounds[64]) as part of France's major intelligence expansion after its dependence on American material during the Gulf War.[65] It has some Italian and Spanish support, though German participation in follow-on systems is said to have been cancelled through defence economies. Israel has a programme of some kind, India may have one, and Japan has apparently decided to move into the field.[66]

There have also been ambitious proposals for international projects. International satellite monitoring for arms control and confidence-building was first proposed at the United Nations in 1978 and has subsequently been brought occasionally off the back burner. This has been followed by the more realistic Western European Union (WEU) proposals for a European effort of some kind. A WEU (now EU) interpretation centre has been in operation in Torrejon in Spain since 1991 and now uses a mixture of commercial imagery, French Helios output and some Russian material, and there has been regular pressure to develop it as a basis for a European collection system of some kind. The last ten years have demonstrated Europe's dependence on the US for this material, and there have been hints of problems when it was not forthcoming; it has been claimed that in the period of Western disunity before the mounting of IFOR there was American reluctance to supply imagery bearing on its alleged breaches of the Bosnian arms embargo.[67] According to the WEU Assembly some years ago:

> Both France and Germany are prepared to share their satellite cooperation programme with other WEU member states.... It will be necessary to quickly acquire an independent space capability to free Europeans from their dependence on the United States for intelligence which may be given or withheld but which in any event is selective and sifted by NATO.... WEU must acquire an independent satellite data-acquisition system.... It must at least be a ground segment sharing resources with other national programme users or using them on a cooperative basis.[68]

Europe committed itself at the 1999 Cologne Summit to creating a military capability that will make NATO a more equal US–European partnership, with greater European participation in political and military decision-making and an ability to operate if necessary without US participation. There is the familiar argument that Europe with two-thirds of the US's GNP could produce a better defence capability through more integration. If this is applicable to defence, why not to intelligence imagery? Despite its sensitivity, it could be an important test case.

British Policy

Britain has been fortunate in receiving the output from the wide variety of American satellite programmes without having any of its own. Its access to these American efforts is not uniformly robust and complete, but the overall relationship with them has indeed continued to be 'special', on a par with the rest of the intelligence relationship. For many years Britain has taken substantial steps to ensure the service in the Sigint part of the field. An ambitious attempt in the 1980s to develop a British Sigint satellite was found to be too costly, but was reportedly superseded by 'buying in' in various ways to parts of the American Sigint system to ensure access to the whole. It has been claimed that this is a long-term and recurrent commitment.[69]

By contrast, there has been no similar UK action over imagery. Thanks to an association going back to RAF participation in overflights of the USSR early in the Cold War, Britain has received most of the American satellite material, and has performed its own interpretations of it at JARIC.[70] There has been collaboration in this analysis, but not in the expensive business of collection. The service of this material therefore remains relatively fragile, without any irreplaceable contribution to the US. The material itself is particularly relevant to military operations of all kinds. There is no guarantee that it will be available to meet British needs if British and American priorities differ, or if the US is not involved in joint operations and not necessarily a supporter of them.

With the international move towards satellite collection some greater stake in it now seems a UK necessity. It may well be assumed that the UK–US arrangements are adequate for satellite Sigint, but in imagery it seems contrary to the rest of national policy to be no more than a country member of the growing satellite imagery club. Britain has relied on the US service and trusts that it will continue, but on a longer view there appear to be three options. One would be to have a genuine national imagery programme; a satellite with echoes of Bevin's determination in 1946 to have a nuclear weapon 'with a bloody Union Jack flying on top of it'.[71] Another would be to make a demonstrably important contribution by buying in to the American imagery capability, on the lines reported for Sigint. The third would be to participate in a European project, presumably based on the French Helios satellite and its successors, and the existing Torrejon centre.

The first seems unrealistic in the present climate of cooperative international initiatives. Of the other two, the British instinct would be to take the transatlantic route of an increased contribution to American imagery, though the problems of doing so should not be understated; the culture of sixty years of UK–US Sigint cooperation could not be created easily in this quite separate field. On Continental collaboration there would be British resistance to joining as a subordinate in a French-led programme, and there is the deep fear that close Anglo-European collaboration might be seen by the US as a betrayal of American secrets, including technological ones of value to Europe's space industry.[72] On 8 December 1999 a former Defence Secretary joined with a

Field Marshal and a retired head of the FCO to warn that in their view the 'unique' UK–US intelligence cooperation would be threatened by the pooling of defence intelligence with the French; 'we will lose a vital pillar of our relationship with the United States, and NATO will be severely undermined'.[73]

Yet the transatlantic and European routes may not be mutually exclusive. Top-level American opinion has always favoured British collaboration with Europe, promoting transatlantic links while increasing Europe's ability to contribute more to NATO. There is no reason why satellite imagery should be regarded as an exception. Indeed a framework reconciling national, transatlantic and European approaches to intelligence satellites may exist in the proposals by the Brown Commission, presumably reflecting professional US opinion: that there should be a satellite policy of two-tiered international burden-sharing and exchanges of product, with the US providing the more sophisticated systems and its allies contributing to the less costly, bread-and-butter coverage. In this policy,

> The United States would retain in the first tier its own high-end classified systems which involve the most sophisticated technology and techniques and are used to collect against the most critical consumer needs. The second tier would be developed in conjunction with friendly and allied governments and would consist of capable, but technically less sophisticated, reconnaissance systems that would emphasise the application of commercially available technology where possible as well as the application of existing industrial capacity. Foreign partners would be able to build, operate, and control their own satellites and ground stations, which would form part of a larger overall system.[74]

It is implicit, though unstated, that this proposal refers to imagery, and not Sigint. Underlying it in the concept of the 'information umbrella' of US power is the view that security constraints on satellite surveillance should be loosened, and that for international security purposes this intelligence should be seen as 'a public good, but not a free one'; those able to make a contribution should have to do so.[75]

One possible result could be some form of EU–US imagery satellite agreement on these lines, dedicated to the support of international security, with UK participation. An agreement of this kind would be a matter of great complexity. Yet it is a logical development of NATO intelligence and an EU/WEU identity within it. For Britain it is difficult to see any other means of providing an affordable stake in satellite imagery collection, buttressing the transatlantic connection while providing some guarantee of imagery support for deployed British forces and other national needs. In the light of current policy towards the European Strategic Defence initiative, Britain seems bound to move eventually in this direction.

Hence the issue arises of how policy matters of this importance are handled. Mention has already been made of the intelligence community's devolved structure, far removed from the single service originally postulated by Churchill. Satellite policy has implications for the whole community and needs central leadership. It is by no means the only issue of this kind. The remainder of this paper therefore considers central management and its development.

MANAGEMENT OF THE NATIONAL CAPABILITY

Responsibilities

Churchill's 1940 minute about the Intelligence Service posed another question: who was the man responsible for it?[76] Despite all the changes, the question remains, sixty years later: who's in charge? The remainder of this paper discusses the answer. The management forum is usually seen as the JIC and discussion must start with the part it plays.

The Committee evolved at the beginning of the Second World War with two distinct functions, joined almost by accident: the production of agreed national assessments, so that government action 'should be based on the most suitable and carefully co-ordinated information available', and intelligence management, or 'the consideration of any further measures which might be thought necessary in order to improve the efficient working of the intelligence organization as a whole'.[77] Setting aside the points made earlier in this paper about detailed analysis and expertise, the Committee has a distinguished record on the first of these functions. Warts and all, JIC assessment is like democracy: the least bad arrangement yet invented.

Its record on the second function is less impressive. It was effective in the Second World War in sorting out disputes between the three armed services, but had limitations where the civilian agencies were engaged. It kept out of disputes between the Security Service and SIS, and (more surprisingly) the management and priorities of wartime Sigint. After 1945 the wartime machinery for the management of Sigint remained (and remains) in use, distinct from the JIC. Nevertheless the JIC's management got broader, inspired perhaps by a seminal recommendation that the intelligence attack upon the opaque Soviet target should be mounted and coordinated as a campaign. It developed a network of sub-committees to coordinate and stimulate collection and analysis (for example a Scientific and Technical Intelligence Sub-Committee and its subordinate Guided Weapons Working Party), and saw itself as a principal management forum. Thus for over ten years after 1945 it is said to have maintained the Second World War machinery for the provision of pigeons for clandestine wartime communication; as part of the contingency planning of that time for a Soviet occupation of Western Europe this does not deserve the ridicule it might now receive. It illustrates the Committee's continued management role on a wealth of interdepartmental matters, including the activities of the JICs and LICs (Local Intelligence Committees) established where British forces were deployed overseas.

But it was still a coordinating committee, with a neutral Foreign Office chairman holding the ring. It did not – could not – control the ultimate levers of management: money and appointments. And eventually the network of sub-committees atrophied, particularly after the three single-service intelligence departments and the Joint Intelligence Bureau were subsumed into the DIS. The Committee's original *raison d'être* of knocking military heads together had disappeared, or at least been transferred to the MoD.

This does not mean that the JIC has not been useful for sorting out specific managerial problems. Many of these are best settled by consensus and give-and-take, and successions of chairmen have brought intellect and impartiality to them. The Committee has always played a part in reviewing formal intelligence requirements and priorities, though arguably the result has been a legitimization of what is already happening.

However the emphasis in central management has gradually shifted towards the role of Intelligence Coordinator. The post was originally created in 1968 on a part-time basis, but soon became involved in the managerial issues posed by the Irish situation in 1969. Successive incumbents have expanded its role to include the presentation of the intelligence budget to the Permanent Secretaries' Committee on the Intelligence Services (PSIS), and other community issues. They have developed considerable managerial clout, not entirely exercised in the JIC forum, and have significant achievements to their credit.

Nevertheless some features need comment. First, Churchill's question 'Who's in charge?' still has no clear answer. The JIC Chairman has clear responsibility for the Committee's intelligence output, but the post's institutional weight has varied. From 1985 to 1992 it was held by a retired diplomat in combination with the influential role of Prime Minister's Foreign Policy Adviser, but after a brief tenure by his successor it reverted to being the part-time responsibility of a succession of busy FCO officials on secondment as heads of the Cabinet Office's Overseas Secretariat. Intelligence Coordinators have had greater continuity but lower profiles, concentrating on the professional efficiency and priorities of the covert agencies. When next there is an intelligence failure, those conducting the post-mortem may find it hard to allocate responsibility between the JIC's dyarchy.

Second, the Coordinator's own remit is enigmatic in a typically British way. Most Coordinators have been former Heads of Agencies, on retirement from single-agency careers; the British system does not breed multi-agency professionals.[78] Others were appointed in earlier years without professional intelligence experience; not necessarily a handicap. In recent years the professional status of the post has been reduced relative to its Heads-of-Agency peers. In short, although the post is senior and important it has never been seen as intelligence's national Head of Profession. Finding future Coordinators worked for many years on the principle that it would be all right on the night.

The basis of the post is influence and advice, not executive responsibility. The Coordinator sits as a member of the JIC, and is influenced by the ambience of committees and consensus. The official description of his functions is in terms of advice, coordination and chairing committees; his clearest responsibility is establishing intelligence requirements and advising on the allocation of resources to meet them.[79] He has only a very small staff to help him. It is a very personal job, dependent on his own observations, initiatives and relationships. Elsewhere the author has likened his position, not entirely in jest, to a strong-minded Head of an Oxford College: able to achieve a great deal, but dependent on being able to carry colleagues with him.[80] In the collegial ambience of British intelligence it might be slightly more accurate to compare him with a college's much-respected and influential Vice-Principal.

Neither analogy is quite accurate. They overlook the Cabinet Secretary's concern for intelligence matters, and the Coordinator's position as the conduit of his power. But they convey something of the way in which central management has evolved on subfusc lines. The Coordinator's reflection of the Cabinet Secretary's authority carries limitations with it, reminiscent of those inherent in the position of the Head of the Civil Service in the old Civil Service Department of the 1970s: dependent on Prime Ministerial interest and backing, and powerless – and abolished by Mrs Thatcher in 1981 – when deprived of this support from above.[81]

Budgets

These untidy features are reproduced and accentuated in the key instrument of policy: budgets. JIC management in the Second World War
involved coordination of the three services and the joint-service organizations set up to meet their needs, and the establishment of the DIS lessened
the need to bring inter-service issues to the JIC table. As part of this trend
for MoD to settle its own intelligence affairs, its intelligence budgets are
now divorced from the central budget-setting, resource allocation and
policy oversight procedure through which the PSIS 'scrutinises the agencies annual expenditure forecasts, management plans and intelligence
requirements, as part of the Public Expenditure Survey arrangements'.[82]
Budgets for the DIS and other national-level military intelligence are
vested in CDI and determined as part of the Defence Budget. Despite its
name, the SIV is not a single intelligence vote, but a single vote for the three
covert agencies.

The result is another duality in top-level management and oversight.
The whole political and official structure for this purpose – the
Coordinator's annual reviews of performance and initial advisory scrutiny
of bids and budgets; the PSIS; the Ministerial Committee on Intelligence
Services; the Parliamentary Committee – is formally limited to the three
agencies. It is not charged with responsibility for the national intelligence
capability as a whole; specifically not the DIS, or imagery analysis based on
JARIC, or even the JIC's performance. The futures of the DIS and JARIC
are determined within MoD, not in the intelligence structure. At the level
of budgets, strategy, planning and oversight, it would now be correct to
speak of the management not of one intelligence community, but of two:
the main community responsible to the Cabinet Office on one side of
Whitehall, and CDI's defence intelligence community based on the MoD
on the other. The pattern was symbolized in the newly instituted annual
House of Commons debate on intelligence in 1998 in which the Foreign
Secretary led and the Home Secretary wound up; the Defence Secretary
was not involved. To sum up, there is fuzziness about central responsibilities and about the community to which these responsibilities apply.

Case for Central Overview

Too much should not be read into these managerial disjunctions. The
Whitehall machinery is flexible and closely knit; in 'the Whitehall village'

everyone knows everyone else, and values a reputation for interdepartmental cooperation. CDI and the DIS are constant participants in the JIC's assessment process, and are in regular contact with the rest of the community, in the Committee and bilaterally. The JIC's remit 'to give direction to, and keep under review, the organisation and working of British intelligence activity at home and overseas' still provides a setting for coordination extending well beyond the three agencies.[83] The present combination of the JIC forum together with the elastic relationships between the Cabinet Secretary, Coordinator and CDI provide some balance between central influences and devolved responsibilities. The Parliamentary Committee pragmatically stretched its mandate in 1999 by criticizing the JIC's performance over Sierra Leone.[84]

Nevertheless some issues seem too big for a system that depends so much on cooperation, consensus and influence, especially when issues affect community members' own territories and budgets. The centre needs some ability to take a national view that cuts across institutional interests and boundaries, with some supra-agency capacity rather greater than 'co-ordination'. Intelligence everywhere has this problem; the verdict of the Brown Commission on the US community was that 'the process for allocating resources to intelligence is severely flawed'.[85] Britain is not above such criticism. The present government's concern for achieving 'joined-up government' through an enhanced Cabinet Office role is as relevant to intelligence as to other things.

All source analysis and satellite policy as discussed here illustrate the problems. The present machinery is not called upon to review the balance between collection and analysis, either in quantity or quality, and is not capable of doing so. For the whole of the Cold War everyone grumbled about the DIS, but helping it to pull itself up by its bootstraps was not seen as a national, PSIS-worthy issue; the substantial increases in intelligence budgets under Mrs Thatcher were directed towards the Cabinet Office side of Whitehall, not the MoD. A similar imbalance has applied to satellite collection. Imagery has been regarded as MoD's business, not a matter of intelligence policy. There has been no forum for forming an intelligence satellite policy.

Two other historical examples can be quoted to make the same point. One was the delay in developing a community-wide architecture for information technology, to facilitate a common bank of knowledge, accessible by intelligence and its users. (The US community has recently stated the objective as developing 'interactive data bases to enable the policy maker to initiate a single request, search all community databases, and receive the requested data'.[86]) There were many difficulties, not least the importance of agencies' individual transatlantic connections. Nevertheless although the concept of community IT was articulated nearly thirty years ago, its implementation repeatedly ran up against institutional interests. Contributing towards a community system was in no single organization's immediate interest, and there was rarely sufficient central power to push towards co-ordinated planning. Some of Scott's findings on intelligence handling can be traced back to this origin.

A second issue needing a community perspective was intelligence on Irish terrorism. Despite major operational successes the effort was replete with organizational problems, and it took twenty years from the first bomb on the mainland to resolve (in 1992) the divided responsibilities of the Security Service and the Metropolitan Police Special Branch for intelligence on IRA threats there.[87] Even after that, a former Prime Minister (Sir Edward Heath) advocated the need for a more centralized effort; 'there is not one EC country that has succeeded in defeating terrorism without first establishing a proper, national central agency'.[88]

Heath's was a simplistic solution for a complex problem. The focal point for operational/tactical intelligence on the IRA had to be Belfast, just as the focal point for operational intelligence on the Desert War was Montgomery's Eighth Army and not the War Office. Yet London also had to cope with the tactical requirements posed by the IRA's campaign on the British mainland and by the search for a political solution, plus the 'foreign intelligence' dimension added by the IRA's sanctuary in the Irish Republic and arms acquisition elsewhere. Britain had a well-established model for intelligence on colonial insurgency; but Northern Ireland is not a colony, and intelligence there did not fit any neat model. Yet this made it all the more necessary to maintain some continuous, central, non-departmental oversight of the system – to search for improvement and conduct intelligence as a campaign, waged in the spirit of Churchill's 'action this day' response to junior staffs' complaint in October 1941 that administrative delays were handicapping the breaking of German ciphers.[89]

Organizational Changes

Even if all these problems have been solved, they illustrate the need for central management. Since the creation of the Coordinator's post its influence has been on an ascending curve, but should be rising further.

The management of defence provides a parallel. Over the last fifty, years military power has gradually come to be seen as a unity, rather than independent land, maritime and air elements. British defence policy has moved towards more responsibility for individuals, with rather less reliance on committees. The responsibility and influence of the Chief of Defence Staff (CDS) has grown, at the expense of the Chiefs of Staffs' Committee, and operations have come increasingly under individual Joint Force Commanders. In the 1980s it became accepted that 'CDS was to be the principal military adviser to the Government in his own right, and not just as Chairman of the Chiefs of Staff Committee'.[90] Power shifted from single-service staffs towards his strengthened 'purple-suited' central ones, after decades in which the CDS had only 'a small personal briefing staff of his own, which left him, in effect, with little power and no executive responsibility'.[91] The process has been gradual and partial; centralization is still set in a framework provided by the three single services. Though CDS 'must rightly have the ultimate responsibility for advising the Government on military policy', he 'is not there to ride roughshod over them [his professional colleagues], but rather to provide the central dynamic'.[92] US military arrangements have evolved in the same direction. Less is now said in both countries about 'coordination' and 'collective advice', and more about personal roles and responsibilities.

In Britain the management of intelligence is moving in the same direction as military power, but some thirty years behind. This points to further evolution, not revolution; but deliberate evolution nonetheless. The present arrangements at the centre are personality-driven and workload-driven. The roles of the JIC Chairman and the Coordinator are derived from Cabinet Secretaries' special concern for intelligence, an inheritance from Hankey's position as the first holder of the post. But intelligence issues with a political content – intelligence legislation; political oversight; cases of leaks and unauthorized intelligence publications *à la* Peter Wright; intelligence and trades unions – are bound to take priority with busy Cabinet Secretaries over matters of professional organization and effectiveness, especially if these are long-term. Cabinet Secretaries are now additionally Heads of the Civil Service, besides being directly responsible for a clutch of modern Executive Agencies. With such a workload it would be unrealistic to expect holders of the post to reproduce Lord Trend's position as Cabinet Secretary caricatured in his obituary as 'intelligence's chief shop steward'.[93]

Hence the need for some underpinning of the centre *vis-à-vis* the Heads of Agencies and CDI. Large national and international conglomerates in the private sector take great trouble to avoid over-centralization, and balance the requirements of corporate strategy and planning against the need to keep operating units' accountability for their own success and failure. But responsibility for performance is vested somewhere at the top of the organization. British intelligence should move in this direction.

This might be achievable without organizational tinkering. As a practical matter, the Coordinator in his present role may need some small reinforcement of his central staff to match widening responsibilities. Possibly (but more controversially) he might also have some small 'seed-corn' budget at his disposal to launch programmes like community-wide IT compatibility that are in no agency's immediate interest and attract no agency sponsorship. Signs, symbols and procedures may be even more significant. If the three Heads of Agencies need their publicly declared right of access to the Prime Minister, the Coordinator should also have it. If the JIC is to keep its dual assessment-producing and managerial roles, the Coordinator should chair it as a managerial forum. His post should be demonstrably the summit of an intelligence career, military or civilian.

Despite the attractions of these modest revisions, it would be braver to make a more substantial change. The dual responsibilities for intelligence assessment and management do not sit easily together, since the first always seems more urgent than the second. Yet the US Director of Central Intelligence has always been both the President's chief intelligence officer and his central intelligence manager, admittedly with major problems of exercising authority over the largely DOD-financed American community. More relevantly, the UK for two years, just after the Falklands War, had the same arrangement, with the Coordinator's post combined with JIC chairmanship and occupied (full-time) by an officer with unusual energy and ability.[94] The experiment was a great success. Having found a winning formula once, it seems perverse not to seek to repeat it. It is defeatist to assume that Britain cannot find a successor for the combined Chairman-Coordinator role, with appropriate support.[95] By comparison, responsibility for the collection and analysis of national statistics (plus headship of the Government Statistical Service) were combined in 1996 in a new, single post, the Director of the Office for National Statistics. If this can be done for statistics, why not for intelligence?[96] It has been convenient to write here of intelligence's management. But what perhaps is even more important is leadership.

Irrespective of the central management post, there should be some means of reviewing the national capability as a whole. The 'policy' and budgeting responsibilities of the Ministerial Committee and PSIS should be broadened to include the defence intelligence component, and the same should apply to the Parliamentary Committee. MoD intelligence funding should remain part of the Defence Budget, with defence intelligence competing there with other military requirements. But it should also be considered by the PSIS-Ministerial machinery, to optimize the balance between it and the single-agency investments. Other parts of the Defence Budget (for example the Meteorological Office, and air-sea rescue) are influenced by more than strictly military considerations, and there is no intrinsic reason why this should not apply to MoD intelligence. Despite all the problems, US intelligence has a genuine national intelligence budget, and there is no reason why the UK on its smaller scale should not follow suit.

COMMUNITY-MINDEDNESS

Structure is linked with community culture. Since 1945 most civilian intelligence practitioners have spent their careers in their own, single organizations. There are indeed exceptions. GCHQ has recently had three Directors in succession brought in from outside intelligence; most of the intelligence organizations provide some staff with non-intelligence exposure; the few available secondments to the Assessments Staff and other JIC machinery also widen experience. Intelligence is now quite good at promoting knowledge of the 'outside world'. It has been less good at exchanges within the community itself. There has been no system for 'broadening' postings for promising officers between the agencies and the DIS, or between the agencies themselves. Half a century of professional intelligence in peacetime produced sets of leaders without inside knowledge of each other's professional disciplines, or the community-mindedness that springs from it.

Here again something can be learned from armed forces' experience of modifying single-service tribalism by inter-Service training and postings. Since 1945 there have been consistent attempts to encourage inter-Service 'jointery', as in the foundation of the Joint Services Staff College 'to nourish and to disseminate among the higher commanders of all Services and their staffs that mutual understanding and Inter-Service comradeship in arms which, in war, were the very basis of our success'.[97] Single-service cultures are deeply embedded, and the Canadian attempt at a unified defence service was not a success. But it is recognized everywhere that armed forces' senior commanders need to shed single-service blinkers. Experience in joint staffs or with another service has become required for the CV of an ambitious officer.

Intelligence is too small to have a joint staff college on military lines. Nevertheless it could introduce community-oriented training and 'broadening' postings as part of career development. (It is interesting that for the US the Brown Commission came to the conclusion that 'intelligence agencies should function more closely as a "community"',[98] and recommended rotation between agencies and the creation of a common list of senior posts). A British initiative in this direction would need a push from the centre. In this, as in other things, someone needs to take a view of the national capability as a whole.

SUMMARY

British intelligence has a unique 'upper second class' status in world terms. This status underpins the transatlantic relationship and a service from it of almost the total US product. From its national effort plus the US relationship, HMG receives a quasi-superpower level of intelligence support. Factors governing the value of this support include:

- The continuing need for covert collection, despite the world's generally increased openness and the growth of other information sources; and the increasing technical scope for this covert collection in the modern electonic world.
- The direct value of some of this single-source covert material, particularly in providing 'diplomatic support' for HMG's overseas relationships.
- The critical importance, nevertheless, of the relatively small effort in all-source analysis and assessment, integrating both covert and overt material as inputs to high-level policy and decisions; and of the rather larger military intelligence effort needed for peace-making, peace support and other use of military forces.

These reinforce long-standing British expectations of intelligence and public assumptions about the high-profile foreign policy world and the defence roles set out in the 1998 Strategic Defence Review.

The intelligence community is well managed by world standards, but its devolved and pragmatic style runs the risk of being driven by events. Three issues merit attention. One is the balance of investment between single-source collection/exploitation, about 90 per cent of the total, and the remainder in detailed, all-source analysis. More emphasis should be given to the latter by a variety of managerial and administrative measures. Their costs would be trivial compared with total intelligence budgets, but the measures would reflect the increasing importance of the all-source effort.

Another is the challenge posed by the development of intelligence satellites, at a time when a group of second-class intelligence powers are moving into what is now no longer a superpower preserve. The UK receives the product of many American satellite programmes. Among these it is reported to be contributing on Sigint to an extent sufficient to assure continued UK access. But it makes a less self-evident input on imagery, and there is no guarantee that this American material will continue to be available in all circumstances, such as any EU operations taking place without US participation. Britain should play an active part in this modern spacefaring. A concept put forward by the American Brown Commission in 1996 of overseas partnerships and load-sharing on satellite imagery provides the possibility of US–European collaboration in which the UK could join at affordable cost, reconciling its transatlantic and European imperatives.[99]

The third is the need for more powerful, less lopsided central management – or, rather, leadership. The JIC is a forum without managerial teeth. The Intelligence Coordinator has influence rather than responsibility. The formal structure of official, Ministerial and Parliamentary oversight is geared only to the three civilian agencies, not the wider community. Hence:

- under existing arrangements the Coordinator should have the status of intelligence's professional head; but an effort should be made to repeat the successful experiment of the 1980s of combining this post with chairmanship of the JIC.
- the strategic-level elements of the 'defence intelligence community' should be clearly recognized as an element in the national community, subject to some degree of national resource allocation and planning.
- the remits of the Ministerial Committee on Intelligence and the PSIS should be amended accordingly, to provide oversight of the national intelligence capability as a whole. The statutory status of the Parliamentary Intelligence and Security Committee should at some stage be modified in the same way.

- With the same objective of viewing intelligence as a national entity, 'broadening' postings among the agencies and the DIS should be planned as normal forms of career progression.

NOTES

1. Published privately in January 2000 by the UK Defence Forum. An earlier version was published by the London Centre for Defence Studies in 1997, as *British Intelligence in the Millennium.*
2. *Annual Report 1999–2000* (London: The Stationery Office, 2000), paras 20–7.
3. For a fuller definitional discussion see M.E. Herman, *Intelligence Power in Peace and War* (Cambridge: Cambridge University Press, 1996), Chapters 1–3.
4. F.H. Hinsley with E.E. Thomas, C.F.G. Ransom and R.C. Knight, *British Intelligence in the Second World War,* Vol.I (London: HMSO, 1979), p. 291.
5. As set out in *Central Intelligence Machinery* (London: HMSO, 1996). Note that a later version is *National Intelligence Machinery* (Norwich: The Stationery Office, 2000).
6. It is not clear how the collective label 'intelligence and security' came to be used. 'Security' relates to the Security Service's roles in security intelligence and in defensive security measures; but it could also cover GCHQ's role in supporting communications and other electronic security.
7. *Central Intelligence Machinery*, p. 23.
8. For discussion of the subjects see Herman, *Intelligence Power*, Chapter 7. The author's conclusion is that the core of all-source intelligence is likely to remain 'national security' subjects (including warning, threats, foreign forces and armaments) plus foreign affairs with elements of instability, violence, obscurity or concealment. It is less often seen as the authority on close allies or more open aspects of world international affairs.
9. *Central Intelligence Machinery*, p. 24. See the previous note for the emphasis in practice. A popular Whitehall perception is that the JIC 'puts covert intelligence into context and assesses it', but this is too limited.
10. *Central Intelligence Machinery*, p. 11.
11. Ibid., p.23.
12. JARIC is now a devolved agency with its own published *Framework Document* (London: HMSO, April 1996). There is a (mainly MoD) Advisory Board, a Chief Executive, Customer Agreements and a Business Plan, but 'the Secretary of State for Defence has ultimate responsibility for determining the policy, financial framework, delegations and freedoms within which the Agency operates' (paragraph 1.2).
13. For the definitions of 'strategic' and 'tactical' intelligence and Electronic Warfare, see Herman, *Intelligence Power*, Chapters 5 and 7.
14. Ibid., pp. 37, 38, for indications of the reductions in this period.
15. *Treasury Supply Estimates 1999/2000,* Cm 4221. Slightly lower figures appear in all cases in the 1998–99 *Annual Report of the Parliamentary Intelligence and Security*

Committee (Cm 4532, November 1999), with some technical deductions; the trend is however the same. Figures given from 1997/98 onwards are (millions) £703.3, 695.4, 742.9, 744.8 and 746.7 (2001/2002).

16. JARIC document at Note 12 above.
17. *Military Survey Defence Agency Annual Report and Accounts 1997/98* (London: HMSO, 1999).
18. For indications of Special Branch totals see Herman, *Intelligence Power*, p. 12. The wide variety of Special Branches' law-enforcement and public order commitments must be emphasized.
19. Figures for 1999/2000 are £765 million on diplomacy, £1,794 million as the total budget of the Department for International Development, and £22 billion for defence (*Treasury Supply Estimates, 1999*).
20. E.A. Cohen, 'A Revolution in Warfare', *Foreign Affairs*, 75, 2 (March/April 1996), p. 46.
21. For the scope for terrorists see J. Welch, 'The International Money Market: A Weapon in Waiting?', *RUSI Journal*, 141, 2 (April 1996).
22. Quoted by J.S. Nye, 'Redefining the National Interest', *Foreign Affairs*, 78, 4 (July/August 1999), p. 26.
23. Sir David Gillmore, 'Representing Britain Overseas', *RUSI Journal*, 138, 6 (December 1993), p. 14.
24. Cohen, 'A Revolution in Warfare', p. 40.
25. Accounting for 6 per cent of world output in 1990, according to M. Clarke in 'Constraints on United Kingdom Foreign and Defence Policy', in B. Bond and M. Melvin (eds), *The Nature of Future Conflict: Implications for Force Development* (Sandhurst: Strategic and Combat Studies Institute, Occasional Paper no. 38, 1998), p. 45.
26. Cohen, 'A Revolution in Warfare', pp. 44–5.
27. R. Hibbert, 'Intelligence and Policy', *Intelligence and National Security*, 5, 1 (January 1990), p. 112. His generalization was probably intended to exclude military details.
28. S. Rimington, *Security and Democracy – Is There a Conflict?*, Richard Dimbleby Lecture 1994 (London: BBC Educational Developments, 1994), p. 9.
29. C. Tugendhat and W. Wallace, *Options for British Foreign Policy in the 1990s* (London: RIIA/Routledge, 1988), p. 118.
30. Clarke, 'Constraints on United Kingdom Foreign and Defence Policy', p. 50.
31. Lord Hurd, 'British Foreign Policy in the Aftermath of the Cold War', *RUSI Journal*, 143, 6 (December 1998), p. 10.
32. *NATO Strategic Concept*, 23–24 April 1999, paragraph 53 (d).
33. As put for example by Sir Percy Cradock, BBC TV programme *Panorama*, 22 November 1993.
34. It has been suggested that the Cabinet's Overseas and Defence (OD) Committee really needs an OD (Resources) sub-committee to consider these complementary but competing investments.
35. M. Urban, *UK Eyes Alpha: The Inside Story of British Intelligence* (London: Faber and Faber, 1996), pp. 239, 103.
36. C. Andrew, 'Churchill and Intelligence', in M.I. Handel (ed.), *Leaders and Intelligence* (London: Cass, 1989), pp. 190, 191.

37. Hinsley *et al.*, *British Intelligence in the Second World War*, Vol.2, p. 16.
38. General Strong wrote in 1970 that the JIC was 'still a long way from the ideal of an interdepartmental committee to control intelligence, with an independent chairman divorced from any department and responsible directly to the Prime Minister' (Major General Sir Kenneth Strong, *Men of Intelligence* (London: Cassel, 1970), p. 150).
39. For the rationale and the Gulf War influence see Defence Committee Session 1993–94, Fifth Report, *Implementation of Lessons Learned from Operation Granby* (London: HMSO, 1994), evidence of 24 November 1993, questions 23–37.
40. But see R.V. Jones, *Most Secret War: British Scientific Intelligence 1939–1945* (London: Hamish Hamilton, 1978); D. McLachlan, *Room 39: Naval Intelligence in Action 1938–1945* (London: Weidenfeld and Nicolson, 1968); and N. Annan, *Changing Enemies: The Defeat and Regeneration of Germany* (London: Harper Collins, 1995).
41. Lord Hunt, quoted by P. Hennessy, *Whitehall* (London: Fontana, 1990), p. 227.
42. A.D. McLennan, 'National Intelligence Assessment: Australia's Experience', in D.A. Charters, S. Farson and G.P. Hastedt (eds), *Intelligence Analysis and Assessment* (London: Cass, 1996), p. 84.
43. R. Tomkys, 'The Financial Management Initiative in the FCO', *Public Administration*, 69, 2 (summer 1991), p. 263.
44. Rt Hon. Sir Richard Scott, *Report of the Inquiry into the Export of Defence Equipment and Dual-Use Goods to Iraq and Related Prosecutions*, Vol.2 (London: HMSO, 1996), D8.11, p. 814.
45. Cabinet Office press release, 15 February 1996. Some improvements in Cabinet Office communications were however included, and the DIS was said to be conducting 'co-ordinated assessments of proliferation in particular regions and countries'.
46. Urban, *UK Eyes Alpha*, p. 6.
47. *Report of the Commission on Roles and Capabilities of the United States Intelligence Community (the Brown Commission), Preparing for the 21st Century* (Washington, DC: US GPO, 1 March 1996), Executive Summary, p. 5.
48. Urban, *UK Eyes Alpha*, p. 262.
49. S. Dedijer and N. Jéquier, 'Information, Knowledge and Intelligence', in their *Intelligence for Economic Development: An Enquiry into the Role of the Knowledge Industry* (Deddington, Oxon: Berg, 1987), pp. 18–19, quoted by J. Sigurdson and P. Nelson, 'Intelligence Gathering and Japan: The Elusive Role of Grey Intelligence', *International Journal of Intelligence and Counterintelligence*, 5, 1 (1991), p. 21.
50. Herman, *Intelligence Power*, Chapter 14.
51. Malcolm Smith, 'Sir Edgar Ludlow-Hewitt and the Expansion of Bomber Command', *RUSI Journal*, 126, 1 (March 1981), p. 55.
52. For example, 'the CIA as a whole adopted a hands-off attitude towards the concept of joining in the organised support given combat commanders. It refused to join the Joint Intelligence Center (JIC) located in the Pentagon.... Agency officials asserted that... they needed to remain outside the JIC so they could provide independent assessments for senior policy makers' (Committee on Armed Services, House of Representatives, *Intelligence Successes and Failures in Operations Desert Shield/Storm* (Washington, DC: US GPO, 1993), p. 6).

53. S. Jenkins and A. Sloman, *With Respect, Ambassador* (London: BBC, 1985), pp. 49–50.

54. Foreign and Commonwealth Office Scrutiny, *The Need to Know: Research and Analysis Department and Library and Records Department* (FCO Report), p. 27.

55. Quoted at the Council for Arms Control seminar on the Scott Report, 28 March 1996.

56. For the earlier investigations see Note 54, Annexe C.

57. Herman, *Intelligence Power*, Chapter 15.

58. All-source intelligence analysis 'had a major impact on the shape of scholarship in American universities in the first two decades after World War II' (R. Winks, *Cloak and Gown* (London: Collins, 1987), pp. 114–15). See also the review by B.F. Smith, *Intelligence and National Security*, 6, 2 (April 1991), pp. 498–9, of B.M. Katz, *Foreign Intelligence: Research and Analysis in the Office of Strategic Services* (Cambridge, MA: Harvard, 1989): 'Katz makes a strong case for the view that the R and A [the Research and Analysis Department of the wartime OSS] experience exerted a profound influence on aspects of US post-war academic life.'

59. A.J.P. Taylor, *English History, 1914–1945* (London: Penguin, 1970), p. 409.

60. Using satellites to 'see' terrestrial targets, literally or for electronic interception; not to be confused with the ground-based interception of communications relayed from communications satellites. It is the difference between looking down and looking up.

61. For the British lessons drawn from the importance of imagery (in all its forms, including infra-red and radar images) in the Gulf War, see the official evidence in House of Commons Defence Committee, *Implementation of Lessons Learned from Operation Granby* (London: HMSO, 1994), evidence of 24 November 1993, questions 19–22.

62. *New Statesman*, Supplement, 4 November 1995, p. 12.

63. J.S. Nye, Jr., and W.A. Owens, 'America's Information Edge', *Foreign Affairs*, 75, 2 (March/April 1996), p. 28.

64. K. Hayward, *British Military Space Programmes* (London: RUSI, 1996), p. 60.

65. After the humiliation of depending on American intelligence in 1990–91, the French volte-face over intelligence produced a 1996 'prevention' sector of the defence budget (covering intelligence, space and communications) of 23.1 billion francs, claimed to provide for 57,555 staff, at 12.2 per cent of the defence total; plus expansions of the French equivalents of the British Agencies. The intelligence elements are not clear in all the French figures, and international comparisons are in any case confusing; nevertheless the figures give some impression of a modern Continental scale (Western European Union Assembly Defence Committee Report, *A European Intelligence Policy* (13 May 1996), p. 5).

66. For Japanese intentions to launch four intelligence satellites see *The Times*, 16 June 1999.

67. Hayward, *British Military Space Programmes*, p. 61.

68. Western European Union Assembly Defence Committee Report, *A European Intelligence Policy*, 13 May 1996, paras. 40, 69(iii), 97.

69. Hayward, *British Military Space Programmes*, p. 45. An account (not necessarily authentic) is given in Urban, *UK Eyes Alpha*, Chapter 5.

70. P. Lashmar, *Spy Flights of the Cold War* (Stroud, Glos: Sutton, 1996).

71. P. Hennessy, *Never Again: Britain 1945–1951* (London: Vintage edition, 1993), p. 268.
72. Though press comment suggested that European collaboration in imagery was under active consideration by the UK in 1995 (*The Times*, 20 September 1995).
73. Correspondence, *The Times*, 8 December 1999.
74. *Brown Commission Report*, Chapter 11, pp. 1–2.
75. See Nye and Owens, 'America's Information Edge', particularly p. 35.
76. Hinsley *et al.*, *British Intelligence in the Second World War*, Vol.1, p. 291.
77. Ibid., p. 43.
78. The exception has been Sir Dick White, who was successively Director-General of the Security Service, Chief of SIS and Intelligence Coordinator. His appointment to SIS resulted from prime ministerial anger over the Agency's unsuccessful operation by Commander Crabb in 1956.
79. *Central Intelligence Machinery*, p. 4.
80. Herman, *Intelligence Power*, p. 309.
81. For a brief account see the obituary of Lord Bancroft, *The Times*, 21 November 1996.
82. *Central Intelligence Machinery*, pp. 11, 12.
83. *Central Intelligence Machinery*, pp. 24.
84. Intelligence and Security Committee, *Sierra Leone*, Cm 4309 (London: HMSO, May 1999), pp. 3–4.
85. *Brown Commission Report*, Executive Summary, p. 1.
86. *National Security Agency Objectives 1999*, Goal 3.
87. Rimington, *Security and Democracy*, p. 8. It is interesting that in 1966 the Director-General of the Security Service, resisting a DIS proposal for a central point to handle IRA intelligence, had maintained that it was a police problem. The JIC agreed (R.J. Aldrich, *Espionage, Security and Intelligence in Britain 1945–1970* (Manchester: Manchester University Press, 1998), pp. 128–9).
88. Sir Edward Heath, 'Outflank the IRA Bombers', *The Times*, 10 June 1993.
89. As described in P.S. Milner-Barry, 'Action This Day', *Intelligence and National Security*, 1, 2 (May 1986).
90. The history of the British evolution is set out in General Sir William Jackson and Lord Bramall, *The Chiefs* (London: Brassey's, 1992), quotation from p. 400.
91. Ibid., p. 296.
92. Ibid., pp. 447, 449.
93. Obituary, *The Times*, 22 July 1987. A subsequent letter from Lord Hunt of Tanworth and Sir Robert Armstrong (*The Times*, 30 July 1987) criticized this choice of words, but affirmed Trend's special concern for intelligence matters. See also Chapter 10 in this volume, 'Up From The Country: Cabinet Office Impressions 1972–75'.
94. Sir Antony Duff, GCMG, DSO, DSC, PC.
95. There is now no reason why the Chief of the Asssessments Staff, since 1983 a full member of the JIC, should not be a formal deputy.
96. This happened in 2000 when it was announced that Michael Pakenham was the holder of both posts (*National Intelligence Machinery*, p. 16). But the Parliamentary Report cited in Note 2 argues that the post should be associated with greater intelligence background and status.

97. Chiefs of Staff message on its foundation in 1947, in *The Chiefs*, p. 462.
98. *Brown Commission Report*, Executive Summary, pp. 1, 6.
99. According to two American writers the idea of transatlantic 'partnering' in the development of 'cheap' satellites was also put forward by John Deutch as US Director of Intelligence at the same time (D.M. Gormley and D.M. Hart, 'Extending Network-Centric Warfare', *RUSI Journal*, 145, 2 (April 2000), p. 68).

5

The Joint Intelligence Committee in Perspective[1]

The Joint Intelligence Committee (JIC) is held to epitomize a 'British way in intelligence', akin to Liddell Hart's often-quoted 'British way of warfare'; but like the British way of warfare it needs critical appraisal. I have suggested elsewhere, tongue-in-cheek, that it was Britain's last constitutional export to the United States and the Old Commonwealth,[2] but it now has an even wider salience. For the last half-century other Western counties have admired it while feeling that they could not follow suit, yet its concept of 'national assessment' is now central to the intelligence dimension of Europe's Common Security and Defence Policy. The system needs to be properly understood.

This chapter casts some light upon it through an historical snapshot of its operation in the 1950s, for which committee papers and minutes are now available. 1955 has been chosen as the snapshot year.[3] By then the committee was well established in its post-war form, but had not yet been tested by the Suez and Hungarian emergencies which led to its re-subordination among the 'lessons of Suez' in 1957. The snapshot is therefore of the JIC in its post-1945 'Mark I' form, and its place in the committee's subsequent development.

The snapshot is however by no means complete. The committee minutes of that period give relatively full accounts of discussion, but some of them have been withheld from release, as have some of its most important papers.[4] So too have the Secretary's files recording business handled outside formal meetings.[5] Nevertheless the available records provide a basis for some reasonably firm conclusions.

THE JIC'S REMIT

The committee's terms of reference were first set in 1939, adapted to peacetime in 1948 and updated in November 1955 after discussion in the course of that year. After subsequent revisions the current version was made public in 2000. Throughout the whole period the committee's four post-war functions – producing intelligence itself, managing intelligence as a whole, international liaison, and aspects of security – have remained substantially unaltered. As set out in its 1955 charter they can be summarized as follows, with the latest version for comparison:[6]

1. *Intelligence production*: in 1955 'to assemble, appreciate and present intelligence' to meet the requirements of the Chiefs of Staff, or 'as may be required', or as the committee itself 'may deem necessary'. In the present day the Chiefs of Staff (COS) subordination is ancient history, and the remit has been expanded 'to monitor and give early warning of developments of direct or indirect threats to British interests, whether political, military or economic' and 'to assess events and situations relating to external affairs, defence, terrorism, major international criminal activity, scientific, technical and international economic matters'.
2. *Management*: in 1955 the JIC was to 'give higher direction' to intelligence operations and 'keep under review the organisation and working of intelligence . . . as a whole . . . to ensure efficiency, economy and a rapid adaptation to changing requirements'. This is now substantially repeated with two additions: coordinating interdepartmental plans 'as necessary', and presenting 'requirements and priorities for intelligence gathering and other tasks to be conducted by the intelligence Agencies' for Ministerial approval.
3. *Liaison*: in 1955 'to maintain liaison with appropriate intelligence agencies . . . in the self-governing Commonwealth countries and the United States and other foreign countries' and with 'international defence organizations of which the United Kingdom is a member'; now it is 'to maintain and supervise liaison with Commonwealth and foreign organizations as appropriate'.
4. *Security*: the 1955 JIC was accorded almost the same responsibilities for 'defence security' as for intelligence. It now has a more generalized responsibility for reviewing 'threats to security at home and overseas', and dealing with 'such security problems as may be referred to it'.

The committee's activities in 1955 are examined here under the first three headings and not the fourth. By that year the security role, largely of information security with an emphasis on NATO regulations, had been mainly delegated, and much, though not all, of it subsequently moved in practice elsewhere.[7] Security business is therefore not covered here in detail.

STRUCTURE AND *MODUS OPERANDI*

Members of the 1955 JIC were the Foreign Office Chairman, the Director of Naval Intelligence, the Director of Military Intelligence, the Assistant Chief of Air Staff (Intelligence), the Director of the Joint Intelligence Bureau (JIB), and the heads of the Security Service, the Secret Intelligence Service (SIS, described in the 1955 charter as MI6) and Government Communications Headquarters (GCHQ). The Colonial Office often attended and became a full member during the year. The Commonwealth Relations Office also attended sometimes, though in discussion of the draft 1955 charter a suggestion that it should become a full member was treated rather cavalierly: 'its function was liaison, not production', and it 'has nothing to offer in the way of intelligence'.[8]

As a COS committee the JIC issued its papers under Ministry of Defence headings, though its charter was endorsed by the Foreign and Colonial Secretaries as well as the Minister of Defence. The COS subordination determined much of its character. Its two drafting teams of the Joint Intelligence Staff (JIS) were mainly military, each with representatives of the three services plus one civilian. Its minutes suggest that the weightiest contributors in its discussions tended to be the three (still independent) military Directors; the JIB seems less prominent, and GCHQ, SIS and the Security Service seem to have kept low profiles except on matters in which they were directly concerned. The papers do not record the attendance by US and Commonwealth representatives that became routine in later years. The general impression is therefore that military matters and military interests loomed large. The committee was still to some extent a device for knocking senior armed forces' heads together.

Yet, as in wartime, this was combined with the distinctive feature of a Foreign Office Chairman, not only injecting non-military dimensions but also acting as something more than an inter-service arbitrator. A seminal review in 1947, the Evill Review,[9] had focused on the importance of leadership: a Chairman was needed who had an 'assured position, adequate time and sufficient supporting staff' to provide 'the added authority that is needed to give more forcefulness and influence to our intelligence organization as a whole'. Ministers should have 'a single individual to whom they could refer any general issue . . . and would equally give to intelligence as a whole a spokesman well placed to voice its possibilities and its needs'. The choice offered by Evill was between a whole-time Chairman based on the (new) Ministry of Defence and continued Foreign Office chairmanship with enhanced status. In the event the Foreign Office option was chosen: a decision that has influenced the character of British intelligence ever since.

Hence in 1955 the committee's military character was balanced by civilian influences. The Foreign Office Chairman was then in the third year of what was to be an unusual, seven-year period of office.[10] Below him the Foreign Office's Head of the Permanent Under-Secretary's Department (PUSD), handling intelligence matters, was influential in the JIC though not a full member,[11] and the Colonial Office and the three civilian Heads of Agency added to the civilian weight.

The committee was attended by Directors and met every Thursday. It was supported by one junior committee (nominally of Deputies) meeting less regularly on Wednesdays under the Head of PUSD's chairmanship, and another on security business, meeting on Fridays.[12] The Wednesday meetings tended to concentrate on those management and organizational affairs that did not merit Directors' own attention. Intelligence production was therefore usually a matter for the Directors, and made up the main part of the Thursday agendas. The draft weekly Summary of Intelligence, produced by the interdepartmental Heads of Sections meetings on Tuesdays, was always included, plus drafts of one or more longer intelligence reports produced by the JIS. Management business was usually less substantial, though there would normally be at least one paper of this kind. Liaison subjects also featured frequently, sometimes arising out of other items. Thursday meetings began at 1030 and presumably ran most of the way to lunch.

PRODUCTION AND ASSESSMENT

The weekly Summary of Intelligence was the direct predecessor of the modern weekly 'Red Book'. It usually contained about a dozen separate, very brief items, with more substantial (but still short) notes sometimes appended to it. An abbreviated version seems to have been prepared for a top-level readership. The Soviet Union was central, but considerable attention was given to threats of Chinese action over Quemoy and Matsu and communist activity everywhere. Each week the Summary began with a statement that there were no Soviet indicators of war, followed by a similar (but often slightly expanded) paragraph about Chinese activity, plus occasional Indo-Chinese forecasts. The body of it contained items on the USSR and Eastern Europe, China and Indo-China, and the Middle East (with an emphasis on Egypt), in that order. Over the first six months of 1955 the count of individual items was 90 on the USSR and Eastern Europe, 50 on China, 57 on Indo-China and 82 on the Middle East, with only a few others. Some of the content was of a rather mundane military kind. The general impression of these summaries is of unsophisticated reporting by modern standards, with the appearance of a rag-bag.

The 53 longer-term reports over the complete year ranged from notes of two or three pages to large reference works. More than three-quarters were on Soviet subjects. Among the shorter of these were assessments covering Soviet disarmament proposals; hypothetical Soviet attitudes towards partial disarmament; German reunification and demilitarized zones in central Europe; Soviet courses of action in 1956; and communist policy towards Afghanistan. The changes in the Soviet leadership in that year were reported in the Weekly Summary but do not seem to have been the subject of a separate assessment. Other short Soviet pieces were surveys of the Soviet ballistic missile threat, the Soviet merchant fleet, the importance of East German uranium, the Soviet Bloc's campaign for émigré repatriation, and the threat to Greenland, Spitzbergen and the Faroes.

Bigger reports on the USSR were mainly compendiums, some of them updates of regular surveys, some looking ahead as far as 1959 or 1960. They included periodic intelligence summaries and order of battle data for NATO, an annual account of world communism (mainly covering party strengths and activities, legal and illegal), and summaries of Soviet Bloc war potential, research and development, economic growth, amphibious capabilities, and economic activities in the Middle East and South and South-East Asia, plus a six-monthly digest of 'developments in the Soviet Zone of Germany' and Soviet missile intelligence. The minutes refer to a report on 'Assessments of the Threat by Communist Forces' though it is not clear whether this was ever produced. There was to be JIC involvement in a steering committee assessing 'the effect of Allied nuclear attacks on Russia and China'. Another major commitment was the annual update in consultation with the US of the large NATO paper on Soviet military capabilities, and there were similar inputs to ANZAM (Australia, New Zealand, America) and other politico-military conferences. Other basic papers dealt with Soviet intentions and capabilities in war, mainly in a time-frame up to

1959; the estimated Soviet conduct of its land, maritime and air campaigns; Soviet logistic problems in nuclear war; the nuclear threat to the UK (a brief paper); Soviet oil supplies (two reports); the wartime threat to the Middle East; and the submarine threat to NATO sea lanes in 1960–65.

China was also covered in reports, though less so than in the weekly Summaries. Its activities figured in the surveys of communism worldwide and of the communist powers' activities in the Middle East and South and South-East Asia. Other Chinese subjects were the threat to South-East Asia in the event of war in 1956–59 (also covered in a paper for ANZAM planning), the effect of allied nuclear counter-action, and (briefly) the repercussions of a Chinese attack on the offshore islands, including possible US nuclear or non-nuclear intervention. There were three papers on Indo-China, and one, surprisingly, on the threat to New Zealand.

By later standards the rest of the world received relatively little attention, though some of it figured in the Soviet and Chinese 'threat' papers. There was only one substantial Middle East paper – on Israeli courses of action in the event of war with the Arab states, apparently originating in British planning for military assistance to Jordan – plus a short piece late in the year on 'the likelihood of Israeli–Arab war in the near future'. The Israeli threat to Cyprus appeared once as an agenda item. There was however a succession of relatively short reports dealing on situations and outlooks elsewhere: in Turkey, Libya, French North Africa, Somaliland and (all in one report) Sarawak, Brunei and North Borneo. Other similar papers were produced on the Guatamalan threat to British Honduras and on Yemeni interference in Aden. Quite outside this mould, a report on the future of West Germany was commissioned, but not completed before the end of the year.

Hence this pattern of output reflects the priority of communist targets, and the committee's role in providing the detailed threat assessments of them needed by military planners, including those in NATO, CENTO, SEATO and other bilateral and multilateral forums. In all these respects the product reflected the committee's COS subordination, and its origin as an adjunct to Joint Planning Staffs. Ministers were not formally listed as principal customers until the 1957 revision of the terms of reference.

On the other hand the committee took a reasonably wide view of its role. On the Soviet target it dealt with the political subjects just described, and produced forward-looking assessments. 'Likely Soviet Courses of Action up to 1st January 1957', intended as preparation for the Geneva Foreign Ministers' Conference, demonstrated its tackling of major subjects of this kind. Soviet military capabilities, too, were themselves examined in the round, with papers on raw materials, industry and science and technology, probably reflecting the joint-service influence of the JIB. Committee minutes show concern with nuclear and missile threats and a questioning of earlier ideas about a long war. The weekly reassurance about indicators of Soviet aggression was ritualistic, but at least recognized the increased importance of warning in the coming missile age. Similarly the full membership given to the Colonial Office was an indication of a broader range of geographical coverage then beginning, and no doubt rapidly accelerated in the following year by events in the Middle East.

The committee also did not confine itself to written production. The Thursday meetings included discussion of current items not included in the Summary, including some relatively new interests; examples were the outbreak of Cypriot terrorism and the threat to the British base there, a warning from the Security Service that IRA activities were expected to increase in the coming winter, and (most unusually) communist influence in UK strikes. Periodic discussion with the military Directors of Plans was also part of the routine. So too were the discussions with senior foreign visitors and British officials and commanders from overseas, described below under 'liaison'. The committee also tabled and discussed fifteen American National Intelligence Estimates (mainly on Sino–Soviet Bloc subjects, but with forecasts for West Germany, Austria and Japan) and similar papers from the Canadian and Australian JICs, though it is not clear how far these discussions were intended to produce feedback to the originators.

So the JIC as an intelligence assessor reflected the realities and assumptions of the time: the widespread British Empire and the worldwide deployment of British forces, the overarching concern for the USSR as part of a monolithic and worldwide communist threat, and the place of China and South-East Asia among its manifestations. The accuracy and influence of its product is not considered here. But on Soviet attitudes and intentions it addressed at least some of the important questions of the day. It was a piece of Second World War military machinery adapted without great change to the Cold War; yet, whatever the eventual verdict on its analysis, it was more than just a cog in a conventional military machine. Its formal output was considerable, and in so far as some of its other discussions of world affairs gives an impression of a talking-shop, a recent comment by a member of the modern Assessments Staff should be borne in mind: that in some ways the *process* of interdepartmental assessment is more important than the *product*. Committee discussion helped to ensure that diplomats, military officers and intelligence practitioners saw the world through roughly the same eyes.

MANAGEMENT

The committee's managerial responsibilities can be traced back to its 1939 charge with 'the consideration of any further measures which might be thought necessary in order to improve the efficient working of the intelligence organization of the country as a whole' – a concept of 'intelligence as a whole' that the Official History of British Intelligence subsequently identified as a major landmark.[13] JIC business of this kind in 1955 can be conveniently examined here in terms of its remits for 'higher direction' and effectiveness ('efficiency, economy and a rapid adaptation to changing requirements'), plus some specific issues.

Higher Direction

In 1955 there were three major studies falling under this heading. In the first part of the year the committee considered 'The State of our Intelligence on the Sino Soviet Bloc and Measures to Improve It', revisiting a subject previously dealt with in 1953. The report itself is not available and there is no indication of its content. The only clues in the minutes are references to the possibility of penetration flights over the USSR, and to establishing a working party to coordinate the briefing and debriefing of travellers there.

The second study was of 'defence intelligence targets'; the limitation to defence reflects what was then thought to be the committee's role. This paper is also not available, but the minutes suggest that it was not a routine exercise. They record the tension between the military requirement for detailed order-of-battle intelligence, and the civilian agencies' view, as put by the GCHQ Director, that the time had come for 'more emphasis on intelligence which would help us in the "cold" war, rather than in the "hot" war'.[14] The collectors disliked the military insistence that they should provide the detailed intelligence for what they denigrated as 'bean counting', and argued instead for broad guidance supplemented by close working contacts. Underlying the argument was the basic question, discussed further in Chapter 12, of where collectors should draw the line between reporting everything to the all-source analysts and performing analysis and selection themselves.

The third was of colonial intelligence arrangements after General Templer's study of 'colonial security'. The JIC report on Templer's recommendations is also not available, but subjects covered included the colonies' Local Intelligence Committees (LICs) (first established in 1950), their relationships with the JIC, and the arrangements for Security Service advisers to colonial governments. The Colonial Office's full membership of the committee was one outcome.

Another element of higher direction was, implicitly, the committee's attention to warning of Soviet attack. In the course of the year it produced a brief report on 'Indications of Soviet Preparations for Early War' up to the end of 1957 (superseding a 1951 report on the subject), and sponsored a discussion of indicators with the Canadians. It revised its own interdepartmental procedures for intelligence alerts, and produced a list of special collection operations that might be undertaken in times of tension. The minutes record Air Ministry speculations about having one or two specially prepared reconnaissance aircraft available in a crisis, and a subsequent brief reference to the possibility of having 'airborne satellites' to assist American surveillance.

Effectiveness

At the beginning of the year the committee found itself considering what remained a major issue forty-five years later: the need to study overt as well as covert material, and to balance single-source collection against all-source analysis. As first recorded in 1955, 'good intelligence depended to an increasing extent on expert evaluation of information obtained from overt sources'.[15] Subsequent minutes refer to deficiencies, unnecessary analytical duplication, and the problems of adequate career prospects for specialist analysts; clearly something was felt to be wrong.

A working party was called, but delayed by initial disagreement over who should chair it. Not surprisingly the Foreign Office Chairman of the Wednesday meetings eventually took it on. Its work occupied most of the year and its report was to be taken early in 1956. One can guess that it became in effect a battle involving the new-fangled JIB and the three independent service Directorates, a battle that went on until the creation of the DIS nine years later.

On its own output the JIC in October discussed the form of its weekly review, aiming at something broader that 'would present the important developments of the week so as to make an impact on the reader'.[16] Suggestions included more colonial coverage, more supplements in the form of short notes (which in later years became a separate line of JIC output), and the inclusion of internal security information from the Security Service – possibly domestic intelligence, but more probably on matters of colonial security. Further consideration was deferred at the end of the year until 'the organization of our intelligence' had been discussed.[17]

One other item was a portent, unrecognized at the time. Those attending a SHAPE conference had been exposed to American enthusiasm for 'machines' for processing and recording intelligence, and wondered if the UK should join in. A Wednesday meeting sought advice from the Treasury Organization and Methods Department and the National Physical Laboratory, but then kicked the idea into touch. American-style machines were distrusted, and one objection was that adopting them would push the UK into a 'combined' (presumably UK–US) organization. Thus were the beginnings of information technology ignored.

Specific Issues

Most of the committee's management business, including Wednesday items, was concerned with more specific matters of organization, procedures and plans. Sub-committees on Intelligence Mobilization Plans, Defectors and Service Attachés generated some business, though not very much, and there were regular presentations from the sub-committees on nuclear and scientific and technical intelligence. The most consistent preoccupation was however with the effects on in-theatre intelligence arrangements of the Federal Republic's entry to NATO and the withdrawal of occupation forces from Austria. Over Germany a special JIC meeting was called in November before the Chairman's visit. Finding a new basis for the British intelligence structure established under the post-war Control Commission may have been one topic. On Austria the committee paid similar attention to the intelligence effects of the British withdrawal.

Other detailed items of organization and planning included joint-service training for the provision of more Russian linguists, mainly national servicemen; the position on Chinese linguists; language training for service attachés versus Treasury obduracy; and standardized terminology in foreign translation, with the Joint Technical Language Section at GCHQ as the interdepartmental authority. There is a brief reference to the allocation of responsibilities between the service ministries and the JIB over the deployed Soviet missiles: another issue of Whitehall strife for some years to come. Interdepartmental procedures for handling Soviet Bloc and other defectors were issued or reissued, and provoked discussion about the proper handling of defectors. On war planning there were papers on the principles of intelligence mobilization, a peacetime cadre for a Joint Service Defence Interrogation Centre and its wartime expansion, and an Air Ministry initiative for joint service escape and evasion training.

Other business revolved around the British JICs overseas. JIC (Germany) hardly figured, but the Middle East and the Far East bodies (JIC(ME) and JIC(FE)) raised issues through their international connections. London had to deal with a NATO request for contacts between JIC(ME) and NATO intelligence staffs in the Mediterranean, guidance for JIC(ME)'s support for UK–US–Turkish discussions, and JIC(FE)'s inputs to ANZAM and SEATO meetings. There was also a purely national tug-of-war with JIC(ME) over Middle East intelligence arrangements following the British withdrawal from Egypt to Cyprus. The Prime Minister wanted work pulled back to London, but JIC(ME) had a trump card in the official doctrine that overseas theatres had to be able to function in war without counting on reinforcements. Another working party was established, yet again under the Foreign Office's Wednesday Chairman. Later in the year the JIC Chairman and the Director of Military Intelligence visited Cyprus for discussion.

The Effect on 'Intelligence as a Whole'

Since the most important papers are not available the committee's efforts on higher direction and overall effectiveness cannot be properly judged, but as a board of management it was certainly active. The Chairman visited Germany, the Middle East and the Far East; and there was the succession of Foreign Office-chaired working parties. The committee was by no means coasting.

Yet the consistent impression is that its responsibility for the review of 'intelligence as a whole' was interpreted with some tacit limitations. The Security Service, SIS and GCHQ were no doubt involved in the work on intelligence targets and the 'measures to improve' study, and the Security Service must have taken a major part in the review of colonial intelligence. But hardly any business appeared on the committee's agenda concerned specifically with these three intelligence agencies, either individually or collectively. Managing the secret intelligence activities of civilian agencies probably did not fit easily into the operation of a COS committee.

This was consistent with the committee's origins and wartime record. Despite its wide terms of reference in 1939, the wartime JIC was concerned mainly with arrangements between the three armed services and the wartime joint-service organizations; the affairs of SIS and the Security Service remained to a considerable extent outside its purview. The Official History refers to SIS's 'historic aloofness' from the wartime JIC machinery, and to the surprising consequence of a separate supervisory structure for Sigint, with the only rare JIC involvement.[18] These wartime features had been carried over into peace. The assumption that the affairs of secret agencies were not really suitable for the committee is reflected in an opinion, recorded in its discussion of the 1955 charter, that the wording should 'exclude [intelligence] procurement operations that were not the responsibility of the JIC'; though no exclusion of this kind is apparent from the final version.[19]

Of course the three agencies were not loose cannons. The Security Service was linked with the Home Office, and SIS and GCHQ came under Foreign Office supervision from the senior officials involved in the JIC. Arguably PUSD was, up to a point, a central authority for the oversight of foreign intelligence. Sigint also had its own superintending Board, meeting periodically, in some respects as an expanded JIC. There were also the intangible effects of the JIC's collegiality. Collectors came into regular contact with their principal customers; discussing substantive intelligence each week encouraged common views, and helped the civilian Directors to fine-tune their priorities. The JIC ethos encouraged cooperation and lessened inter-institutional conflict. The committee's direction of intelligence as a whole was to some extent an illusion, yet indirectly it was a powerful cultural influence in the community's self-management.

LIAISON

Something of the same can be said about the JIC's liaison responsibilities. Relations between the single-source agencies and their foreign equivalents were not JIC business. Neither did the committee review total relationships with particular countries, though it did discuss a tricky request from South Africa for intelligence on African countries, including British colonies.[20] The UK–US relationship was taken for granted, though there was one discussion of transatlantic exchanges of nuclear intelligence where special sensitivities arose. Essentially the JIC looked after its own liaison, or military liaison with a joint-service flavour, and left the individual agencies to develop their own overseas relationships. Guidance probably came from the Foreign Office and not the committee.

With this limitation it dealt with the succession of particular issues that appeared to be its business. NATO matters loomed large, and the committee coped with the problems of releases at SHAPE's naval and air intelligence conferences and with a succession of other SHAPE and SACLANT (Supreme Allied Command Atlantic) requests. It discussed a conference with SHAPE on the principles of NATO's intelligence war planning, and dealt on other occasions with NATO's wartime photo–interpretation, counter-intelligence and processing of captured documents. NATO's complexities even extended to the difficulty of exchanging information on the alliance's own members' ports, beaches and other features. Outside NATO the committee made arrangements for intelligence at ANZAM and SEATO conferences and meetings with the Baghdad Pact planners.

The problems posed by these issues are obvious enough. NATO's intelligence structure was partly UK–staffed, and national intelligence inputs were essential for its viability. Intelligence was also part of the currency for promoting CENTO and SEATO and other regional arrangements. Yet security was the obstacle; it was assumed, correctly, that penetration by Soviet intelligence was so widespread that intelligence releases of these kinds could well be releases to Moscow. In 1955 the JIC held that in NATO the imminent integration of German officers was increasing the risks. The committee was therefore balancing intelligence use against the protection of national sources, in the light of the basic NATO principles that intelligence collection was not a multinational NATO activity and that the Alliance depended on national inputs: principles that still apply in NATO, and have been carried over into concepts for intelligence support of the EU and UN.

Otherwise the committee's main liaison business consisted of entertaining senior foreign visitors to London for *tours d'horizon* at its Thursday meetings, as part of the 'intelligence diplomacy' of the day with the US and Commonwealth. The succession of visits that took place or were projected in 1955 included those by Allen Dulles the American DCI, Canada's JIC Chairman and (separately) its JIC members, and Australia's JIC Chairman, DNI, DMI and First Assistant Secretary in the Prime Minister's Department. The committee also endorsed bilateral discussions with the US, Canada and the French on NATO matters. The committee's discussions with the US/Commonwealth visitors were complemented by those already mentioned with senior UK visitors from overseas, and on one occasion by a session with a leading academic expert on the Soviet economy.

SECURITY

Relatively few security items reached the main committee from the Friday meetings, but some did. They included restrictions on the Soviet mission in the UK, the security of economic and industrial information, announcements of NATO exercises, and the threat posed by the distribution of propaganda in 'Soviet News' to army units. A Wednesday meeting considered the protection of key points in the UK from sabotage.

SUBSEQUENT DEVELOPMENTS

This, then, was the peacetime JIC Mark I. The committee's 1955 members would still find much that was familiar to them in the present committee's routine, with its weekly meetings and their juxtaposition of the Weekly Summary, other more substantial reports, and matters of intelligence management. Some other features have disappeared. The subordinate Wednesday and Friday committees are now long gone; the Tuesday interdepartmental Heads of Sections meetings have been replaced by the Current Intelligence Groups; the JIS has been replaced by the Assessments Staff; the JIC is no longer at the hub of the set of complementary JICs overseas. The committee's post-1955 history has combined continuity with step-changes at intervals of ten years or more.

Hence the committee's development falls into four phases. The first was initiated by its post-Suez transfer to the Cabinet Office in 1957; the substantive link with the COS was broken and the committee became more clearly linked with top government, though without other changes at that time in its membership or structure. The second phase began with the major structural changes of 1968, probably the biggest in the committee's history: the replacement of the JIS teams by the much larger Assessments Staff; the initiation of a separate 'economic' JIC of equal status to the main committee (though it did not survive as a permanent feature); and the creation of the post of Intelligence Coordinator. The third phase, from 1983, followed the post-mortem on the Falklands invasion and included a more specific warning role, a more tightly controlled assessment programme, expanded membership, and – most significantly – enhanced status and independence for the Chairman. For nine years after 1985 the post was filled by an ex-diplomat who also acted as the Prime Minister's Foreign Policy Adviser. The fourth phase began in 1994 when this Adviser post lapsed, and the Chairman became once again a serving diplomat combining the job with other, operational responsibilities. Through all the phases since 1968 the post of the Intelligence Coordinator developed as a focus of central management, and possibly a new phase began in 2000 when the post was amalgamated with the chairmanship, and filled full-time by a Foreign Office official; though at the time of writing little is publicly known of the effects.

To some extent these changes represent a process of increased civilianization. The amalgamation of the JIB and three service Directorates into the DIS in 1964 reduced the four military/JIB seats to two.[21] After 1957 the JIC Secretary (whose role had been described the previous year as 'very much what the engine and steering gear are to a ship'[22]) was always a civilian, usually from the Foreign Office, and after 1968 the Coordinator provided more senior civilian influence. The Assessments Staff created at the same time has almost always had Foreign Office secondees at its head and as its most powerful element. Civilianization of these kinds mirrored, and at the same time accentuated, the committee's changing role compared with 1955: to produce politico–military–economic assessments reflecting worldwide British interests, no longer (even during the Cold War) with a concentration on communist targets or special attention to military needs.

Despite these shifts of balance some basic features have survived. One is the continued Foreign Office (or ex-Foreign Office) chairmanship. Related to this is the continued importance in the committee's intelligence production of those who are in a sense intelligence 'amateurs' – mainly professional diplomats, but also senior military officers and other Whitehall officials – rather than career intelligence professionals. The JIC is a bulwark against powerful intelligence agencies with policy axes to grind. A third feature is the combination in the same committee of responsibilities for top-level assessment and for community management, with the first tending to take precedence over the second. A fourth is the unevenness of the committee's performance in 'reviewing intelligence as a whole'. Its attention has shifted from the 'defence intelligence' that concerned it in 1955, but the effect has been for management to rest increasingly with the Intelligence Coordinator rather than the committee; though the system as a whole still remains open to the criticism of 'weakness in the centre' recently made by the Parliamentary Intelligence and Security Committee.[23]

THE FUTURE

JIC assessment has quite a good record. Its general quality is better than in most countries. The fact that its output is interdepartmentally agreed gives a special edge to its use in decision-taking. The committee has avoided political commitment; on the whole it has not consistently backed MoD preconceptions against those of the Foreign Office, or vice versa. It has had spectacular warning failures, but no more than those of the US and others.

Linking this role with management has been less successful; the committee has been better at producing than managing. Its direction and overview have been selective. Yet its collegial, consensus-seeking atmosphere has encouraged cooperation and negotiation. This author has argued elsewhere that more central influence is needed.[24] But, at the very least, the British community's internecine strife is much less than the international norm. The JIC has encouraged a useful degree of community self-management.

These achievements notwithstanding, more radical thoughts may now be in order. Governments in the information age have ever-increasing appetites for assessment at a greatly accelerated pace. Assessment in the JIC committee style is Rolls Royce in the effort put into it, particularly in the opportunity costs of the time that its top members give to it. Perhaps in intelligence production the system will move to increased reliance on the central Assessments Staff, more delegation from the main committee to its subordinate Current Intelligence Groups, and a high-profile Chairman; on this last, Evill's 1947 recommendations about the value of a 'single individual' and an intelligence 'spokesman' may have renewed relevance. On matters of policy and management it may be sensible to see the JIC more clearly as a useful forum, but not an authority. The electronic revolution in business, commerce and information services has already moved into other aspects of government; the British Cabinet has committed itself to the slogan of 'information age, joined-up government', with all government services available electronically by 2008.[25] There should be a similar objective of a joined-up intelligence community, with all its customers served interactively by a 'one-stop' electronic system. It will need central vision and power to set it and reach it.

With the combined Chairman JIC/Coordinator post the British community may already be moving in new directions.[26] The JIC committee system inherited from the second half of the twentieth century remains a considerable asset, but needs some de-mythologizing.

NOTES

1. Amended from a paper 'Role of the British Joint Intelligence Committee: an Historical Perspective' given at the XXVI International Colloquium of Military History on 'Intelligence after World War II' at the Norwegian Institute for Defence Studies, 9 August 2000, as part of the 19th International Conference of Historical Sciences; being published by the Institute in 2001 as one of the conference papers, (ed.) Lars Christian Jenssen.
2. M.E. Herman, *Intelligence Power in Peace and War* (Cambridge: Cambridge University Press, 1996), p. 277.
3. Public Record Office (PRO) sources for 1955 are CAB 158/19-22 in date order for reports and papers, and CAB 159/18-22 in date order for committee minutes. Sources are to these papers unless otherwise stated.
4. In most cases, however, the length of the minutes withheld can be deduced, and subject headings are sometimes shown even when minutes and reports are not available.
5. Files in CAB 163 series, PRO; they have been extensively weeded.
6. The references are to JIC(55)74, CAB 158/22, PRO, and *National Intelligence Machinery* (Norwich: The Stationery Office, 2000), p. 19.
7. Some security responsibilities were transferred to the Security Policy and Methods Committee on the JIC's resubordination to the Cabinet Office in 1957. Details are in CAB 163/9 PRO. The JIC remained particularly involved in inter-departmental questions of *intelligence* security, for example the release of wartime intelligence records.
8. Minutes of 11 August. In the event the CRO became a full member the following year.
9. *Review of Intelligence Organizations, 1947* by Air Chief Marshal Sir Douglas Evill, Misc/P 4781 6 November 1947: CAB 163/7, PRO. Quotations in this paragraph are from p. 12.
10. Sir Patrick Dean chaired the committee from 1953 to 1960 (R.J. Aldrich, *Espionage, Security and Intelligence in Britain, 1945–1970* (Manchester: Manchester University Press, 1998), p. 232).
11. G. McDermott; author of *The New Diplomacy and its Apparatus* (London: Plume Press, 1973), published after an early and contentious retirement from the Foreign Office.
12. Great emphasis had been laid in the 1947 Review on the establishment of sub-committees to free the main committee for major items of business; separate sub-committees were then envisaged for intelligence, organization and security. It should be noted that the 1955 minutes do not reflect the difference in status between the main JIC and its two subsidiaries.
13. F.H. Hinsley with E.E. Thomas, C.F.G. Ransom, and R.C. Knight, *British Intelligence in the Second World War,* Vol.1 (London: HMSO, 1979), p. 43.
14. Minutes of 28 April.
15. Minutes of 6 January. Just over thirty years later the present author criticized the inadequate attention still given to overt Soviet military publications in 'Reflections on the Study of Soviet Military Literature', *RUSI Journal,* 133, 2 (summer 1988).

16. Minutes of 13 October.
17. The outcome for the committee itself was the replacement of the Weekly Summary in June 1956 by a weekly 'Grey Book' (issued after 1957 by the Heads of Sections meetings, not the main committee) plus the higher-level weekly 'Red Book', issued by the committee itself with material of higher classification. In 1966 the Grey Book was discontinued and the Red Book was split into Part 1 for Ministers and Part 2 for a wider readership.
18. Hinsley *et al.*, *British Intelligence in the Second World War*, Vol.2, p. 271. Disputes between the SIS and SOE however became JIC business.
19. Minutes of 11 August.
20. Minutes of 2 November.
21. In the 1983 expansion the MoD was given an additional seat, but for a civilian policy-making post. The Home Office became a full committee member in 2000.
22. *JIC History*, JIC/1/56 (and in various other versions), CAB 163/8, PRO.
23. *Intelligence and Security Committee Annual Report 1999-2000* (London: The Stationery Office, 2000), paras. 23, 41.
24. See Chapter 4.
25. For an account of British (non-intelligence) government plans and problems, see C. Bellamy, 'Implementing Information-Age Government: Principles, Progress and Paradox', *Public Policy and Administration*, 15, 1 (spring 2000).
26. But note the doubts about the status of the new post expressed by the Intelligence and Security Committee, *Annual Report 1999–2000*, para. 23. Perhaps a more important issue is to ensure some continuity in its tenure. The announcement in September 2001 that the post of Chairman and Coordinator is to be held by a member of the SIS (MI6), 'the first occasion since its formation that the JIC has been chaired from outside the Foreign Office', marks a significant development in the committee's evolution.

6

British and American Systems: A Study in Contrasts?[1]

My subject was intended to be the contrasts between UK and US intelligence. But in reflecting on it I was struck not only by the differences but also by the similarities. At a basic level, for example, both countries think in terms of communities of specialist agencies, rather than monolithic intelligence services on the KGB pattern. Both assume that 'intelligence' has two complementary facets: it is both the collector/exploiter of special single-sources, usually covert in nature, and also government's all-source expert on some subjects. By no means all other countries view intelligence in these lights. There is also the degree of UK–US interaction; each has learned from the other, and continues to do so. So I have inserted a question mark in my title. Is it a study in contrasts or similarities?

SIZE AND STRUCTURE

It may be useful to begin with size. The latest US intelligence budget is said to be of the order of $30 billion.[2] When defence expenditure on strategic intelligence is added to the declared British Single Intelligence Vote, the total there is probably somewhat over £1 billion. Among other things the difference between the two reflects US expenditure on intelligence satellites, but a comparison is unfair for other reasons; tactical military intelligence finds its place in the American figures in a way it does not in the British. My guess is that a ratio of around 12:1 or 10:1 might be a fair reflection of the two states' relative expenditure, but that is no more than an informed guess.

Differences in size also affect the two communities in some not entirely obvious ways. The US community constantly worries about problems of intelligence's access to policy, of the need to work hard to get its messages home. The British on the whole have fussed less. The difference is partly a result of the sheer size of US government and the dispersion of its intelligence – CIA at Langley, NSA at Fort Meade   compared with the smaller and more compact British system, with most of the main elements (except the Sigint and imagery centres) in walking distance of each other. But it is also bound up with the British culture of what has been called the small 'Whitehall village', caricatured as one in which all the senior officials have grown up together since knowing each other in their student days at Oxford or Cambridge.

Next, the obvious equivalences and differences between the corresponding institutional bricks in the two countries. The British Secret Intelligence Service (SIS) equates with CIA's Directorate of Operations, with its remit of Humint and covert action. The opposite number of the Government Communications Headquarters (GCHQ) is the National Security Agency (NSA) with almost the same offensive and defensive responsibilities for Sigint and electronic security; both are in a sense federations of civilian and armed forces efforts. NSA as founded in 1952 and its predecessor the Armed Forces Security Agency were both closely modelled on the British example; the US organization of Sigint is the clearest and most long-standing example of direct British influence. The third of the three British civilian agencies, the Security Service, appears at first sight to be equivalent to the intelligence department of the FBI, but this is not as clear-cut as it seems. Unlike the FBI, the Security Service is not a law-enforcement authority; it works closely with police services but is very distinct from them. My impression is that in this area of terrorism and counterintelligence – where responsibilities are tangled enough in the British system – the Security Service's equivalents are parts of both FBI and CIA, plus elements of the armed forces' security organizations. Finally, the UK's Defence Intelligence Staff (DIS) can be roughly equated with the Defense Intelligence Agency, except that historically the DIS has also controlled the Joint Air Reconnaissance and Intelligence Centre,[3] the British analogue of the American National Imagery and Mapping Agency.

INTELLIGENCE'S CENTRE

One missing brick on the UK side is any equivalent to the US National Reconnaissance Office, since there have been no corresponding British satellite programmes. Far more significant in comparing the two national systems is the absence of a British equivalent to the CIA's Directorate of

Intelligence for the production of finished intelligence. There is a small central Assessments Staff serving the Joint Intelligence Committee (JIC)[4] in the Cabinet Office, but the concept is quite different from that of the large CIA analysis, research and production effort. It is indeed an oddity that Britain, priding itself on intelligence, does not have a central analytic agency on the CIA pattern. The explanation lies in the British attachment to departmental rather than central arrangements, and to interdepartmental consensus as epitomized in the working of the JIC which I shall discuss shortly. But it is of interest that in a high-level review of British arrangements in the autumn of 1947, the reviewer expressed admiration for the US system that had only just been put on a statutory basis in the National Security Act, and expressed some regret in deciding that he could not recommend it for the UK.[5] Historical orthodoxy has it that at that time the UK was the intelligence teacher and the US the learner; but on this evidence the position on central arrangements in 1947 might have been reversed. It should be added, to balance the oddities, that the CIA's subsequent evolution to combine its central analysis with permanent responsibility for one form of covert collection (Humint) still strikes the foreigner as strange, however understandable this was in the Cold War circumstances in which this developed.

This brings me to the place of a committee, the JIC, in the British system, combining the two central responsibilities for producing assessments for the top level of government and managing intelligence as a whole. Its actual effectiveness in the second role can be debated, but it undoubtedly has this formal responsibility and acts as a forum for the community's managerial matters, though not all of them.[6] These two functions came to be joined in the one committee almost by accident in 1939 and the early wartime years, and have been a feature of British arrangements ever since. Everyone now refers to it as 'the JIC', but for much of the post-1945 period the JIC system included a constellation of overseas JICs and Local Intelligence Committees in colonies or other areas where Britain had forces deployed, with the London committee at the centre. Hence the simplistic answer to the question asked by Churchill about intelligence in 1940 – 'Who's in charge?'[7] (and, he might have added, 'Who is government's chief intelligence officer?') – is the committee, or sometimes its Chairman; Chairmen have themselves varied in the personal stamp they have left on the system. The textbook answer to the same questions about the American system would be the Director of Central Intelligence, the DCI. Here, then, is a principal difference between the two systems. The difference between the JIC and the DCI represents the difference between the British system of cabinet government based on consensus and the American Presidential system of greater personal power and responsibility.

Of course reality is more complex, and to discuss it it is convenient to separate the centre's provision of top-level intelligence from its managerial role. It is misleading to see JIC assessment as just the work of a committee, or a principal committee sitting over its subsidiary London committees, the Current Intelligence Groups (CIGs). It has always been serviced by a central staff who do the important drafting and effectively lead the system, sometimes short-circuiting committee procedures and producing items direct for senior readers. Equally on the American side the personal responsibilities of the DCI grew up alongside the system of National Intelligence Estimates – descended from the wartime procedures insisted on by the British to ensure agreed intelligence inputs to UK–US Grand Strategy – and these have incorporated community views formalized via various Board-like institutions. The two systems are not as radically divergent as they may seem.[8]

Nevertheless there are considerable differences. Whatever the central influence, what goes to British Ministers represents an interdepartmental view, and there is constant search for consensus; to present radically diverging interpretations of the same situation is usually felt to be a failure in the JIC's process of discussion and persuasion. Moreover the JIC product represents the views not only of 'intelligence' but also of operational departments. Non-intelligence officials from the Foreign Office and elsewhere play a full part in the committee process; the intelligence community for this purpose is a remarkably elastic one. The American assessment system, by contrast, leaves three impressions on the outsider. One is that it is 'intelligence', not a combination of intelligence and non-intelligence judgements. Another is the personal position of the DCI and the central influence of the CIA; the President's Daily Brief is, I understand, written by the CIA, as compared with the interdepartmental nature of the Prime Minister's weekly Red Book. A third feature, apparently contradicting the second, is the retention of some community procedures, especially the formalization of dissenting views, as in the traditional device of 'taking a footnote' to record departmental disagreement with a National Intelligence Estimate. In this the system perhaps mirrors a feature of US government – the value attached to disagreement, dissent and exposure to a marketplace of ideas – not found to the same extent in Whitehall. If the British system is a committee modified by a strong central backbone, its

US counterpart is more centralized advice, greatly modified by the national respect for diversity.

Of the centre's second role, management, the two systems present similar appearances though for different reasons. The DCI's nominal powers are considerable but it is common ground among American commentators that holders of the office are frustrated because most of the levers of power – control of budgets and appointments – are in the hands of the Secretary for Defense. Perhaps the appointment of a succession of new DCIs by incoming Administrations has worked in the same direction; Robert Gates was the last professional to be appointed from inside. In the UK the JIC's management role has taken second place to its intelligence production, and central management has developed since 1968 around the more personal role of the Coordinator. But this is based on advice and influence rather than any direct responsibility; his position depends on the persuasion of colleagues and backing from the busy Cabinet Secretary.

Hence neither country has strong central management of its intelligence community. The UK does not really believe in it, though actually might now be moving some way towards it by repeating the successful arrangement of nearly twenty years ago of concentrating the central production and management responsibilities on one incumbent. The US wants stronger management, or at least says it does, but has no way of getting it, in a nation in which government has been likened by Peter Jay to the effects of a field of forces rather than well-established institutional power. In reality both countries probably need incremental tinkering rather than sweeping reform. A factor in both is probably an instinctive libertarian fear that a powerful Head of Intelligence might become like the Chairman of the KGB. Americans probably feel that the CIA is powerful enough already, and the British distrust the CIA model anyway.

QUESTIONS OF INFLUENCE

A common factor to both countries is that intelligence has considerable influence and on the whole is held in high regard. By world standards both countries are big spenders on it relative to national income, defence spending and size of diplomatic services. Though it is a sitting target for media criticism and exposures in both counties, public opinion tends to support it. In the UK the record of Bletchley successes in the Second World War has coincided with Irish terrorism from 1969 onwards to make it seem important. Perhaps the memory of Pearl Harbor has similar effects in the US. Within the UK the official Whitehall culture is receptive to intelligence, and politicians, including Labour Ministers, tend to be fascinated by it. It is significant that, among the violent and long-running political controversy over the Conservative government's banning of national trade unions at GCHQ in 1984, the need for GCHQ and the size of its intelligence activities were not questioned.[9] I have the impression that American intelligence has to work harder to make itself heard in Washington; perhaps it meets more disrespect or inexperience there than in London. But good intelligence is generally recognized in both countries as necessary for their world roles: the US as the superpower and Britain, with its continued belief in its world influence, as the coordinator and fixer of international efforts.

This does not mean that intelligence in either country has been a power player in its own right. The only DCI who has been an active policy-maker with Cabinet status was Casey, and he was exceptional. But there is an interesting difference between the two in the external influences upon it. Both systems are of course lobbied by interest groups, particularly in the defence area. But the special characteristic of British intelligence is the remarkable influence of the Foreign Office within it. As part of the post-First World War settlement the Foreign Office assumed some overseeing of the SIS and hence an oblique responsibility for the predecessor of GCHQ. There was then the Foreign Office Chairmanship of the JIC in 1939. The 1947 inquiry into the JIC put forward the alternatives of Foreign Office or Ministry of Defence chairmanship, but the decision was predictably in favour of the Foreign Office.[10] Since the new JIC Assessments Staff was created in 1968 the Foreign Office has almost always led it and has supplied much of its intellectual muscle. The SIS and GCHQ continue to report to the Foreign Secretary. Two out of the three Directors recently brought to GCHQ from outside came from the Foreign Office. The major participation of Foreign Office members in the JIC and its CIGs has already been mentioned.

I believe that this Foreign Office influence has been on the whole beneficial, but it is unusual, and must seem odd to Americans. The US community is no doubt under many external influences, particularly from the Congress, but probably not from permanent officials of another government department in the British style. US intelligence as a whole is more defence-oriented than the British, and if there is any departmental influence of the kind discussed it may come from Defense; but not from State. A difference between the two intelligence systems is that while the State

Department may have been undermined by the development of intelligence, particularly by the CIA, the UK's Foreign Office has probably been strengthened by it.

DEMOCRATIC ACCOUNTABILITY AND LEGALITY

Here the flow of influence has been clearly West-to-East. The issues emerged in the US in the 1970s and made their way to the UK with the usual time-lag. The British intelligence legislation which began in 1985 owed something to the effects of the European Convention on Human Rights, but was triggered mainly by the American example and the way it was drawn on by the Old Commonwealth countries. The same is true of the Parliamentary Committee on Intelligence and Security created in 1994. Despite the very different UK and US governmental systems and legal constraints the issues are very similar.

However one difference should be recorded. The British community now follows the American model in being governed by law, and account-able (to a very limited degree) to the Legislature. But it has operated in the long, and perhaps rather different, tradition of legitimacy via autho-rization by Ministers of the Crown. The tradition originated partly by arrangements for Ministerial authorization for communications intercep-tion by Royal Warrant, with a basis in ancient Crown Prerogative; it should be remembered that a Warrant signed by a Secretary of State is a royal command, not an authorization. It then received some additional force from the Commander Crabb affair in 1956 when a covert operation was mounted against a Soviet cruiser bringing Soviet leaders to the UK, with disastrous results. The outcome was to reinforce the habit of refer-ring sensitive operations for Ministerial authorization, usually by the Foreign, Defence or Home Secretaries. Though additional legal constraints now apply, I have the impression that this basic requirement for authorization by elected Ministers distinguishes the operation of the British system from the more complex obligations of its US equivalents to Federal law and the Congress as well as the Executive. If there are accusations of acting as rogue elephants, as in Senator Church's criticism in the 1970s of the CIA, it is perhaps clearer in the UK than the US whether responsibility lies at the door of intelligence or the government directing it.

WHAT DOES EACH SYSTEM THINK OF THE OTHER?

Given this mixture of differences and similarities, it is interesting to consider what each system thinks of the other. Of course there is no single set of UK–US relationships: only the bilateral liaisons of individual agencies with their opposite numbers. I can only speak from my own limited experience. You naturally believe that your own agency, with all its faults, is better that your ally's. In my recollection the British view of the quality of US analysis was rather patronizing for perhaps the first fifteen years of the Cold War, but much less so thereafter. We envied the scale of US resources. Increasingly we admired US drive and skill in harnessing technology. Despite the duplication, rivalry and waste we could see in the system, there was vision, a gift for getting the big things right; the intelligence satellite programme typified many others. We admired the hustle and the recognition that intelligence should be a 24-hour activity; perhaps, again, the Pearl Harbor effect. We wondered sometimes if speed was pursued at the expense of reflection. But some of us admired above all the seriousness and sense of dedication. My American colleagues really acted during the Cold War as if the security of the West, indeed the fate of the world, depended on them.

What did the Americans think of us? I believe there was recurrent surprise that relatively small British resources could produce good results: the advantage of being small for 'getting things together'. Despite the numbers and specialist knowledge of CIA analysts, there was US admiration for the British JIC product, often largely achieved by the small team of Foreign Office amateurs (in intelligence terms) seconded to the Cabinet Office. But I did once hear the question asked: was it not just that the British wrote better? Both sides got about as much right and wrong. The list of joint warning failures is familiar. It is worth remembering that the surprise at the Argentine invasion of the Falklands was a spectacular American failure as well as a British one, on an area we regarded as an American intelligence back yard.

Probably our US colleagues felt that the UK was wimpish over some provocative operations, under the influence of the Foreign Office's political control; though this was not invariable. It must be remembered that at one time the British undertook overflights of the USSR in US aircraft, because President Eisenhower would not authorize them. The British view combined professional admiration of US willingness to take political risks, with reservations, sometimes, about the consequences of gung-ho American approaches. Here we may again have intelligence mirroring national characteristics; in this case the British reaction to what we see as the echo in the American attitudes of the moral sheriff in a frontier society. But this is reflecting on limited experience in what is now the distant past. Both countries' view of each other in the present more legalistic, transparent and risk-averse age may be quite different.

This has been only a superficial account of a fascinating subject. I draw no grand lessons. My only general conclusion about these differences and similarities is that intelligence is not an isolated activity. It is an integral part of government. It reflects the character of national constitutions and the societies in which it is set. Despite the differences, what strikes me is how much more British and American intelligence have in common than British intelligence has with the European systems that begin only twenty miles away across the Strait of Dover. That of course is British intelligence's version of the growing national dilemma about Europe.

NOTES

1. Given to the Institute of International Studies, Yale University, September 2000.
2. L.K. Johnson, 'Spies', *Foreign Policy* (September/October 2000), p. 18.
3. JARIC is now the Defence Geographic and Imagery Intelligence Agency, incorporating Military Survey.
4. This should not be confused with the official American use of 'JIC' in recent years to denote Joint Intelligence *Centers*, not committees. See also Note 8.
5. The investigation by Air Chief Marshal Evill was completed in late 1947. His comments on the US system are on PRO file CAB163/7, reference JIC 1017/47 of 26 September 1947.
6. For discussion see Chapter 5.
7. F.H. Hinsley with E.E. Thomas, C.F.G. Ransom and R.C. Knight, *British Intelligence in the Second World War*, Vol. I (London: HMSO, 1979), p. 291.
8. Note also that the US had its own Joint Intelligence Committee formed in December 1941 avowedly to mirror its British opposite number. As a committee reporting to the Joint Chiefs of Staff this remained in existence until 1958, but with declining influence outside purely military circles. For an account, see L.A. Valero, 'The American Joint Intelligence Committee and Estimates of the Soviet Union, 1945–1947', *Studies in Intelligence* (Washington: CIA, Center for the Study of Intelligence), no. 9 (summer 2000).
9. For discussion of this episode see Chapter 11.
10. PRO CAB 163/7. The Evill report is Misc/P 4781 dated 6 November 1947. JIC comments and the record of decisions are JIC(47)34(O)Final and JIC(47)84(O)Final of 3 January 1948.

7

Norway as an Intelligence Ally[1]

All modern intelligence services engage in transnational cooperation. This is not completely new; in the eighteenth century there were regular cryptanalytic exchanges between the British and Hanoverian Black Chambers. Military alliances in the first half of the twentieth century encouraged intelligence exchanges, culminating in the pooling of British and American material on the enemy in the Second World War. Yet the idea of formal agreements and wholesale peacetime interchanges is a relatively recent one, a product of the Cold War. Here I discuss Norway's participation in the patchwork of bilateral and multilateral intelligence cooperation that developed inside and outside NATO. For the details I draw on Olav Riste's and Arnfinn Moland's officially commissioned account of the Norwegian Intelligence Service between 1945 and 1970, published at official request in 1997.[2]

ELEMENTS OF NORWEGIAN COLLABORATION

More than in most countries, Norwegian intelligence was a response to the Cold War. NATO intelligence was based on national contributions, not on a supranational effort. The Alliance's formal bedrock was its agreed estimate of the Soviet threat and its annual updating, and this depended on the regular circulation and discussion of intelligence between nations, both bilaterally and within NATO channels. Europe viewed the American inputs with great respect, yet some suspicion; and Britain was seen sometimes as the honest broker between New World and Old, and sometimes as Perfidious Albion, manipulating Europe for transatlantic ends. So NATO members who took the Cold War seriously needed a genuine national view of the Soviet target and some access to the evidence on which it could be based. Though historians may take it for granted, an unspectacular part of Norway's intelligence collaboration to the Alliance was therefore the continuous exchanges with its allies of final, 'finished' intelligence.

Norwegian inputs to NATO carried some weight – and served Norwegian national interests – in ensuring that the threat to Scandinavia had sufficient prominence.[3]

One other inconspicuous set of international contacts also underlay Norway's effort. The pattern of formal military threat assessments of NATO (and briefly CENTO and SEATO) was matched by the worldwide but quite different network of *ad hoc*, mainly bilateral contacts that developed to exchange detailed information on Soviet espionage, subversion and covert action. The network was secretive, insulated from most other cooperation, and rarely featured in any national intelligence audits. Yet it should be recorded that Norway was an active ally in this and other aspects of defensive intelligence. Its competence and cooperation in resisting Soviet penetration in this way underwrote its other intelligence collaboration.

Nevertheless in resource terms the Norwegian investment was not in finished assessment or counterintelligence and counterespionage, but overwhelmingly in the collection and processing of covert intelligence on Soviet military targets; and it was on this that Norway international relationships centred. Some underlying factors influencing these relationships were not specific to Norway, or even to the Cold War. The appetite for intelligence is inexhaustible, and even the biggest power cannot meet all its own needs. Small powers cannot cope on their own with big and complex targets, yet want some collection of their own to avoid complete reliance on what they are given by their Big Brothers. Countries can almost always bring some special assets to the common table. Professionals naturally tend to seek cooperation with like-minded foreign colleagues, and institutional relationships between them develop their own momentum. Yet this is always offset by caution over the costs of collaboration and the need to protect sources and methods; by a constant re-calibration of the partner's competence and reliability; and for small powers by the risks of becoming a major power's satellite. Despite the effects of political stimuli and constraints, intelligence liaisons tend ultimately to be sets of hard-headed professional bargains.

This temper is also reflected in the forms they take. International collaboration tends to be through bilateral or multilateral contacts between functional authorities, often with a minimum of central coordination. The historical pattern is of specific arrangements between individual agencies rather than national Grand Strategies.[4]

This was the background to Norway's Cold War intelligence collaboration. NATO Commands received national intelligence inputs and provided NATO assessments, but these remained something of a façade;

the important players remained the national agencies, judging their foreign peers in terms of their competence and reliability, preferring bilateral relationships to all-embracing 'clubs'. The Norwegian Intelligence Service (NIS) had more central influence than many of its foreign equivalents, but its overseas liaisons were still complemented, sometimes rivalled, by those of the Air Force and the Navy. To some extent Norway's central coordination of its international cooperation was necessarily a mirror-image of the coordination – or lack of coordination – that existed in its principal collaborators, particularly the US.

A PARTNER IN COLLECTION

Norwegian covert collection sprang from the threat from across the Soviet frontier, and the opportunities it presented. Norway was starting from scratch on targets whose size and technical difficulty posed problems well beyond its own resources, and support from overseas allies was natural on all sides. The resulting relationships were however moulded by two more specific factors. One was the way in which trends in global strategy and intelligence technology coincided to give a particular importance to North Norway and the seas and airspace beyond it. The other was the Norwegian policy of avoiding permanent foreign deployments on national territory. The two combined to make Norway a special, perhaps unique, intelligence ally.

Strategic and Technical Factors

The strategic factors and resulting intelligence requirements are well known. From NATO's early days the North was an avenue for Western land-based and carrier-borne strategic air attack, and intelligence on Soviet targets and defences was of prime importance. The USSR's development of its own capability for strategic air attack on North America intensified the intelligence requirements. Soviet nuclear tests and missile firings added to the area's importance. The Northern Fleet developed by the early 1960s to become the main naval threat to the West, and the Cold War was played out in maritime terms in the monitoring of Soviet naval incursions into the Atlantic and in Western penetrations of the nuclear 'bastion' of the Barents Sea for the Soviet SLBM force. Throughout the Cold War it was assumed – correctly – that Soviet military planning included the occupation of North Norway in the event of war. For all these reasons intelligence requirements on the area ranked high, with special links with the nuclear strategy of both camps.[5]

North Norway's value in meeting them was partly as a base and observation point for traditional intelligence methods. It provided visual surveillance across the Soviet frontier, and facilities for observations by sea and air of the Barents Sea, Novaya Zemlya to the east and the maritime exits to the Norwegian Sea and the North Atlantic to the west. Riste's History records Norwegian frontier-crossing in the early days of the Cold War, cross-border surveillance, and observation and photography from fishing and other Norwegian vessels in the area.

But the History brings out the extent to which intelligence-gathering of these kinds, important as they were, came to be overshadowed by North Norway's role in technical collection. The area provided radar inputs to intelligence as well as operational warning, and shore bases for chains of acoustic sensors detecting underwater submarines. By far its main contribution to technical collection was however in the interception of radio communications and other electronic emissions, in a period which was perhaps the high-water mark of collection of this kind from fixed ground stations. Interception sites were needed within some hundred of miles of their Soviet targets, or in some cases at much closer ranges to match the development of naval, airborne and terrestrial radars, weapons guidance systems and short-distance communications. The United States itself was too distant for interception and, while its allies could offer useful geography in other areas, Norway was specially placed for the High North. Temporary airborne and shipborne platforms could provide some specialized coverage, but were no substitute for the continuous operation of North Norway's terrestrial sites, which became a unique window on the north-west USSR and on Soviet naval and air activity in and over the ocean area. As an intelligence base, Eastern Finmark on the Soviet Northern Fleet and its associated forces was roughly what West Berlin was on the Group of Soviet Forces in Germany and its Air Army. Technical trends as the Cold War progressed did not alter this value. Riste claims that North Norway's special geographic value survived the advent of military satellites, and describes its access to communications and other data dumped from Soviet satellites over Soviet territory.[6]

All this technical collection involved high technology as well as considerable manpower, both on scales which became increasingly out of Norway's league. Exploitation of Norway's position came to depend on overseas backing, and in the event technical collection became predominantly

US-equipped and principally US-financed. Technology and target trends combined to put Norway in the position of an American subsidiary.

National Autonomy

Nevertheless the opportunities and challenges were met in what became a characteristic Norwegian intelligence style. Those developing the NIS did so with considerable self-confidence, determined to make a full contribution to the Western alliance, not tied exclusively to Norway's geographical position. Riste records the energetic use of what emerged early in the Cold War as a valuable but unexpected national asset: the heavy involvement of the Norwegian merchant navy – the fourth largest in the world – in trade with the Soviet Bloc, with commensurate opportunities for *de visu* and other intelligence collection.[7] Similarly there was some covert collection in Iron Curtain countries, and a network of intelligence relationships extending more widely than to Norway's Scandinavian neighbours and the UK and US. Though Norwegian intelligence was built on its position as the Arctic listening-post, it was determined not to be parochial but to develop at least an element of world reach.

Allied with this was the policy that, despite the close overseas connections, permanent collection on Norwegian territory was to be Norwegian-manned. With some small exceptions, jointly manned operations remained off the agenda. Similarly the regular use of North Norwegian bases was on the whole denied to mobile allied collectors, adding thereby to the importance of airborne and shipborne Norwegian operations.[8]

The stranger cannot say whether this exclusion of foreign forces was imposed on a reluctant NIS, or favoured by it. One suspects at least an element of the latter, contributing as the policy did to Norwegian intelligence's growth and status. It ran its own show, and could be seen as a distinctive, irreplaceable contribution to the Western cause.

Hence the special character of North Norway among the front lines of Western intelligence operations. Other key territories around the Soviet periphery provided intelligence bases not only for the host countries but also for their allies, sometimes in unexpected variety; for some countries, not Scandinavian, hosting foreign intelligence operations became almost a primitive tourist industry. By contrast the intelligence collection which loomed large in Finmark was an indigenous occupation, without foreign faces.

This reflected but also reinforced the spirit of Norway's liaisons. Even if national self-sufficiency were impossible, the appearance of dependency was to be limited as far as possible. Riste records recurrent Norwegian pressure for feedback from its allies in return for the collection provided and for a full part in analysing it. For a small organization this may have been unrealistic at times, but it reflected a vigorous instinct. The status of an American subsidiary, merely a collector of raw material, was to be avoided. One result was to support national attempts to maintain dialogues elsewhere, and Britain, with its status as a top-table NATO intelligence power, was naturally included.

THE BRITISH CONNECTION

Close relations were only to be expected. Britain and Norway were particularly close allies in the Second World War. Collaboration in human intelligence and covert operations was forged then, and by the denazification that followed the British participation in Norway's Liberation. The mutual respect developed in war was reinforced after 1945 by geographical propinquity and common maritime interests.

Close collaboration indeed developed after 1945, particularly in the use of human sources. Riste demonstrates that in the organization and manning of technical collection in the early post-war period Norway was heavily influenced by the British example, in preference to American practices. He records regular British contacts throughout the Cold War, including occasional RAF bids to use Norwegian airfields.[9] Yet the picture presented by the History is that, compared with the Americans, the British remained rather distant allies, not as close as might perhaps have been expected.

This was partly just a matter of resources. The US could supply technical equipment and financial backing on a scale quite impossible for Britain. But it may also have reflected differing US and British strategic priorities in the Cold War's formative years when relationships were shaking down. US defence planners recognized the Arctic quite early as the area of most immediate contact with the potential adversary, for both attack and defence. Britain on the other hand was a touch ambivalent about it. As NATO evolved, Britain shared US interest in northern waters, filled the CINC-NORTH (Commander Allied Forces North West Europe) post, and eventually provided a major part of the amphibious force trained to reinforce North Norway (with remarkable results for Britain in the Far South).[10] On the other hand, in early planning for the V-force British eyes tended to wander towards bases in the Middle East and CENTO area. In the early Cold War period the Soviet naval threat had been seen as Baltic-based; the first out-of-area projection of Soviet naval power into British waters – the visit of the cruiser *Sverdlov* to the Coronation Review in 1953 – was from the Baltic, not the Northern Fleet. The Royal Navy became closely involved with Norway, but after the Defence Review of 1957 shifted its focus east of Suez,[11] and throughout the Cold War British strategy was based on the British Army of the Rhine and the Central Region. Oslo figured as part of the defence of the Baltic exits, but the Far North was a long way away.

Whatever the policy background, Riste claims that one provision of the official US–Norwegian agreement of the early 1950s was that the US would represent the UK in liaison with Norway on some technical collection, and would ensure that Britain received the Norwegian material.[12] It is not clear from his account whether this reflected differing UK and US priorities, or was no more than a convenient division of effort between close allies; perhaps it was a mixture of the two. Bilateral UK–Norwegian relationships continued on all other matters and were notably close and harmonious, but the centre of gravity had shifted to the US.

This may need no other explanation than the recognition of the combined effects of resources, geography and strategy. But perhaps, despite its military investments in support of NATO, it may also have reflected in intelligence a British caution typical of its traditional uncertainty towards 'the continental commitment'. This had been a feature of British intelligence in the 1930s, and throughout the Second World War intelligence exchanges with the Continental governments in exile remained understandably limited. Then and thereafter the transatlantic relationship became paramount. Intelligence in the Cold War mirrored Britain's historical ambivalence over the relationship with Europe; perhaps it still does.

If Britain was on the whole content with American primacy, was Norway? One's impression from Riste's account is that Norway resented any impression of American exclusivity, but accepted the realities of the relationship as one of the facts of life. In any case Norway, as a more peripheral European power than Britain, may have shared the fear of excessive European commitments. Perhaps it still shares Britain's problem over European entanglements.

CONCLUSIONS

Cold War intelligence was a Norwegian success story. Geo-politics, technical trends and the physics of electromagnetic propagation combined to deal Norwegian intelligence a strong hand. The hand was played with skill, determination and self-reliance. A grumpy but well-informed American intelligence professional described the British as 'superb intelligence diplomats', 'making an extraordinarily astute investment buying into the US system, particularly in Sigint'.[13] *Mutatis mutandis* something of this can be said of Norway's success as recorded by Riste. It got American funding for much of its technical collection equipment and some 70 per cent of its running costs, while successfully maintaining its national identity.[14] But, unlike some other NATO members, Norway was much more than just a good bargainer. The bottom line for its status was its professional competence, good security and sense of independence.

The result had an epic quality, rather different from the intelligence war in other areas. The war in many other places was equally intense, literally or technically eyeball-to-eyeball. But the wastes of Eastern Finmark and the waters of the High North were far removed from the fleshpots of Berlin, and climate and terrain left their mark. I have said elsewhere, pejoratively, that nations get the intelligence services they deserve. Norwegian intelligence was nurtured by the experience of war and occupation, the proximity of the Soviet threat, the harsh conditions in which it had to operate, and the realities of bargaining for forty years with the US superpower. None of this left much room for posturing.

Thus as an intelligence ally Norway was hard, serious, dependable, realistic, without pretence. In a January 1999 special survey of the Nordic countries the periodical *The Economist* emphasized Norway's sense of independence, and concluded that 'the Norwegians win the Nordic prize for nationalistic prickliness'.[15] As a comment on the Norwegian intelligence role within NATO, as a small power combining a determination to contribute with a sense of its own worth, the description has some resonance. I intend that as a compliment, given with admiration.

NOTES

1. Paper for a conference at the Norwegian Aviation Museum in June 1999 for NATO's fiftieth anniversary, and published in K.L. Kleve (ed.), *50 Years with the Cold War* (Bodø, Norway: Norwegian Aviation Museum, 1999).
2. The English translation is O. Riste, *The Norwegian Intelligence Service 1945–70* (London: Cass, 1999). For other background see M. Berdal, *The United States, Norway and the Cold War, 1954–60* (London: MacMillan/St Antony's College, 1997), and R.Tamnes, *The United States and the Cold War in the High North* (Aldershot: Dartmouth, 1991).

3. Riste, Chapter 13.
4. For discussion of these factors see M.F. Herman, *Intelligence Power in Peace and War* (Cambridge: Cambridge University Press, 1996), Chapter 12.
5. For Soviet military objectives in this area see M.K. MccGwire, *Military Objectives in Soviet Foreign Policy* (Washington: The Brookings Institution, 1987), pp. 146–56.
6. Riste, Chapter 10.
7. Riste, Chapter 4, pp. 74–81.
8. For a discussion of this policy see Berdal, pp. 7–8.
9. Riste, Chapter 5, pp. 95–6; Chapter 6; and Chapter 11, pp. 227–8. See also Berdal, p. 31.
10. If the Battle of Waterloo was allegedly won on the playing fields of Eton, the Falklands were certainly reclaimed in 1982 through the military experience gained in amphibious exercises in North Norway and the logistic planning geared to operations there.
11. Berdal, Chapter 5.
12. Riste, Chapters 5 and 11.
13. Mark Urban, *UK Eyes Alpha: The Inside Story of British Intelligence* (London: Faber and Faber, 1996), pp. 239, 103.
14. Riste, Chapter 12, p. 242.
15. *The Economist*, 23 January 1999, 'Nordic Survey', p. 15.

8

New Zealand's Intelligence Alliance: An Antipodean Dilemma[1]

A review of Nicky Hager, Secret Power: New Zealand's Role in the International Spy Network, *an attack on New Zealand's participation in the UK–US–Commonwealth Sigint project nicknamed 'Echelon'. The criticism of Echelon has subsequently been taken up elsewhere, most recently by the European and French Parliaments in 2000.*

The reader – at least, this reader – groans at the book title: surely not another work of investigative journalism and revelation? Can books about intelligence really attract readers only by having labels of secrecy and espionage? The publisher's blurb that the aim is 'to generate debate about the secret workings of supposedly accountable government departments' makes one expect another run-of-the-mill 'exposure'.

The author certainly sets out to condemn intelligence, but the result is one of the more informative and thought-provoking examples of the genre. Despite its grandiose title, it is actually a detailed study of New Zealand's Sigint organization and its collaboration with other parts of the UK–US–Old Commonwealth (UKUSA) Sigint alliance. It traces the way the New Zealand operation developed after 1945: from contributing some manpower to its partners' efforts in Australia, Singapore and Hong Kong, to building up in the late seventies and eighties a national institution of some two hundred civilians, developed to create a New Zealand Sigint identity and make a bigger and more identifiable contribution to the alliance.

Along with this account of the organization as a whole, the book pays particular attention to its move in the late 1980s into the interception of traffic sent via INTELSAT and other commercial communications satellites (Comsats), along with the use of sophisticated computer dictionaries to select material of intelligence value. States have always intercepted international communications, from the Post Office's service carrying diplomatic despatches to Europe in the eighteenth century to the international telegraph companies operating from the mid-nineteenth century onwards; interception and selection from the billions and trillions of messages now sent via communications satellites is this long-standing intelligence activity updated to the modern age. It now has a special salience for current targets like nuclear proliferation, terrorism, international crime and others using international communications. The Comsat technology needed is increasingly complex and challenging, but is not beyond the resources of smaller Sigint powers; most states with viable Sigint organizations now attempt some effort of this kind. (Using big dishes in this way on the ground, pointing *up* to monitor signals coming down from communications satellites, should not be confused with the vastly more expensive activity of using intelligence satellites for interception and surveillance from the sky, with aerials pointing *down* to intercept terrestrial communications and other emissions.)

The author describes the New Zealand decision to move into this field through collaboration and division of effort within the Sigint alliance, depicted in this context as a worldwide enterprise tightly controlled from Washington. He argues that in this way the enhanced New Zealand Sigint identity of the 1980s has in fact tied its governments more tightly to doubtful and often reprehensible US foreign policies, and to Australian attitudes tarred with the same brush. Oddly enough, the political effects of the UK link hardly get a mention, despite its major historic influence on the New Zealand organization; perhaps Britain is too distant for its policies to be worth condemning. Be that as it may, Hager believes that 'By leaving the [Sigint] alliance New Zealand would have more integrity in its international relations and could, over time, set a much needed example for other nations'.[2]

This is in effect a re-run in intelligence of the debate of the 1980s about the orientation of New Zealand's foreign policy, brought to a head by its Labour Government's non-nuclear policy, breach with the US administration, and withdrawal from ANZUS; but the book's criticism of Sigint is wider-ranging. Indeed there is overkill in it, hanging New Zealand Siginters several times over. Thus their product is not much use; it failed to give warning of the Fiji coup in 1987 or the French *Rainbow Warrior* operation. 'The publicly claimed benefits of intelligence cooperation, such as that New Zealand receives vital economic intelligence and information on terrorism, do not stand up to examination.'[3] The legality of intercepting international communications is ambiguous, and the 1982 Nairobi International Telecommunications Convention is cited to this effect (though in this as in previous agreements there are let-out clauses). Except perhaps as a small adjunct to its armed forces, New Zealand needs neither its own Sigint effort nor the access to all the UKUSA product it secures. If national Sigint continues at all, it should be independent, uncorrupted by relationships with more powerful allies, and reformed to give Ministers, Members of Parliament and the public fuller information about it. It should be purged of the threats to the privacy of the overseas communications of 'the individuals, businesses and government and private organizations that innocently [*sic*] entrust their communications to these [international communications] companies'.[4] The body politic should no longer be corrupted by the intelligence's excessive secrecy.

It is easy to lampoon this as a liberal, idealist vision of New Zealand in a state of innocence, half-way to the South Pole, untainted by international politics; a world forgotten by the world forgot, in which elected and electors are both capable of prudence and discretion in handling any genuine secrets still needed amid otherwise universal transparency. It implies an old-fashioned, rather isolationist view of New Zealand's ability to pick and choose its contacts in an increasingly interdependent world.

It is also a pity that, after all the rubbishing, the author does not say more precisely what he wants. The book's impact is not improved by its Foreword by David Lange, the Prime Minister from 1984 to 1989, who now complains that he was misled about Sigint while in office and calls for 'a rational debate on security and intelligence'. Surely a cop-out; how did he spend his time while in power? And it is irritating that one has to look elsewhere to put the criticism into proportion. The official New Zealand handbook for 1996 puts the annual cost of civilian Sigint as the equivalent of about £8.5 million, or about 1.5 per cent of defence, itself about the same percentage of GDP. Even allowing for some additional military elements, this is small beer by world standards: hardly a mark of a police state or an intelligence mercenary. It is interesting that the author does *not* claim that America foots the bill.

Yet behind all the rhetoric there are interesting questions about small powers, the role of alliances, and the impact of sophisticated modern Sigint. Should small powers depend completely upon big ones, as was to some extent New Zealand's position for many years after 1945? Should they work their passage via alliances, in the way Hager describes, using their geographic and other assets to provide a quid pro quo? Should they do their best on their own, and try to manage without access to state-of-the-art advice? Or is the right course just not to bother at all? The author raises issues for New Zealand that are not irrelevant to the US's other allies – including Britain.

He has certainly done his homework. Along with good human sources he has also used classical intelligence methods including the analysis of government staff lists and home addresses to penetrate official secrecy. The KGB is said to have had quite good access within New Zealand, but probably did not know half as much. The result is an elaborate, almost excessive account of the minutiae of organization, people and even rooms and layouts; anyone wanting to blow up a New Zealand Sigint installation would find it an indispensable primer. More substantially, it gives an interesting impression of the sheer volume and diversity of the Sigint available from Sigint outside the traditional Cold War targets. What then is the reader to make of it all?

This reviewer guesses – it can be no more than that, especially on recent events – that many of the details are correct, subject to the usual distortions of individuals' access and memory. It is a pity to see the old canard trotted out yet again about American tapping of British Telecom circuits at Menwith Hill.[5] Some of the background (for example that 'the Directors of the five UKUSA agencies meet once a year to plan and coordinate the activities of the global intelligence alliance')[6] sounds exaggerated; it may be true, but reads like something out of a novel. The broad picture of New Zealand's modern Sigint is probably accurate in some respects, misleading in others.

America is certainly the Sigint superpower, and is now at the centre of a remarkable (and remarkably enduring) English-speaking alliance. Yet the impression of a coherent, deliberately planned, US-controlled network – an American Grand Design – distorts the pragmatism of real life and the relationship between big and small partners. In practice America's collaborators have something unique to bring to the table; relationships are a mixture of clout, national independence and institutional and professional habits and drives – especially the professional element. The complexity and durability of institutional relationships is brought out in Hager's description of how, over the American decision at the political level to break off the intelligence relationship to punish New Zealand's non-nuclear stance, so many complications and repercussions were adduced by the American and other professionals that it all turned out to be a damp squib. The description of an American visit to New Zealand as 'not too far from that of a giant United States parent company visiting its New Zealand office'[7] has more than a grain of truth in it, but does not capture the nuances.

Similarly the author's generalizations about international tasking and information-sharing – who targets what? who gets what? what limitations are there on tasking partners and their individuals? what 'rights' do junior partners have? – probably fail to reflect the complexity of the activities he describes and the diversity of the arrangements bound up with them. As in other transnational relations, there is the risk of reading too much into systems which have grown up piecemeal. Arrangements develop a technical life of their own; they are rarely planned and reviewed *de novo*. The author gives a good overall impression of the extent of exchanges and collaboration (and their limitations), but it would be unwise to take his details as gospel. The reader should be on the watch for an undeclared conspiracy theory about US motives and influence.

On his conclusions, Hager is right to argue that secrecy can give covert intelligence an exaggerated importance. Its value needs to be tested against other sources of information and analysis. New Zealand's intelligence budget should of course be weighed against the value of the information gathered by the Ministry of Foreign Affairs and Trade. One can argue endlessly about gauging the worth of any information service, intelligence or otherwise. The varied local targets quoted by Hager – the independent South Pacific countries; French activities in the area; incoming and outgoing diplomatic communications; Russian shipping; reports on non–UKUSA bases in Antarctica – seem relevant to New Zealand interests, and his verdict of uselessness to policy-making is surprising. One wonders whether he reflects the views of most senior policy officials, or just those of selected ex-Ministers. Perhaps he does not accept that intelligence can be prosaically useful without being dramatic and exciting.

Usefulness in any case needs to be considered broadly. The main value of intelligence is through accretion, education, reduction of surprise, and support for armed forces when needed; not in the linkage of specific items with particular governmental decisions. Similarly it is difficult to draw intelligence boundaries. New Zealand in the 1990s aims for a special position in the South Pacific, but has not exactly turned its back on the rest of the world. It was a member of the Security Council in 1993 and 1994, and is currently active in a fistful of regional and international bodies. Its military have been recently involved with UNSCOM in Iraq and in peacekeeping, verification and other missions in the Middle East, the former Yugoslavia, Cambodia and Mozambique.

No one can prove that this stance needs support from UKUSA Sigint, but it is surely a reason for seeking to have a fairly well-informed foreign policy – if public opinion wants a policy at all, and cares how well it is executed. What does New Zealand really want? Exploring this is perhaps what Lange means in advocating the 'rational debate' he should have organized himself; but condemning the intelligence effort in advance of it is easy and rather vacuous, putting the horse before the cart.

Perhaps Hager's objection to Sigint is less that it is not cost-effective – though he forcibly makes this claim – than that the alliance limits New Zealand's national freedom of action and offends the national conscience; and here there is a serious question. Most intelligence is now an internationally collaborative business. How indeed is a small power with limited resources to manage without surrendering its political virginity? To Hager, 'the foreign policy significance of this system [of Comsat collection] is immense.... When the subject is the internal politics of Vanuatu or the economy of the Solomon Islands, and the intelligence New Zealand collects could affect the way these countries are treated by one of the UKUSA countries, no one in the [New Zealand organization] has the job of judging whether or not it *should* be passing on this report.'[8] The professional can argue in reply that his job is to provide the best information and forecasts he can; as put in the current GCHQ graduate recruitment brochure, 'government cannot make the right decisions unless it has the full picture'. Even for the biggest powers, national intelligence resources, opportunities and competences are always incomplete; allies can provide additions and share loads; in unequal relationships the small participant has something to offer, though he has far more to gain. One may be influenced by one's allies' selections, translations and interpretations of material, but at the 'raw', single-source Sigint stage the information content is relatively 'hard'. It is less influenced by national preconceptions or deliberate manipulation than the exchanges of 'finished', all-source JIC and similar assessments. Like the statistician of world trade, the single-source intelligence officer can feel that his information has an apolitical, international quality about it, likely to make all recipients – not just his own government – wiser and better-behaved than if they did not have it.

In practice different national policies can proceed on this basis of shared information, as in the violently conflicting UK–US attitudes in the Suez crisis, and over the US invasion of Grenada. One does not necessarily sell out politically to the bigger intelligence partner. Nevertheless intelligence collaboration does give the big battalions some tangible and intangible leverage over the smaller ones. The alliance's intelligence pool – including one's own contribution to it – *can* be used by others for policies of which one disapproves. 'Intelligence sharing arrangements are not neutral; by their nature they involve taking sides in political, economic and military conflicts and competition between nations.'[9] Hager does not object specifically to the support New Zealand coverage gave to the UK in the Falklands War, but one senses that the principle worries him; he cites as undesirable the Australian use of New Zealand intercepts on Papua New Guinea. His attitude to intelligence is at the same time ultra-liberal, deploring covert information covertly obtained, and distinctly nationalistic, prizing political independence rather than international cooperation and consensus.

Surely it is a matter of swings and roundabouts. For a foreign and defence policy of any substance, New Zealand gains from having much better intelligence from the alliance that it could produce on its own. Its special intelligence responsibility within the alliance for the South Pacific area enables it to exert some influence on the others' policies there. Nevertheless he is right to see intelligence collaboration as a conduit of national influence; it is not insulated from international politics. A wise British liaison officer in Washington wrote after 1956 that though the UKUSA Sigint relationship had survived the Suez crisis it would probably not survive more of them. The English-speaking countries tend to have roughly similar views of the world, and the intelligence alliance both reflects this situation and buttresses it. If New Zealand seeks a consistently anti-American policy – which one feels Hager favours – it will eventually have to seek new intelligence allies in the Pacific, if indeed there are any worth having. *Mutatis mutandis*, something of the same would now apply to Britain if the Labour Government's agonizing over the transatlantic and Continental pillars of policy, and a more 'ethical' foreign policy, led eventually to jettisoning the American connection at a political level.

Such issues are implicit in this work of revelation and (largely) denunciation. It also leaves the reader with another question: should books of this kind be written? Certainly this one will do nothing to enhance New Zealand's reputation with its allies for good security; they may nudge its organization a millimetre or two towards the international isolation which the author seeks. But not far; revelations of this kind are now an international norm.

How much damage will it do to sources and methods? Probably very little. The French will not care about the interception of communications connected with their nuclear tests; the references to coverage of Fiji and the other tiny South Pacific states are very generalized; there have been other references to the interception of Japanese diplomatic communications, though the press coverage of this book in New Zealand may well have drawn attention again to this vulnerability.

But no one ever knows what actually causes intelligence's sources or methods to be lost until it is too late. What accretion of evidence is needed to force any bureaucracy to worry about the security of its communications? What is the last trickle that breaks the dam of complacency and inertia? The *Chicago Tribune's* revelation just after the battle of Midway that the American Navy had detailed foreknowledge of Japanese plans was never picked up by the enemy; but it might have been, or so it seemed to American leaders at the time. Security has to play safe over quite remote risks.

It also has to cope with indirect penetrations and inferences. The Cold War in which every intelligence practitioner was a KGB and GRU target may be over or at least attenuated, but intelligence's secrecy continues to act as a magnet for investigators. Where does a genuine concern for open government become overtaken by the intellectual buzz of beating the security system? This book is an excellent demonstration of how to use apparently quite unrewarding evidence to construct a good picture of a secret organization and its activities. Like other investigators of this kind, Hager is potentially a good intelligence officer lost to the profession. Security consists of protecting real secrets behind a defensive glacis, often maintained less for the value of the information in it than to hinder penetration beyond it. One paradoxical conclusion to be drawn from the plea for greater openness is that New Zealand's security glacis might well be made wider and steeper.

From this aspect of the book the best one can conclude may be simply that governments should exercise commonsense and avoid appearing pigheaded. Security does not lend itself to simplistic distinctions between what is potentially damaging and what is not, and pursuing policies acceptable to allies adds greatly to the complications of release. But clearly it is no longer sensible to be driven by minuscule risks about the present that reinforce inertia over the past. In America the Gates initiative set new benchmarks for openness in recent years, notably in the release of satellite imagery extending well into the Cold War. The record of British governments is actually better than they are credited with; the decisions to release Enigma decrypts in 1974 followed by the volumes of the Official History were the most significant developments for intelligence historiography anywhere in the West, and now we have the release of the Venona decrypts (jointly with the US) and the early Cold War JIC material.

This suggests concentrating on serving history. It is not the same as Open Government, and certainly not what Hager and others want for current transparency. But this reviewer is inclined to put his weight behind opening up the past, while keeping sizeable security protection for the present.

NOTES

1. A review of Nicky Hager, *Secret Power: New Zealand's Role in the International Spy Network* (Nelson, New Zealand: Craig Potten, 1996), published in *Intelligence and National Security,* 12, 4 (October 1997). More recent information about New Zealand Sigint, including its personnel strength, interception facilities and collaboration with the UK–US–Canadian–Australian alliance, was published by the New Zealand Government in December 2000 in 'Securing our Nation's Safety' (www.dpmc.govt.nz/dess/securingoursafety/index.html).
2. Hager, *Secret Power*, p. 17.
3. Ibid., p. 15.
4. Ibid., p. 56.
5. Ibid., p. 39.
6. Ibid., p. 22.
7. Ibid., p. 139.
8. Ibid., p. 208.
9. Ibid., p. 201.

Part III

Historical Lessons

9

The Cold War: Did Intelligence Make a Difference?[1]

In recent years we have had a spate of American intelligence releases, the appearance in the Public Record Office of British Joint Intelligence Committee (JIC) estimates, the publication of Soviet and other documents in the Washington Cold War International History Project, and even an officially sponsored Norwegian intelligence history. To young Cold War historians Wordsworth's words must apply:

> Bliss was it in that dawn to be alive,
> But to be young was very heaven!

They will soon be able to decide whether intelligence made a difference. Did it produce better knowledge and understanding, and a safer world? Or was it playing out and intensifying the Cold War as a self-serving game between opposing intelligence agencies? Did it simply use its cachet of special secrecy to reinforce governments' preconceptions and serve their domestic political requirements? Did it contribute its own *déformation professionelle*, demonizing the enemy and exaggerating threats in a destabilizing way?

A starting point for any answers is that the Cold War was peculiarly an intelligence war. Both sides gave intelligence an importance unprecedented in peacetime. The USSR with its conspiratorial view of the world was wedded to secrecy about itself, and to covert intelligence for reliable information about others, and the West moved to its own reciprocal investments in intelligence and counter-intelligence. One can only guess at the number of people on both sides engaged in coverage of the adversary, but a grand total of rather more than a quarter of a million might not be too wide of the mark.[2] There were heavy intelligence investments in satellites, specialized ships and aircraft, computers, electronics and other equipment. Political alliances on both sides were interwoven with intelligence liaisons. Intelligence had an almost wartime intensity.

But the intelligence war was not a symmetrical contest between similar bodies. Intelligence was part of the two sides' very different systems. Soviet intelligence was bound up with covert action to a far greater extent than in the West. From its covert information-gathering it presented its results direct to the Soviet leadership; there was none of the Anglo–Saxon philosophy of all-source interdepartmental intelligence assessment, integrating covert and non-covert sources, presented as JIC reports or American National Intelligence Estimates. Heads of the KGB and its predecessors were at the heart of the Soviet autocracy, with no separation of intelligence and policy.[3] In the West the Baconian dictum so often quoted about intelligence – 'knowledge is itself power' – did not actually fit the record of intelligence leaders and institutions. With one exception, American Directors of Central Intelligence did not seek to be major policy-makers. In Britain successive historical flukes since the First World War caused intelligence to be dominated by the Foreign Office, pre-empting any private intelligence-run foreign policy, even when Number 10 was at loggerheads with the Foreign Office.

So historians must be careful in tracing reciprocal effects of the intelligence war. Here I ignore the intelligence/policy relationship in the USSR and concentrate on the West.[4] Historical writing tends to present Western intelligence collection as a success story with a happy ending. Starting with great ignorance about the adversary, intelligence worked its way towards redressing the balance between Soviet secrecy and the more open Western societies. The deployment of American imagery satellites in the 1960s can be seen as one landmark; the Western credit balance by the 1980s in the recruitment of human agents (and the identification and periodic expulsion of Soviet intelligence officers from embassies) as perhaps another.

Western collection was indeed a remarkable story. American resources and technology were major factors, but so too were the ingenuity and determination shown by both parties in the transatlantic relationship. Intelligence cooperation also extended far more widely. Some of its aspects had the romance of a multinational Great Game, played out not only along the German border, but also in Berlin and around the rest of the Soviet periphery – the Baltic, North Norway and the Barents Sea, the Black Sea, the Sea of Okhotsk and elsewhere: tough men rolling for weeks on station in small ships; patient monitors on quiet islands; aircraft of many nations flying every day, packed with technical equipment; and much else. There was a remarkable alignment of national and alliance interests.

Yet the triumphalist picture of Western rags to riches needs to be qualified. The contest with Soviet secrecy remained a dynamic one to the end, with fluctuating balances between offence and defence. The USSR's ferocious security was periodically strengthened not only by Washington leakiness about intelligence successes, but also by Soviet penetrations of Western agencies. It was a game of snakes and ladders; every ladder of success was followed by a snake through insecurity or Soviet espionage. Complete intelligence victory was impossible. On a medical analogy, the West by the 1980s had become well informed about Soviet anatomy and physiology; but the windows on to the antagonist's mind remained largely opaque.

What difference did it all make? Much of the immediate intelligence produced by the West was, strictly speaking, totally useless; its twenty-four-hour surveillance was a precaution, for warning of an attack that never came. Yet the reassurance this provided contributed to what John Gaddis has called the Long Peace. American Presidents never believed that they were about to be Pearl Harbor-ed. Western confidence in intelligence warning provided some stability in Cold War management; in contrast, for example, with the hasty British reaction in early 1939 to the rumours and reports of imminent German action, which in those pre-JIC days there was no machinery for evaluating and assessing. And on occasion timely intelligence helped to contain crises and strengthen Western positions.[5]

As for long-term effects, the most important were probably intelligence's inputs to the Cold War's basic parameters of military threats and defence planning. One can argue about whether Western views of ultimate Soviet objectives were determined by intelligence or other sources of policy.[6] But defence decisions did not skip the intelligence stage of assessing Soviet capabilities, present and future. This was where intelligence assessment really counted in Whitehall, at least up to 1957 (when the JIC ceased to be a Chiefs of Staffs' committee) and arguably much later; and probably the same was true of Washington. Intelligence in all its aspects – hard information; best guesses and worst cases; objective and politicized; used and abused by decision-takers – was the currency for debating defence issues and all that sprang from them. Not the least of these, and possibly the most significant, was strategic arms control.[7]

How accurate was it? Did it inform governments, or echo their prejudices? I will leave it to experts to discuss the top-level effects. All I will do here is comment from a different level, from those parts of the trenches that I occupied from time to time. It never occurred to us there that we were not being as objective as possible in our selections, interpretations and comments. We had never heard the academics' warnings about mindsets and cognitive rigidity, and would have been rather dismissive of them if we had.

We were not ideologues. I cannot think why the BBC some years ago felt it had to give a sensible programme about intelligence the misleading title 'My Country, Right or Wrong'.

There was indeed rather more Whitehall excitement over evidence of increased Soviet capabilities than in evaluations of Soviet weaknesses – though interest in the weaknesses increased the nearer one got to the command levels where battles had to be planned. Our collective psychology probably had an element in it of the warner, the Cassandra; but I do not count it as a *déforma-tion*. In any case a bigger element can be put, grandiloquently, as the search for truth, free from policy – or, put with more humility, as the urge to disagree with one's predecessors, collaborators and customers, or beat them to the punch with new discoveries. Assessing the character of intelligence in the West would be incomplete without recognizing the role of dialogue and disputa-tiousness, within national communities and between transatlantic partners. Intelligence had its equivalent of the 'invisible colleges' of modern scholarship.

Intelligence as information and assessment made a difference to policy; but so, too, did some intelligence activities. Soviet espionage had a special place in the Cold War's origins and continuation. Both sides' short-range technical collection became worldwide, but it was heaviest around the Soviet periphery; in geo-political terms, the Soviet Union was looking out, the West looking in. Often this collection was ritualized, but sometimes not, with effects on mutual threat perceptions. Some 14 American intelligence aircraft were destroyed by Soviet defences around the periphery up to 1970, and others not on intelligence missions were also victims. Deep penetrations of Soviet territory up to 1960, including the twenty-four U-2 flights, were seen by the regime as reconnaissance for Western nuclear strikes. Later in the Cold War, two civilian passenger aircraft were shot down as intruders over Soviet airspace, with grievous casualties; 269 civilians were killed in the South Korean aircraft which flew over Kamchatka in September 1993.[8]

Writing in the first half of the 1980s, Raymond Garthoff pressed the need for a Soviet–American 'code of conduct'.[9] Intelligence was in some ways the Cold War waged by other means, but some of its collection was not far from war in its methods and effects. But Garthoff at the same time stressed the need for knowledge and understanding of the Soviet Union.[10] I believe that on this, all things considered, historians will give Western intelligence estimates reasonably good marks, at least in restraining the wilder thinking of politicians and opinion-formers.

But intelligence's impact on the Cold War was complex. Two very differ-ent systems had varied effects on two very different regimes. We look to future historians for research and synthesis.

NOTES

1. Paper for RIIA/BBC conference on 'Cold War: Heroes, Villains and Spies', London, 10 September 1998.
2. Not counting the vast KGB and other efforts on border control and other internal security. For some figures see M.E. Herman, *Intelligence Power in Peace and War* (Cambridge: Cambridge University Press, 1996), pp. 37, 48–9.
3. The KGB's influence in Soviet decisions to invade Czechoslovakia in 1968, and its distortion of evidence to achieve this end, is summarized in M. Kramer, 'The Prague Spring and the Soviet Invasion of Czechoslovakia: New Interpretations', *Cold War International History Project, Bulletin 3* (Washington: Woodrow Wilson Center, fall 1993), pp. 6–8. For Andropov's pressure, as its head, for intervention in Afghanistan in 1979 see O.A. Westad, 'Concerning the Situation in "A": New Russian Evidence on the Soviet Intervention in Afghanistan', *Cold War International History Project, Bulletin 8–9* (winter 1996–97), pp. 128–32.
4. Though I pose one puzzle in passing. There is widespread agreement that the KGB presented a warped and hostile picture of American and other Western activities and intentions, but we know little of the GRU's estimates of Western military capabilities. At operational levels Soviet military staffs were trained in 'scientific' appraisals of the balance of forces. There was what appeared to be a realistic Soviet formula for assessing the relative fighting power of American, West German, British and Soviet divisions, incidentally with a rating not flattering to BAOR (K.S. Brower, *The Warsaw Pact – NATO Military Balance: The Quality of Forces* (Camberley: Soviet Studies Research Centre, 1988)). But did any of this scientific approach survive at the top level of Soviet defence planning? Was the Soviet defence effort derived from accurate intelligence estimates of NATO's nuclear and conventional capabilities, or exaggerated ones?
5. American pressure based on intelligence warnings probably played some part in the Soviet decision not to proceed with a military solution in Poland in 1980–81 (Herman, *Intelligence Power*, p. 224).
6. As an historical layman, I have the impression that in Britain the official judgements about Soviet objectives that carried weight in the crucial 1940s and early 1950s were those of the Foreign Office and its Embassies, rather than those of the JIC *per se*, though Foreign Office chairmanship of the committee complicates historical assessment. Intelligence's influence in Washington was perhaps even longer delayed.
7. Progress with strategic arms control turned almost entirely on intelligence's ability to verify, *inter alia* by the extraordinary US–Soviet agreement in SALT II, to limit the encipherment of missile telemetry. For discussion see Herman, *Intelligence Power*, pp. 160–1.
8. Details of airborne operations from P. Lashmar, *Spy Flights of the Cold War* (Stroud: Sutton, 1996).
9. R.Garthoff, *Détente and Confrontation: American–Soviet Relations from Nixon to Reagan* (Washington: Brookings, 1985), pp. 1073–82.
10. Garthoff, *Détente and Confrontation*, pp. 1118–23.

Up from the Country: Cabinet Office Impressions 1972-75[1]

I was once a modern Dick Whittington, travelling to London to explore its mysteries – though without a black cat, and not on foot. I was summoned from my provincial civil service department to be the Secretary of the Joint Intelligence Committee (JIC) in the Cabinet Office from 1972 to 1975. My contacts there with the heart of government were intermittent and tenuous; in the cricketing metaphor, I was lucky to get a touch. Yet, like Dick Whittington, I was an impressionable innocent. Recollections of the milieu may be of interest.

IMPRESSIONS

The Cabinet Office was still relatively young. Sir Burke Trend, the Cabinet Secretary, was only the fourth holder of the post. But the Office was already much more than the War Secretariat which evolved from the pre-1914 Committee of Imperial Defence to provide minutes of War Cabinet and Cabinet meetings from 1917 onwards. Even since the end of the Second World War it had expanded. The JIC had become a Cabinet Office committee when it was transferred from the Chiefs of Staff in 1957 after the Suez fiasco.[2] The Central Statistical Office had subsequently become nominally part of it, and in 1970 Heath's Central Policy Review Staff had been based within its building and administered by it.

Nevertheless the Cabinet Office's role was relatively clear and unencumbered. Trend's predecessors' competing responsibilities for the Treasury and as Head of the Civil Service had been eliminated, and the Cabinet Secretary was free to focus on making Cabinet government work. Throughout the Office there was the understated, subfusc but secretly intoxicating sense of being at the centre of power.

The first few weeks brought a kaleidoscope of impressions. One was given a cordial welcome and a folder of useful information, including the history of the building (which I fear I never read). But the institution remained opaque and slightly mysterious, in some ways like the Kremlin. It was a world of common understandings and unspoken agreements. Everything was implicit, nuanced, understated; not exactly secret, but not conveyed by announcements and explanations. I was reminded of my Oxford college just after the war, in which I had lived for five terms before I found that there was a seamstress employed to sew on one's buttons. Useful people find out what they need to know; if they do not, they are not useful enough to be worth telling.

This applied to one's duties. Like my confrères in the Ministry of Defence (MoD) on the other side of Whitehall, I had been brought up to think of well-defined responsibilities and clear chains of command. After the handover week in the Cabinet Office I confessed to my predecessor that I still had no idea who was my boss. A naïve question. He explained to me, as to a yokel, that I would work nominally for three masters, but should not make too much of subordination and chains of command. One was there to get useful things done.

Such was the introduction to the Whitehall policy-making village, in which everyone in the Administrative Class knew everyone else, and had probably been at Oxford or Cambridge together. One of the institutions was the Cabinet Office Mess on the top floor. Originally the Mess used by the War Secretariat, it was by then a modest annex to the canteen, with a waitress service, a bar and a few easy chairs. As befitted the Cabinet Office, it was not a grand organization: two-star, compared with the rival and plusher four-star MoD Mess on the opposite side of Whitehall. It was usually in financial trouble with the Treasury. Subsequently I heard that it was being closed down, after successions of senior civil servants had had to worry about its viability.

It was an exclusive club, used by the senior Cabinet Office officials and Administrative Class people from other Departments, plus a handful of MoD generals; in the Whitehall village it was the saloon bar, not the lower-class public bar. Its barriers were typically implicit rather than articulated – except for a rule that politicians were not admitted as guests. (I understand that some years earlier there had been difficulties over the membership of a senior Cabinet Office lady; gender prejudice had still ruled.) It was an important institution for exchanging information, organizing business, and building up the Whitehall consensus. Security was regarded as a matter of good sense, on Whitehall's 'good chap' principle; I was (yet again) gauche in asking whether the Mess was formally cleared for classified talk, and at what level. Tables were not reserved, except for the corner table at which the Cabinet Secretary sat with his Private Secretary; one wondered what they talked about. There was usually sufficient pressure on places to fill tables where conversations had begun *à deux*. It is a commonplace of modern management theory that efficiency depends on horizontal information flows across vertical organizational boundaries. Encapsulating the Administrative Class's combination of hierarchy and equality, the Mess helped to make government work in this way.

It was also a pleasant haven, retaining some shreds of its wartime origins. Though it was a lunchtime club, the bar when I first arrived was still specially opened on Thursday evenings by the ex-Royal Marine barman who had survived from the war, since this was the day the JIC met and its minutes and weekly papers (including the 'Red Book' summary of intelligence) were issued. After the week's output had been put safely to bed, my Colonel deputy and I would repair upstairs to drink red wine and dissect the day's performance of the JIC's Heads of Agencies. We were keen students of form. The military were particularly unpredictable runners, and we would mark the Chairman for the style and dispatch he had shown in controlling them that morning. Much fortified by appraising our betters, I would repair to my flat; my friend would face the weary Underground journey to his distant military quarters. It was a pleasant life, much different from the provinces.

Other Cabinet Office practices also seemed new and intriguing. The material received on joining included a paper setting out the canons of Cabinet Committeemanship. Secretariats were managers of business, not just scribes. Meetings took papers; never problems *sans* papers circulated beforehand. Minutes were issued within 24 hours, and not cleared with chairmen and participants. They were records of decisions, reasons for them and the main points of argument; never of statements 'for the record'. The classic formulation was the notional chairman's introduction (actually the minute-writer's recapitulation of the paper circulated beforehand); the impersonal summary of the main arguments, in which attributions to individuals were exceptional and discouraged; and the (crucial) chairman's summing-up followed by agreed decisions and assigned actions.

Writing these minutes was an art-form of seductive elegance and attraction never forgotten, like riding a bicycle. In the JIC Secretariat we took a pride in crafting precise conclusions, recording worthy points made in discussion and eliminating what we judged to be irrelevancies. We saw ourselves as jockeys paid to keep our expensive but mettlesome horses on tight reins; we censored from the record the Committee's occasional end to its meetings with what the Colonel condemned as 'the port and nuts stage' of unprogrammed discussion. I never reconciled myself in later life to minutes that did not meet the Cabinet Office criteria of brevity, impersonality, focus on decisions, and immediate issue.

These details are part of the warp and woof of Cabinet government, but encapsulate its nature in two words. Decisions are *agreed* by the meeting, not taken by individuals; and Departments are *invited* to take action, not instructed. Decisions are collective, not personal; the system depends on seeking consensus, not staking out individual positions; decisions must be seen to proceed from discussion and reason, not intuition or conviction. In one of his rare public utterances after retirement, Trend set out the Cabinet Office doctrine that 'There has to be one centre round which the rest of the official machine can come together', but that the Cabinet Secretary had to arrange it 'to deal with that endless upward surge of business, driving it downward as much as he can'.[3] The forms of minutes are part of the organizing and disciplining process.

Another impression of the Cabinet Office was as a microcosm of the wider Civil Service distinction between policy and execution. The Office's role at the senior, 'policy' level needed support from its paper-handling and other apparently mechanical services. Peter Hennessy has referred to some of them as follows:

> So long as Cabinet government survives, the minutes will be taken, typed and distributed, prodding the rest of Whitehall into action after every Cabinet and Cabinet Committee meeting. At eight, one and five precisely, the brown vans will go out carrying the green boxes. Whatever the circumstances, like Wells Fargo, they will always get through.[4]

There was quite a sharp distinction between the policy-related officials and the operators of these supporting services. The so-called 'administrators' of the Administrative Class were birds of passage, on two- or three-year secondments from their own departments, birds being groomed to fly higher; the only non-migratory bird was the Cabinet Secretary himself. By contrast the Executives and other supporting Classes were permanencies. The difference emphasized the distinction made in the Old Civil Service between the clever and the practical. To use a shorthand which I shall later reject, the transient administrators and the permanent regulars had the relative status of officers and troops, or Gentlemen and Players.

Consistent with this was a certain Cabinet Office conservatism. Documents were produced by the typing pool on the wax stencils now long forgotten. Cabinet Minutes in a special typeface looked quite presentable, but the product of official bodies like the JIC resembled leaflets produced on a clandestine printing-press in Occupied Europe. There were regular complaints from seconded Foreign Office officials that the impact of their high-quality analysis was lost through this sub-standard presentation. I suspect that our American allies were rather attached to it, as an example of British quaintness. An offset litho machine had been tried out in the 1960s, found wanting one evening and removed by fiat from Trend; modern technology must not be allowed to wreck the serious business of government.

The Office also seemed old-fashioned in other ways. The Cabinet Secretary had a handsome room, accurately reproduced in the 'Yes, Prime Minister' television series, and there were some grand conference rooms. But the building as a whole was shabby. Clerical staff worked in unattractive conditions. There was a certain vagueness about things like job enrichment, staff appraisals, career planning and training that were then becoming *de rigueur*. Welfare services and fire precautions seemed sketchy. Lectures to junior staff in the JIC were a bizarre innovation. The Cabinet Office did not concede much to fashion.

Yet my recollection is of the high efficiency of all this supporting machinery. The quite small body of regulars was astonishingly flexible and Whitehall-wise. Accommodation and support services for Ministerial reorganizations were fixed at the drop of a hat. One became accustomed to the speed and reliability of the day-to-day services that summoned meetings, organized conference rooms, and carried out the typing, checking, production and distribution of papers and minutes. They were the foundations for the Rolls Royce machine. And it goes without saying that, in those days, it never occurred to us that the Civil Service could leak.

These were my impressions of the policy-related and supporting levels. Four portraits may help to clarify them.

BURKE TREND

Sir Burke Trend was in many ways the quintessential top civil servant. He had joined the Civil Service in 1936 with first-class Oxford Honours in

Mods and Greats, and rose quickly in the Treasury. He became Secretary of the Cabinet in 1963 and retired in autumn 1973 to become Rector of Lincoln College Oxford. He died in 1987 as a Peer and Privy Councillor. The memorial service in Westminster Abbey was a moving occasion, a roll-call of the highest national leadership; mere KCMGs got no further than the North Transept.

He was a prodigious worker, and tough, keeping up with the pressure of government year after year; in appearance carrying unobtrusiveness almost to shabbiness, with a glint of natural authority behind the spectacles. Incisive summaries of complex subjects were dictated without a pause. One's own submissions were returned with gentle, understated manuscript notes in a neat hand. On one imbroglio that I referred to him for immediate solution he wrote 'I could have borne with rather more notice of this problem', but then noted how he had solved it in three or four deft telephone calls. He worked with a small outer office of a young Principal and two young Executives.

But none of this was remarkable. Permanent Secretaries do not bark like generals, or have the same retinue. Indeed his obituary in *The Times* gave a rather colourless impression.[5] Yet there was more to him than that. I admire him more than any other public servant I encountered.

My 'joining interview' with him in January 1972 set the pattern. In reply to the conventional enquiry about what I had been doing, I mentioned a particular project on which I had spent some years, before its cancellation. 'We should have carried on with it', Trend said decisively; he had apparently backed it in Whitehall. I countered that it had been an unrealistic idea from the start. A brisk viva voce followed, and we passed on to other things. But the exchange had made its mark. One's opinion was genuinely worth seeking, not a formality to be endured. I doubt whether over the next 18 months I was alone with him more than half a dozen times, but my memory is of an inspirational quality; the ability of some first-class people to inspire second-class people to raise their sights and perform better.

This was not 'people management' in any modern way. Trend never 'visited the troops', and did not give routine praise and thanks. He was a civil servant of his time, a slightly preoccupied and austere figure, tending to take the Office's supporting machinery for granted. Yet he left a trail behind him of a humanity outside a stock mandarin mould. The Cabinet Office had a 24-hour intelligence watch, shared in those days between five elderly retired military officers. Every Christmas Day the Duty Officer was telephoned by Trend with seasonal greetings, plus the news that one of his wife's cakes was on its way from Blackheath via the official driver. And at his crowded farewell party the customary speeches and presentations had an unusual finale – a bouquet for Lady Trend from an embarrassed, inarticulate office messenger 'for being so kind to us when you used to come to collect him'.

There were other not entirely standard dimensions. There was a hint of the philosopher-turned-administrator about him. The record of his evidence to Lord Franks's review of the Official Secrets Act in 1972 reads like an oral examination in political philosophy, the candidate passing with flying colours.[6] There was also a streak of romanticism and enthusiasm.[7] And what most sticks in the memory is 'spin' in the sense originally coined by C.P. Snow: not exactly unconventionality or eccentricity, but an element of the intriguing and unexpected.

Thus stories about Trend tend to be slightly off-centre. In one, Cabinet Office legend maintained that he had wrestled personally with that first offending offset litho machine on that late evening in the 1960s, before consigning it to outer darkness. In another, an SIS (MI6) acquaintance told me many years later that, on delivering a paper after working on it all the previous night, he was invited to take a nap on Trend's office sofa. No doubt both tales have gained in the telling, but they would not be told about all Cabinet Secretaries.

A third, authentic anecdote comes from one who was then a middle-grade military officer dealing with nuclear policy. Some issue had arisen which kept him late with Trend and others. By two in the morning the problems had been settled, the telegrams dispatched and cars summoned for transport home. At his normal time the next morning the officer met Trend as they walked from Waterloo station. (Why, he asked himself, was Trend mysteriously using the train and not the official car?) The night's events were not mentioned. Conversation developed on some recondite subject, perhaps tribal customs in Borneo. Trend sought information with increasing intensity as they walked up Whitehall. He worried at the subject as a dog worries a bone, and his companion found himself more or less shanghaied into the Cabinet Secretary's office before they went their separate ways. Recounting this episode fifteen years later my informant, by then a retired General, still wondered about Trend. 'Did this mean something? Had his curiosity simply been caught by tribal habits in Borneo? Or was it a coded signal to this officer new to Whitehall, that one must never pick over the previous day's events; a new day brings new challenges?' One never knew, but remembered.

His conduct of affairs was notably direct, but he could be unexpected. My JIC deputy was once summoned to be the secretary at a meeting of high-level, civilian officials about a proposed new Cabinet Office committee. Things did not go well; there were predictable departmental objections. Trend suddenly announced that the meeting needed the Colonel's opinion; for that subject and forum, it was as surprising as asking a member of a Covent Garden audience to step up and sing an aria. 'Just the answer to our problem' announced Trend after my friend extemporized. The meeting acquiesced, demoralized by the flank attack; another piece of interdepartmental machinery was created.

These stories are trivial. Yet they convey the style of someone who, for all his studied anonymity, was far more than a standard-issue bureaucrat. Someone should attempt his biography.

THE EXECUTIVES

As in a set of Russian dolls, the Civil Service's policy-executive division was reproduced not only in the Cabinet Office but also in the JIC Secretariat within it. The Secretariat was housed in a suite of offices linked by an internal corridor. One end was 'policy'; the other execution. The physical divisions mirrored those of an old-fashioned boarding school. The Secretary's office at one end was the headmaster's sanctum. The large, battered, scruffy room at the other end – staffed entirely by young, male clerical officers, among furniture that could have been of First World War vintage – was like the Lower School's classroom. (I never thought to ask why there were no women there; perhaps in those days it was thought that women should not be asked to make their way home after late evening working.) Linking the two ends were the offices of the Secretariat's own small hierarchy: the temporarily seconded Deputy and Assistant Secretaries towards one end, the senior regulars towards the other. The clerical officers at their end were the JIC infrastructure of checking, security classification, proof-reading, collation, publication and distribution of draft and 'final' papers: in effect the publishing house for the JIC and its numerous Current Intelligence Groups. The Secretary from his end was not supposed to interfere. On the school analogy, he dealt with the masters and hobnobbed with the prefects, but had no part in the classroom. If he appeared there it was regarded as an amiable eccentricity, rather out of the mould.

I can hardly exaggerate the scale and intricacy of the routine work of the clerical officers; the complexity of the various security regulations to be implemented; the procedural variations from document to document, and recipient to recipient; the scope for damaging errors, like sending 'UK Eyes Only' documents to foreign allies; the meticulousness needed, day after day and year after year, in emergencies and late evenings as well as normal hours. I found it a marvel that the system responded so well to the demands placed upon it. I cannot recall a serious mistake, or a misprint that seriously distorted intelligence on an important issue. Where was the credit due?

A trio of regulars were in charge: Betty Green, Reg Pullen and Mervyn-Smith, all now long retired. Betty joined the Office in 1938 when Hankey was still in post as the Cabinet Secretary. She was a London graduate, recruited as a lady typist – an illustration of women graduates' careers at that time. In the Second World War she became General Ismay's secretary, travelled with him to the big wartime conferences, supported him again when he became NATO's Secretary-General, then joined the JIC Secretariat and remained there for the rest of her career. She had to be coaxed to produce wartime reminiscences, but recalled that Churchill remarked to her after the war that she must have many secrets locked in her bosom. Reg was a cheerful, rubicund figure who had become a Post Office messenger-boy at the age of 14, and came to the Cabinet Office shortly after wartime military service. Both were Higher Executive Officers who would probably have gone further in most other Departments. I never asked them if they had tried to move. Both received MBEs, and I always think of them when people now advocate fewer honours for civil servants and more for footballers. They were in one sense the archetypal Executive Class officers who knew the precedents and rule-books; but they also ran a complex production machine with initiative, sensitivity and commonsense.

Under them came Mervyn-Smith, who directly supervised the clerical officers and was more of a mystery than the others. He had held a post-war army commission, and rumour had it that he had once passed the Administrative Class entry competition. I never knew how he came to be where he was, as an Executive Officer in late middle age; but he was there, owlishly supervising the young clerical officers from the top corner of the old-fashioned, big room. A wing collar and a high desk would have completed the Dickensian impression he gave. He was a silent man of considerable intelligence, *mutatis mutandis* as enigmatic as Burke Trend himself.

I never knew at first why the clerical officers stuck at their intricate and boring jobs so willingly. The trio's management style was parental rather than populist; but the swinging 1960s had brought no sign of restlessness, no demands to wear jeans. (Though there was one such sign of the times. At the JIC's weekly meeting a clerical officer was always on duty among the Secretariat for various fetching and carrying purposes. For the newly joined, gentle Gary this posed a problem. He did not possess a tie, and could not see his way to buying one expressly for this purpose. What would now cause a great furore was handled otherwise. The Colonel's successor, a Group Captain, brought a tie and handed it over when required on Thursday mornings, rather like a head waiter in a good restaurant supplying suitable neckwear for an improperly dressed client.) There were probably some material incentives in the overtime and 'unsocial hours' payments that the job involved; in those distant days such financial matters were left to the regulars to sort out, not something for the birds-of-passage. Perhaps working in the JIC Secretariat also had an element of status and mystique about it. But I realized quite soon that the motivation came from the influence of the management trio, and the examples they set.

They were not pushovers: Betty, the most correct of civil servants, once met the demand from a young diplomat for a special messenger to carry a document to the Foreign Office a hundred yards away, by remarking gently that he could always carry it himself. But the ethic was of service. I earlier likened the two separate elements of the Cabinet Office to officers and men, and Gentlemen and Players; but the analogies are unfair. If information-handling and communication are central to the battle for effective government, the trio were the front-line company commanders in it; we others were the red-tabbed staff officers back at base. The front line could be relied upon; it would not break.

One incident sums it up. The JIC at one of its weekly meetings had an unexpected policy issue on its hands. It broke up at about 1230, decreeing (unusually) that I was to write a paper to be available at a reconvened meeting at 1700. My first step was to ask about the latest possible deadline for reproduction, checking and collation. Reg replied with a time which seemed to cut things fine. As the deadline approached he hovered with mild anxiety symptoms, then made off at speed with the completed draft. In due course the Great and Good of the JIC began to assemble for 1700. By 1658 a certain restlessness began to manifest itself around the table. Generals prepared to bark; diplomats to assume expressions of hauteur; intelligence Heads of Agencies to mark the Secretary's professional card.

The outcome hardly needs to be recorded. At 1659 Reg entered the conference room, pink-faced, bearing the stack of papers; recovering his breath, he distributed them with butler-like aplomb, and proceedings commenced. There is only one significant thing about this recollection. Normally it is prudent to assume that if things can go wrong they will. Yet I had absolute confidence, in that place and with those people, that I would not be let down.

IMPLICATIONS

These are elderly recollections of middle-aged salad days in Whitehall. I went to London expecting to scorn. In the event I was fascinated, indeed bowled over, by the Cabinet Office and its insight into Whitehall. Like Dick Whittington after his London fling, I never saw things in the provinces in quite the same light again. These impressions are tainted by this nostalgia.

Nevertheless they lead me to two reflections on British public adminis-tration. The first is on the influence of civil servants, specifically the extent to which those in the Cabinet Office influence politicians' decisions. The literature emphasizes the lines drawn between officials' recommendations and Ministers' responsibilities. Anthony Seldon's account of the Cabinet Office in later years, under the first two Thatcher governments, concludes that its marks on the substance of decisions were confined to a relatively small number of episodes; the main satisfaction of most Cabinet Office offi-cials was that 'they had done their work expeditiously, invited the right people to committee meetings, briefed the chairmen correctly, ensured that papers were circulated in good time, that decisions were taken in the light of the fullest information available at the time, and that clear instructions following meetings were sent to the relevant people in Whitehall'.[8] In his view this was nothing new; apart some structural changes, 1979-1987 'in many other ways will be seen as an unexceptional period during which the [Cabinet Office] machine operated along lines already established'.[9]

For the earlier period about which I write, Trend's usefulness to Prime Ministers of both parties is not in question. A JIC Chairman commented to me that he had made himself quite indispensable, in overseas as well as domestic matters.[10] Kissinger while in power in Washington regularly visited him *en route* to senior Ministers and Number 10, and Kissinger was not one to waste his time. A Private Secretary captured Trend's relationship with the Prime Minister in describing how, at the Commonwealth Conference in Canada in 1973, he and Heath would meet after the long evening's proceedings and discuss outstanding London business; Trend would then dictate telegrams into the small hours, in a sense covering for the Prime Minister's absence. At home his weekly meetings on Thursday afternoons organized Cabinet and Cabinet Committee business for the next week, squeezing quarts out of the pint pots of Cabinet and Prime Ministerial time, seeking always for the proper handling of issues (what preparation, in what forum? who needs to comment beforehand? how long should they be given to see the papers? what position on the agenda?). The meeting's tone had the senior civil servant's brevity and lightness of touch; the language was allusive, incomprehensible to the neophyte. But clearly this was the engine-room that kept central government moving.

But was it also one of the rudders that steered? No doubt the wording of Cabinet Minutes has always helped Prime Ministers to get their own way; but has the Cabinet Office itself influenced decisions in particular directions? Perhaps this can only be known when its Steering Briefs become available in the Public Record Office.[11] I can offer only one minuscule bit of evidence from my sole foray through the connecting door into Number 10. It was to do the record of a small 'meeting of ministers' in the Cabinet Room. Some legislation then in hand raised quite incidentally an issue of national security. My recollection is that discussion ran into the sand, with an ambiguous summing-up between alternatives A and B, less through Ministerial disagreement than because all sensed that it fell into a 'too tricky' category. It was a complex but unspectacular issue, taken on a hot afternoon; I have no reason to think the meeting was typical of that government's style.

Nevertheless what followed has the vividness of unrepeated experience. On the way out of the Cabinet Room Trend said to me 'I want a conclusion in favour of A'; no more. I retired bemused; but then realized that a logical progression could be constructed by standing the order of the subjects on its head and selecting a suitable sequence of discussion, summing-up and conclusions. The record was dictated, and ready to go out that evening. For the Cabinet Office this was run-of-the-mill stuff. But it raises the question of the official imprint on policy. Did Trend know the Prime Minister's mind, or was he himself tilting the decision? All I can say with confidence is that historians using my record will have a distinctly synthetic view of the decision process.

I am inclined to think that this particular case illustrated a special role for the Cabinet Secretary on some matters. Hennessy described how Trend felt he had to use his own initiative as 'custodian of Cabinet confidentiality' over Sir Anthony Nutting's book about the Suez Crisis, in a way compared by Crossman with the position of the monarch as arbiter a hundred years earlier.[12] My record was written to favour the requirements of national security. Trend consistently took a special interest in the intelligence and security services, including the protection of their information and sources.[13] In the incident I describe he may have felt it right to influence the outcome in their favour: not to disregard Ministers, but to give national security the benefit of the doubt in a situation of Ministerial ambiguity – rather as a cricket umpire favours the batsman in doubtful cases.

Perhaps things are different now. Personally I hope that this official influence still exists, derived as it is from Hankey's orientation towards security and defence issues and Cabinet Secretaries' subsequent role as chairmen of the Permanent Secretaries' Committee on the Intelligence Services.[14] Attlee's explanation of not involving the Cabinet in the decision to develop nuclear weapons – that he 'thought that some of them were not fitted to be trusted with secrets of that kind'[15] – showed an admirable and not yet outdated realism. Politicians and their associates do not change. Many years later, intelligence professionals were shocked by a former Minister's revelation in Parliament, on the day after the Falklands invasion, that Argentine ciphers had been readable under the previous government.[16] I have no problem over seeing the Cabinet Secretary as a constitutional check-and-balance on certain national security subjects.

Whether or in what degree this influence has extended further I am not qualified to say. But I wonder if some features of the available evidence do not weigh the conclusions drawn from it. Most Ministers write their memoirs or publish their diaries; few civil servants do. Ministers seek to register their mark on history; while, even in confidential recollections, officials are influenced by their lifetime style of understatement and reticence. It is now unfashionable for politicians to blame civil servants for past failures, and arguably the two have a common interest in buttressing the received view of the master-and-servant relationship between them. Perhaps these factors lead historians marginally to underrate Cabinet Office influence on specific decisions, and perhaps the effects of senior civil servants as a whole.

My second, less tentative reflection is about the significance of the Cabinet Office's supporting services and those who provide them. Cabinet government would be impossible without this support. Despite its efficiency, reliability and importance, this part of the machine has never attracted the interest or got the credit it deserves. Those writing about government have neglected it, rather as historians of war tend to overlook logistics. To pursue the military analogy: if government is a continuous battle for coherence against cock–up, chaos and the unforeseen, then masses of paper are like the food and ammunition on which armies depend. War depends on supply systems; the quality of government is set by the paper-work and how it is handled. The JIC section I have described reflected the standards of the Cabinet Office machine to which it belonged, and depended, like it, on Old Civil Service virtues.

This has implications for one's view of the restructuring over the last ten years of the New Public Management.[17] The three Executives I have described had not been specially selected as fliers, in the way that the Administrative Class people were chosen for their Cabinet Office tours. The trio embodied the role and qualities of the Executive Class in the stratified Civil Service that then existed. Subsequently the Fulton reforms of the 1970s moved a little way towards bridging the grading system's institutional-ized gulf between policy and execution. Now we have gone back to an even greater separation, between the policy-making centre and the devolved exec-utive agencies of Next Steps – but with a deliberate attempt to produce a new kind of civil servant (or short-term employee) and destroy the old system.

This is not the place to discuss these changes. But my strongest memory of the Cabinet Office regulars is of their idea of service at the core of government. Institutions have to develop, and information technology is now the catalyst for massive changes. It is to be hoped that the Cabinet Office's Wells Fargo–like system is being electronically transformed. But the system will still be needed in some form, and will still depend on the values held by those operating it. All good organizations have their values, but they are not identical, transferable or creatable in short order. The spirit of the Old Civil Service was not the same as that of other excellent but different organizations. Yet it was there, as the underpinning.

I hope my pen-pictures have hinted at its nature. I am saddened that it is now so little esteemed. Modern public service slogans such as IiP ('Investment in People') are praiseworthy if seeking to build on the best elements of tradition; catchpennies if waved as banners for a state of permanent revolution.

NOTES

The author is grateful to Colonel Murray Petit, Betty Green, Reg Pullen and others for their comments upon his recollections.

1. Published in *Contemporary British History*, 11, 1 (spring 1997).
2. The JIC Secretariat and the Joint Intelligence Staff had been part of the Cabinet Office (which included the Office of the Minister of Defence) in the Second World War. I have been assured that the small permanent civilian staff described in this paper remained titularly within the Cabinet Office in the reorganization of 1945–46, even though the central defence committee structure was then deemed to be part of the new MoD; JIC reports were issued as MoD documents (General Sir William Jackson and Lord Bramall, *The Chiefs* (London: Brassey's, 1992), pp. 192, 268). After the major change of 1957 in which the JIC in all its aspects became a Cabinet Office and not a Chiefs of Staff committee there was still a nod towards its COS origins in its terms of reference, whereby 'special assessments requested by the Chiefs of Staff shall be directly submitted to them in the first instance'. This still stands and is quoted in the official terms of reference, now *National Intelligence Machinery* (London: The Stationery Office, 2000), p. 20. It is a touching bit of British traditionalism, of no significance whatever.
3. P. Hennessy, *Cabinet* (Oxford: Blackwell, 1986), p. 20.
4. Hennessy, *Cabinet*, p. 15.
5. *The Times*, 22 July 1987.
6. *Departmental Committee on Section 2 of the Official Secrets Act 1911*, Cmnd 5104 (London: HMSO, 1972), Vol.3, p. 316 onwards. It must be a matter of historical regret that Lord Franks – the examiner *par excellence* – was (unusually) absent from Trend's session.
7. As described in P. Hennessy, *Whitehall* (London: Fontana, 1990), pp. 214–17, with reference to Trend's special concern for the Commonwealth and US relationships.
8. A. Seldon, 'The Cabinet Office and Coordination', *Public Administration*, 68, 1 (spring 1990), pp. 120–1.
9. Ibid., p. 120.
10. Compare with Crossman's hostile diary notes that Wilson was 'really fond of Burke Trend and sees him as a close personal friend and confidant', and that government had become 'a Wilson–Burke Trend axis' (quoted in Hennessy, *Whitehall*, pp. 217, 218).
11. For the Cabinet Office briefs, and Trend's attitude to them, see Hennessy, *Cabinet*, p. 79. I recall that at one Thursday afternoon meeting Trend reported a complaint from the Prime Minister that the briefs asked too many questions and gave too few recommendations. He had characteristically argued in reply that policy emerged best from the Socratic method, but had not converted the Prime Minister. Trend enigmatically ended the Thursday meeting with the guidance, 'Well, we must do our best'.
12. Because the government of the day could not have access to the earlier papers of the other side (Hennessy, *Whitehall*, p. 214).
13. Thus Trend in the late 1960s had been exercised by the question when and how the code-breaking successes of the Second World War should be revealed, and was engaged in prolonged correspondence with Sir John Masterman over his intentions to publish what eventually became Masterman's *The Double Cross System in the War of 1939–45* (New Haven, CT: Yale University Press, 1972). For the description of him in his obituary as intelligence's 'shop steward' see Note 5 above, and subsequent comment in a letter from Lord Hunt of Tanworth and Sir Robert

Armstrong (*The Times*, 30 July 1987). If there is any truth in pictures in the 1960s of struggles within Number 10 between Trend and Marcia Williams, later Lady Falkender, the issue was probably access to classified information, rather than influence on policy.

14. *National Intelligence Machinery*, p. 12. Sir Robert (later Lord) Armstrong's role in the Peter Wright affair was consistent with this special concern for the protection of intelligence.
15. Quoted in Hennessy, *Cabinet*, p. 131.
16. E. Rowlands (*Hansard*, 3 April 1982, col. 650). A recent claim that this revelation was without effect (Mark Urban, *UK Eyes Alpha: The Inside Story of British Intelligence* (London: Faber and Faber, 1996), p. 68) should be treated with reserve.
17. For the term and its scope see, for example, R.A.W. Rhodes (ed.), 'The New Public Management', *Public Administration*, 69, 1 (spring 1991).

11

The Effects of Secrecy:
GCHQ De-Unionization[1]

A 1993 view, with postscript.

No one needs to be reminded of the government decision of 25 January 1984 to ban national trades unions at GCHQ, the signals intelligence (Sigint) centre at Cheltenham. It has become an entrenched part of British political and trades union mythology; the sight of First Division civil servants marching in Cheltenham with the National Union of Mineworkers in the annual rally of protest sums up its lasting effects. Re-unionization is well established as Labour's policy in opposition and will happen sometime; national unions were all set to offer attractive packages of cut-price membership after the expected Labour victory in 1992. The fact that Cheltenham is a marginal seat now gives the situation extra spin. Politics apart, the affair has a bearing on a raft of issues: trade union structures; patterns of public sector management; control of intelligence agencies; judicial review; the place of 'national security' in law and constitutional practice. In all these contexts a proper account of the affair is badly needed.

The short and readable book *A Conflict of Loyalties* by Lanning and Norton-Taylor – well produced as the first venture of a Cheltenham-based workers' cooperative – might seem to provide it, but the authors' backgrounds give fair warning that it is no dispassionate study. Lanning as a full-time trades union official was, and is, deeply involved in the action against the union ban; Norton-Taylor of the *Guardian* is a former Freedom of Information Journalist of the Year, and a long-term thorn in the side of the intelligence establishment. They have produced a campaigning account of a campaign. Indeed, with their penchant for military chapter titles like 'the battle' and 'the war', it reads rather like an old-style military history of one of the less successful episodes of Empire. Our soldiers die heroically for Queen and Country against overwhelming odds. But the cruel and treacherous fuzzy-wuzzies on the other side remain shadowy creatures. One hardly gets to understand why they attacked – and won.

One-sided campaign history of this sort is still useful, and the account here of union reactions and tactics has the virtues of first-hand recollection. The most informative chapter is on the negotiations of February and March 1984, particularly on the unions' 'no-strike' offer and its rejection by the government. (The full text of the offer – an important document, which may still come back to haunt the unions – is printed as Appendix 2). Union politics and personalities are treated uncritically, as is the question whether a no-strike agreement would have survived criticism from the conference militants. Nevertheless the narrative has the whiff of the battle-field about it, and is valuable on that account.

The causes of war get less satisfactory treatment. The authors demon-strate that union problems at GCHQ went back to 1969 and predated the service-wide pay disputes of 1979-81. They analyse the government's claim that GCHQ lost 10,000 days in strikes in that later period. But, though they have no compunction about publishing a wealth of information about GCHQ's classified facilities and operations, they are surprisingly coy about the details of industrial action. The reader looks in vain for numbers, places and dates. The authors argue that the civil service unions were carried away by their own rhetoric in stating in 1981 that their actions were causing disruption and inconvenience; and they claim that the campaign was designed to cause embarrassment and not damage. This is a disingenuous *post facto* interpretation of history. Maybe no one on the union side now knows what really happened; all the more reason for trying to establish the facts. Freedom of information could start with the union records.

They are also determined not to give the other side an inch. GCHQ management is always shown as inefficient, authoritarian and paranoiac. The American relationship is caricatured as a 'master-servant arrangement of convenience... with GCHQ giving the Americans nearly everything of value, while NSA [its American opposite number] is highly selective in the intelligence it deigns to give to GCHQ'.[2] All the stale and unsourced canards about GCHQ are trotted out – illegal coverage of domestic targets; interception of the communications of Jane Fonda and Benjamin Spock; cooperation with South Africa; and so on. GCHQ is 'a uniquely privileged organ of the secret state. Its powerful position, its total lack of accountabil-ity, can only cause serious disquiet among those concerned with civil liberties.'[3] If only half this stuff were true, the mystery would not be why decent people got the sack from GCHQ, but why they ever worked there.

One example illustrates the rubbishing technique. The authors claim that Geoffrey Prime – sentenced in 1982 to thirty-eight years imprisonment as a Soviet agent – was not detected earlier because a woman who knew he was a spy was put off by a GCHQ investigating officer's manner, with the implication that this was an example of inefficiency. This is presumably the story of Miss Barsby, taken from the Security Commissions's report on the case, but without the Commission's conclusion that her explanation was no more than 'an attempt at self-justification for a disgraceful action'.[4] Good campaign stuff, but is the liberal case best served by this selective use of evidence?

Thus as a source the book should be treated with caution. How then can the historian, the politician or the man in the street reassess this important and continuing affair? It may be helpful to suggest some pointers.

CONSTITUTIONAL SETTINGS

Two issues can be mentioned in passing that did not arise. First, the dispute was not about the need for secret intelligence; there was a surprising acceptance on all sides of Sigint's importance. Public opinion had probably been educated by the decisions taken in the 1970s – with much official hesitation at the time – to release details of Sigint successes in the Second World War. By 1984 the wartime contribution of Bletchley Park had become part of British political culture; without this background, the GCHQ debate could easily have taken a different turn. In this respect public opinion was genuinely and properly informed by official releases of information – a moral, perhaps, for the future.

Second, the affair did not raise questions of constitutional propriety or bureaucratic ineffectiveness. Intelligence agencies are usually portrayed as rogue elephants under inadequate Ministerial control. However, the de-unionization decision was taken by the Prime Minister and a small group of Ministers acting on official advice; it is difficult to fault this in purely constitutional terms. As for theories of bureaucracy, Lanning and Norton-Taylor rightly draw attention to the interview with Sir Brian Tovey, the former GCHQ Director, that made it clear that the initiative came originally from him.[5] Academic writers on British public administration have said for years that they wanted a more proactive higher civil service; here they got it in spades, thanks to the resonance between an official submission and a Prime Minister's instincts.

SECRET ORGANIZATIONS AND PUBLIC BUREAUCRACY

Most countries have Sigint organizations of some kind, often on a substantial scale. In some ways they are more like high-technology production lines than research centres. Secrecy tends to produce high morale and feelings of special value. But it also encourages the intensity of closed organizations, particularly since for most of those involved they are full-life careers without escape routes. Managing them is exhilarating but poses its distinctive challenges.

Secrecy also poses the question of unionization. Some countries have it; others do not. GCHQ after the Second World War adopted the full-scale British Whitley system of national unions, and was rather proud of the marriage of secrecy and respectability. Nevertheless it sometimes seemed an odd arrangement. The author remembers sitting as a young man in a Departmental Staff Side meeting with a full-time union official from London said to be a Communist Party member – a curious situation in a secret establishment in the Cold War. Workable compromises evolved; thus the book claims that one national union secretary was rather quaintly asked by GCHQ on his retirement if he would kindly return all the official material classified 'Confidential' from his files.[6] But it was all slightly anomalous. A few cases before Industrial Tribunals produced similar concerns about publicity and disclosures.

There were also questions about recruitment and staffing. The older intelligence organizations – the Secret Intelligence Service and Security Service – took their shape in the aftermath of the First World War and were not swept up into the standardization of the civil service in the 1920s; in their degree of autonomy they were precursors in some ways of the 'Next Steps' agencies of today. GCHQ on the other hand, taking its modern identity in the late 1940s and 1950s, had aligned with service-wide Treasury-style gradings and conditions as the natural way to go. This had advantages for a new department, but there was some chafing at the constraints: were normal civil service structures and conditions the best basis for a secret intelligence organization? The Security Commission's recommendation after the Prime case for introducing the polygraph illustrated the problem: could that transatlantic instrument of torture really be reconciled with a staid civil service regime? There is no evidence for Lanning's and Norton-Taylor's claim that the polygraph was a factor behind the de-unionization decision; but it certainly encapsulated the underlying problems of GCHQ's status.

INDUSTRIAL ACTION

Nevertheless the central issue was industrial action and the role of national unions in it. Official secrecy still limits an account of the background, and only an outline can be given. GCHQ staff as a whole were singularly unmilitant; GCHQ's reputation was of an efficient and well-managed department; a wide area of management/union relationships were relaxed and reasonably productive. But in one large group of staff (and one similar but smaller one) a set of long-standing problems had existed from the mid-1960s onwards: 'age bulges' through wartime recruitment, and their blight on promotion prospects; the impact of new technology on traditional skills; an 'us' and 'them' division between headquarters and 'outstations'; two unions competing for outstation membership – indeed all the elements of a standard business school exercise on 'managing change'. The two unions concerned discovered in a pay dispute of 1969, described by Lanning and Norton-Taylor, that 'working to rule' could produce more pay. The point was taken in the 1970s.

By the chaotic standards of Britain at the time, the amount of serious militancy in GCHQ was minuscule. Even in the 'problem areas', staff support for strikes, working to rule, and opposition to new technology was not solid, and there was usually some union effort to minimize damage. The managerial style was compromise, not confrontation, reflecting the civil service as a whole and the policy of the responsible Ministers. By the standards of the 1970s industrial action was reasonably well contained and the situation relatively civilized. The book goes out of its way to paint a black picture of management's staff relations, but the real atmosphere is conveyed in its cameo of the GCHQ trades union chairman setting out just before the surprise de-unionization announcement for his regular lunchtime pint with the Head of Personnel. Nevertheless, management's relationships with these two unions and the staff they represented – substantial bodies, but not the majority – had an undercurrent of strain and a long-running threat of industrial action.

In 1979-81 this situation within GCHQ was overlaid by the wider Council of Civil Service Unions' campaign against the abolition of existing pay arrangements. The CCSU's national calls for symbolic 'days of action' evoked mixed, fairly lukewarm responses in GCHQ as a whole. Even token actions went against the grain for most people; one of the senior officials in Lanning and Norton-Taylor's cast of subsequent baddies – a Labour supporter and a former local union chairman – resigned from the First

Division Association in protest. But the two unions which had intermittently threatened action in the 1970s went further and targeted their own members with selective GCHQ action in 1981 as part of the national campaign; and some other groups of staff took some action. It would be interesting to know who decided on this, and why.

No one knows what intelligence was missed as a result. The show was more or less kept on the road. But Sir Brian Tovey's subsequent verdict that GCHQ was not at peak efficiency during the Afghanistan invasion in 1979 or the crises in Poland in 1980–81 is not unfair. It was a risk-ridden world, with heightened East–West tension, terrorism, the taking of Western hostages, *et al*. Intelligence as an insurance policy depends on regularity. No agency can operate properly under threat of lightning strikes. Nor can it command the confidence of allies with whom it cooperates. To Lanning and Norton-Taylor the American connection is of course anathema; but nations cannot cover international affairs without collaboration.

REFLECTIONS

Two questions therefore arise: why did the decision of January 1984 cause such a furore, and was it necessary? The book seeks to answer the first, but one point needs some extra emphasis. When it came to refusals to accept the new conditions, the union campaign got less support than it expected in the areas previously regarded as potentially militant. Where the campaign received unforeseen support was from the traditionally non-militant 'headquarters' areas. To a number of these people – some of them rather unwordly, boffin types without previous union connections – the ban and the way it was imposed touched nerves that the national campaign over pay had missed.

The result was quite impressive. In numerical terms the unions' campaign was a flop, and nothing in the book is more graphic than the description (presumably by Lanning) of the last-minute meetings at out-stations, with support gradually melting away. Yet underneath some politicization and martyrdom-seeking, what emerged was a movement of some integrity. The book paints a surprisingly cheerful picture of the campaigners; but there must have been a quota of unpublicized personal sacrifice. One must respect the stand.

Was de-unionization necessary? The conventional wisdom at the time was that the trauma was worth it for a better organization in the end.

GCHQ acquired its management-approved Staff Federation, said to be effective. After de-unionization there were substantial intelligence pay rises, in addition to the compensation paid at the time; in effect the taxpayer has picked up the bill. Presumably staff relationships have improved, despite the immediate effects of the 1984 affair. On the other side of the ledger there is all the management effort locked up for five years in sorting out de-unionization and all its consequences, including the much publicized dismissals that dragged on for some years; and the equivalent effort that will be needed for re-unionization under a Labour government. Reinstating national unions and providing for the continued existence of the Federation will land some future Director with a dog's breakfast of union negotiations, and the Labour Party and TUC will have no incentive to make things easy for him.

Hindsight makes things clearer than they were, and adds some ironies. We can now see that union militancy was substantially defeated at the national civil service level in the strikes of 1981; de-unionization in 1984 was tackling what had become a non-problem. The issue of GCHQ's place in the 'normal' civil service has been overtaken by Next Steps and devolved agencies; its links with national pay and conditions would have been loosened anyway. On the other hand those who criticized de-unionization at the time because it would soon be reversed by a Labour government have been confounded by two Conservative victories. And the new Staff Federation can now be seen to fit a developing national pattern of single enterprise unions; what is good for Japanese factories on Tyneside may well be good for GCHQ.

In seeing 1984 without this hindsight, history may conclude that it was right to tackle the threat of GCHQ industrial action. Strikes elsewhere – in ambulance and fire services, for example – had been regularly threatening the manifold forms of 'public interest'. But 'national security' produced an additional dimension, and the Foreign Secretary's rationale that 'GCHQ is one of the security and intelligence agencies on which our national security, and to some degree the security of our allies, depends' was not unreasonable in the circumstances of the time.[7] And there is little doubt that national unions – or, to be precise, two of them – had actively and tacitly encouraged staff representatives within GCHQ to regard industrial action as a legitimate negotiating card.

Many people at GCHQ welcomed the fresh start but were unhappy about the authoritarian method. 'Couldn't it have been done by negotiation?' was a common reaction. A 'no strike' agreement could indeed have been proposed to the unions, and what the Treasury subsequently paid out in pay rises could have been the carrot. But it is difficult to visualize a bargain: the Thatcher government was not normally in the business of making pay offers to civil servants, and the national unions had every reason for tough negotiation. Management was probably right to think that a complete exclusion of strikes could only be achieved by shock action. The practical alternative was to take on union militancy by appealing direct to the workforce on selected issues, as at British Leyland. This would probably have been wiser, but still bruising.

Once de-unionization was announced, the unions' 'no strike' offer provided a basis for a settlement. The book quotes a senior GCHQ officer who bore much of the burden in the 1970s as saying privately that 'When the unions put their teeth on the table in February 1984, I cannot understand why the Prime Minister didn't pick them up'.[8] Lord Howe (as he became) said in similar vein in a broadcast that (as the responsible Secretary of State) he personally favoured a 'card in the pocket' solution, presumably a no-strike agreement of some kind.[9] No doubt Ministerial memoirs will tell us more about the arguments. But the reality is that the affair generated too much political momentum to be stopped. In any case the memory of Mr Solomon Binding and other union declarations in the 1970s was too green.

Most people quote the former Head of the Civil Service's judgement that 'What is beyond dispute is that the handling has been breathtakingly inept: a further exploration of the bloody fool branch of management science'.[10] But the affair was really Britain in microcosm. Union militancy of the 1970s was trumped by the 'can do', action-man style of government in the 1980s. Industry recognized the need to question assumptions and explore alternatives; of his time as Chairman of ICI, Sir John Harvey-Jones wrote that 'I have said many times that I do not wish to hire yes-men.... What we are looking for are what I call constructive no-men....It requires a lot of faith to believe that such questioning will actually be recognized, liked and rewarded.'[11] Of his time in the wartime civil service, Lord Franks spoke many years ago of the need for 'rational persuasion'; the difference between an ethos of 'what "They" have ordained rather than of what "We" are committed to carry through'.[12] But in 1984 the watchword in government and government service had become decisiveness above all.

The likely verdict on de-unionization will be that the consequences were not sufficiently thought through, perhaps as was repeated with the poll tax. The two-party system, with conviction politics on both sides, did the rest. The most significant feature of the affair was that consultation with the Opposition seems to have been no part of the plan. It was not the Thatcher style; and there was no chance that the Opposition in 1983–84 would have played ball. But perhaps that was the most powerful reason against the proposal. Intelligence sits ill with political controversy.

The enduring result was a boost to intelligence's public profile and salience in political debate. The real casualty was the older and more subfusc view which saw it as a useful, inconspicuous supporting arm of government; at hand, on the fringes of power, but not using the main stair-case or sitting in the Cabinet Room. Just after the announcement of the union ban, GCHQ's Director issued a circular in which he regretted the public debate and expressed the view that 'the important and unique char-acter of our work [is] such that GCHQ needs to be insulated from external pressures'.[13] Just so. But 25 January 1984 made it a forlorn hope then, and not a much better one now.

POSTSCRIPT

This is one of history's uncommon examples of things coming out right in the end. One of the first acts of the incoming Labour government in 1997 was to announce that the ban on national unions at GCHQ was to be rescinded, with a collective 'no disruption' agreement as part of the settle-ment. Possibly a Conservative government would also have sought a settlement of some kind had it been returned to office, but not so compre-hensively and promptly. After the announcement the management-approved GCHQ Staff Federation that had been established in 1985 moved smoothly towards affiliation as a branch of what eventually became the very large Public and Commercial Services Union, an amalgamation of most of the separate unions that formerly represented civil servants nationally. A 'no disruption' agreement was part of the settlement. The recalcitrants dismissed from GCHQ on disciplinary grounds had symbolic offers of reinstatement or retirement, and the thirteen-year campaign against de-unionization was formally closed. All concerned, including the Conservative Party, breathed sighs of relief. In the 1993 article published above I predicted that re-unionization would produce a muddle, with national unions jostling for position with the GCHQ Federation. Happily this turned out to be wrong – as wrong as my expectation in 1984 that de-unionization would be overturned after a Labour victory in the next General Election, or the following one.

This happy outcome springs partly from the national sea-change in trade union militancy, but partly also from the restructuring of the national civil service unions that began in the 1980s and moved with increasing speed in the 1990s. In 1992, expecting a Labour victory, the national unions that still existed at that time were all set to compete with the GCHQ Staff Federation by offering cut-price membership. But by 1997 they had largely completed their merger into the new mega-union, and it had been established that existing staff associations could retain some separate identity within it. As the 1997 election grew closer the officials of the GCHQ Federation took a crucial and statesmanlike decision: to prepare for affiliation on these lines, rather than fighting to maintain their independence. Through this initiative they solved management's problem of reintroducing national unions without provoking a pitched battle between them and the Federation. It was lucky that the Labour victory was delayed until the Federation had developed quite deep roots in the Department and the national trade union structure was able to absorb it.

Does de-unionization now seem worth it? It can now be maintained that since 1984 the main objective – the continuity of operations at GCHQ – has been secured, and is now guaranteed. Though 'industrial action' in GCHQ in the 1970s and early 1980s was only of marginal significance in any direct ways, the action was real enough, and had wider indirect effects on efficiency, the transatlantic relationship and our own self-respect. I remember my own feelings of sadness and shame when present in the late seventies when a Cold War 24-hour surveillance unit for which I was responsible closed down for a night watch as part of a departmental pay dispute. The closure was no more than a gesture, and our allies were able to take the strain; but it was humiliating nonetheless. The agreement to avoid industrial action of this kind is well worth having.

Yet there have been costs, as set out here. The 1984 decision and its prolonged repercussions produced major distractions for management for much of the period up to 1997. The widespread intelligence salary increases provided by the Thatcher government after de-unionization meant that it was harder to fund the new technological investments needed in the 1990s. Media sensationalism and liberal distrust of the covert intelligence agencies were encouraged. Intelligence needed more openness, but could have done without the adversarial context in which it came about.

A general conclusion is that intelligence does not benefit from being too often handled as an exceptional, 'vital' activity, with special treatment and public excitement about it. It needs to steer clear of publicity and political controversy. A less dramatic appearance suits it better, and is probably a better reflection of its true place in national priorities. Fortunately the Parliamentary Intelligence and Security Committee established in 1994 has made this more practicable than previously; indeed this may be its greatest value. It is a pity that it was not available in the frenetic atmosphere of 1984.

NOTES

1. Review article in *Public Policy and Administration*, 8, 2 (summer 1993), drawing on H. Lanning and R. Norton-Taylor, *A Conflict of Loyalties: GCHQ 1984–1991* (Cheltenham: New Clarion Press, 1991), with a postscript on re-unionization in 1997.
2. Lanning and Norton-Taylor, *A Conflict of Loyalties*, p. 33.
3. Ibid., p. 74.
4. Ibid., p. 49. See also *Security Commission Report*, Cmnd 8876 (London: HMSO, May 1983), p. 22.
5. Lanning and Norton-Taylor, *A Conflict of Loyalties*, p. 43–4; *Sunday Times*, 5 and 12 February 1984. See also letter to *The Times*, 6 February 1984.
6. Lanning and Norton-Taylor, *A Conflict of Loyalties*, p. 86.
7. Sir Geoffrey Howe, Commons Debate, 27 February 1984.
8. Quoted on p. 103, Lanning and Norton-Taylor, *A Conflict of Loyalties*, from the Council of Civil Service Unions' *Warning Signal*, 22, 12 November 1984. The same CCSU piece referred, apparently with approval, to this officer's 'running a tight ship' in the 1970s.
9. A. Howard's radio programme *The Brothers*, BBC4, 19 January 1993. Chapter 23 of Howe's autobiography *Conflict of Loyalty* (London: Macmillan, 1994) gives his views in more detail. 'Card in the pocket' would have meant retaining the right to belong to a national union but not to join in union action.
10. *The Times*, 4 February 1984.
11. J. Harvey-Jones, *Making It Happen* (London: Fontana/Collins, 1987), pp. 89–90.
12. Sir Oliver Franks, Sidney Ball Lecture 1947, quoted in A. Danchev, *Oliver Franks, Founding Father* (Oxford: Oxford University Press), p. 51.
13. Quoted on p. 137, Lanning and Norton-Taylor, *A Conflict of Loyalties*.

12

Collectors, Analysts and Customers in the Cold War[1]

The division of responsibility and resources between single-source collectors and all-source analysts was necessary, but getting the best out of all-source analysis posed considerable challenges. It probably still does.

I spent much of my professional life in touch with the Defence Intelligence Staff (DIS) and its predecessors, and worked in it for a year, and had some experience of its relationships with intelligence collectors and the rest of Whitehall. But I have been retired since 1987. I base my comments on the past, and for those engaged in the present I can only say, 'If the cap still fits, wear it'.

At first sight the DIS fits neatly into the diagram of intelligence architecture and information flows. As an organization for all-source analysis it is a recipient of covert intelligence, a producer for its own customers, and a contributor to the JIC process. Of course the real world is messier; information behaves organically, not mechanistically. Distribution lines actually go in all directions, not least between the national single-source agencies themselves and between them and their opposite numbers across the Atlantic. The DIS is also a major collection agency in its own right. In my lifetime there was a galaxy of military single-sources – the Joint Air Reconnaissance Intelligence Centre (JARIC) for one, but also many others[2] – which the DIS steered as national assets, or should have done.

We also forget how accidental the evolution of the British intelligence community has been. The Foreign Office has a unique, and in my view beneficial, influence upon it, but only through a set of historical flukes.[3] The DIS itself is also not part of any natural order of things. I remember life before it was created in 1964, when the three services and the Joint Intelligence Bureau were independent and often warring institutions; in some respects it was a life of greater vitality.[4] Similarly the role of the collectors has developed historically. The single-source agencies are now not pure collectors of 'raw intelligence'; they are also institutionalized analysts, selectors, and interpreters.

But the conventional diagram of the intelligence process does bring out the difference in responsibility. The single-source agencies' expertise is on their sources, but not (except incidentally) on the subjects that they illuminate. By contrast the DIS in its all-source role is government's authority on subjects, not sources. This difference in responsibility in the British system is as accidental and pragmatic as everything else about it, but I believe quite deeply in it. Among other things, it is democracies' best guarantee against the KGB model of slanted covert intelligence fed direct to policy-makers.

To the military men accustomed to intelligence staffs this is preaching to the converted. What is hard for them to realize is that it is not part of the culture of the civilian world. Diplomats think instinctively of intelligence as the covert, single-source material that adds to their own knowledge. They after all are paid to be foreign experts, and do not have intelligence staffs to do the job for them.

Partly for this reason, the DIS's status has always been squeezed between the wartime prestige of Bletchley Park on the one hand and the JIC on the other. Its military and civilian predecessors came low in the national pecking order in 1945.[5] Intelligence had no particular cachet in the armed services. The civilian Joint Intelligence Bureau was a new organization with no wartime track record, distrusted by the three services, entrusted with tasks they didn't particularly want, and with no top-level patron. Whitehall's desk analysts, both service and civilian, attracted the mundane image of 'collation'. The effects were seen in the DIS's relationships both upstream with the collectors, and downstream with the JIC and Whitehall's intelligence users.

Upstream, in Sigint, those who worked in Room 40 in the First World War felt deeply about the Admiralty's failure to give proper weight to Sigint at Jutland and elsewhere, and in 1939 were determined not to let it happen again. The Second World War saw a long series of successful battles against the armed services to establish Bletchley's position as a central Sigint analysis and interpretation centre, concerned not only with cipher-breaking but also with plain language and non-textual 'traffic analysis' and all it could produce.

Some of these battles had to be re-fought in the first decades of the Cold War. But by the time the DIS was created in 1964 GCHQ's role of drawing inferences was well established, as was its respect for London's all-source responsibility.[6] I have vivid memories of some bureaucratic battles in the 1950s and early 1960s, and have a few horror stories about the institutional relationships then and later. But considering the wide range of people and interests involved, and the intensity of feeling on Cold War subjects, it was a remarkably cordial relationship – unmatched, I suggest, in any other country.

But I must record a reservation. Despite the value of the single-source/all-source distinction, it is still intellectually artificial to chop up into two parts what is in reality a continuous search for truth. There are no pure, objective 'facts' delivered to the DIS's front door. All-source analysis needs some ability to reach back into Sigint to understand the basis for its conclusions, and (especially) to compare it with other sources.

Yet some things militated against this. Security demanded protection for Sigint's methods and successes, and there were other fears – not unreasonable ones – about letting customers loose among 'our' raw data which they were not trained to handle.[7] The distance from Cheltenham to London was a practical factor. But it is perhaps forgotten that in the boundaries that evolved between GCHQ and Whitehall the dominating factors were transatlantic. Washington's pervasive leakiness had to be combated by increasingly onerous sets of security restrictions there. Since US agencies were always in a state of permanent fratricide, agreed lines had to be drawn in the sand about what supporting technical data could be included in Sigint reports or discussed with recipients; and, because transatlantic exchanges were so complete, there was little scope for differences between UK and US practices.

There were also quite proper feelings about our independence; that we must not be bound by our customers' preconceptions. Thus for many years our analysis normally proceeded without much prior discussion with the DIS and its predecessors. Most of the Whitehall officers on normal service tours were too busy and inexperienced to want anything different, and I emphasize that there were good relations both with them and at desk levels.

Yet sometimes, when the personalities were right, I saw an additional dimension being added; a creative and transforming meeting of single-source and all-source minds. I hope that our move quite late in the Cold War towards producing draft annual analysis programmes for discussion and prioritization with the DIS and other customers was the beginning of a closer relationship. Despite this, I think that, if we had all been saints (in both institutions), and if we had worked in a purely national and not a transatlantic framework,[8] we would have had a rather closer relationship –

more of an interdepartmental *jeux sans frontières*, or the more fluid wartime relationships described in R.V. Jones's *Most Secret War*.[9] Instead we tended to treat all 'customers' in rather the same way, without recognizing the very different needs of the intelligence and non-intelligence recipients among them. My bottom line is therefore that 'cordial customer relations' are not necessarily synonymous with igniting creative sparks. In some ways, single-source intelligence needs demanding customers, even querulous ones. They may be more welcome than they think – if they can convince the producers about their intellectual calibre and integrity.

On the DIS's relationships with its own customers downstream, I will only make three points. First, the reputation of the JIC obscures the reliance of good intelligence in some subjects – not all of them – on its all-source corpus of knowledge, in indexes and people.[10] It seemed to me in the Cold War that no one really solved the problem of putting the evidence from Sigint and imagery together in this way. Presumably the need for good all-source data bases, including access to open sources, is now even greater than before. Whose responsibility can they be except the DIS's?[11]

Second, there is the nature of DIS 'analysis'. I like the American term 'data warehousing', which vividly represents the need to store some information and have it available on demand. Yet there is also the need to study some targets in a deeper way. I have criticized the DIS's performance during the Cold War on the grounds that, with exceptions,[12] it did not use the high-quality evidence available on some subjects to develop deeper insights.[13] No one expects the DIS to be expert on everything. But what are the subjects on which government looks to it for world-class, top-table expertise?

This leads, finally, to clarifying the DIS's scope. Its military customers are clear enough. So too is its contribution to the JIC, where it is presumably now accepted *inter alia* as the principal source of all-source intelligence on warring and disintegrating states. But what is it expected to study on the periphery of its defence remit? Traditionally the DIS picks up essential non-military subjects which no one else can do, as with Rhodesian sanctions in the 1960s. It is Whitehall's intelligence fire brigade; but is this recognized?

The same applies even more to its service to non-military Whitehall customers at a sub-JIC level. The JIC is a Rolls-Royce system for dealing with important things expensively for top readers. But there are always some subjects that fall below the JIC threshold, but on which Whitehall desks need analysis and summaries, not just a succession of single-source reports. The Scott report on the Matrix–Churchill affair illustrated an absence of this product, and also quite failed to recognize the need for it. Perhaps fighting in Sierra Leone more recently fell into the same category. Are the FCO and other civilian departments clients and *demandeurs* of the DIS; or does the DIS merely oblige them, resources permitting, out of the good of its heart?[14]

On these issues a ghost still walks. The idea of a national analysis agency was ventilated around 1945, but never realized.[15] Some hoped for it in the DIS's creation in 1964, and indeed the DIS then became the nearest thing to a British all-round Soviet analysis centre. But this was never complete; and on the whole the idea of a national agency never achieved more than a phantom pregnancy.[16] In any case it was stifled in recurrent economy cuts in which the DIS was pared down towards a strict MoD orientation. So in my time the only British intelligence officers formally paid to assess targets and situations holistically – not as political, defence or economic experts in separate segments – were the twenty or so bright people in the Assessments Staff, with no continuity, research assistance or records.

I do not actually think that this calls for root-and-branch reorganization, a life after the DIS. There is no room for both the JIC and something calling itself the national intelligence centre, a replica of CIA's Directorate of Intelligence; and I am a JIC believer. But I would argue that, while doing what it does now,

1. the DIS should be properly recognized and staffed as a 'defence plus' all-source agency – the 'plus' not set in concrete, but a matter of management judgement, in the same way as targeting and coverage of any other intelligence body;
2. it should also be staffed as an accredited all-source producer for non–military Whitehall customers, at the sub–JIC level I have described.

I shall be told that these things already happen. But formal recognition would help it, in image, esteem and getting money and talent. It would also have a bearing on the present eccentric arrangements for intelligence community oversight and budgeting in the Single Intelligence Vote which excludes the DIS, JARIC and similar important intelligence entities; but that is another subject.

Part of my advice to the DIS from old days would therefore be to be proactive towards the single-source producers, a shade less respectful, perhaps with more mutual access – both ways. Mainly however I suggest some clarification of its Whitehall role; complementing the JIC and the Assessments Staff, but staffed as more than the poor relation.

These suggestions hinge on the DIS's own quality. I will not stir the pot again on the issues of civilian pay and careers, continuity in service postings, rewards for intelligence specialists in the armed forces, postings to the DIS for those on the fast track to the top, career planning for potential DIS leaders, and the cultivation of military purple-suitedness within it. Things may have changed more than I know. I would only add, in passing, that one of my chief concerns has always been not with the military versus civilian balance, but over the civilian scientific posts. From the early 1970s onwards it seemed to me that government scientists had very little incentive to become intelligence specialists. Who would prolong his stint in the DIS when he could return to the pleasant pastures of Malvern and the other well–situated research establishments?

One can argue about what should be done *for* the DIS. But what could be done *by* it? My suggestion, with all due hesitation, is that perhaps it might advertise itself and chuck its weight about more than it has done. The current 28-page official publication on 'Central Intelligence Machinery' gives the DIS only two references, plus less than a half-page description; the rest is about the agencies and the JIC.[17] Some of the original dreamers about the DIS's role must be uneasy in their graves.

It has, after all, a remarkable and potent mixture of disciplines and experience. Whatever the arguments for its fine-tuning, its heterogeneity forms an essential basis for high–class all–source work. I have never advocated that the DIS should be civilianized as a set of GCHQ clones. The conventional label of 'analysis' hardly reflects the many more extrovert parts of DIS work: driving collection and cultivating customers, to say nothing of the JIC role, the orchestration of the defence intelligence community, the information-handling challenges, and the direct impact on policy decisions. In terms of job satisfaction the DIS has a good, rounded package to offer entrants, short-term and long-term, service and civilian.

Perhaps all it needs – or needed in my time – is just a little more zing or buzz within it, a sense of corporate identity; the yeast that sets the fermentation process going. Despite its official name, it should not be thought of as a staff. It is an institution, needing to nurture all the intangibles on which institutions depend for success.

NOTES

1. A talk to members of the British Defence Intelligence Staff, June 1998.
2. Including aircraft, surface and sub-surface shipborne collection, military attachés behind the Iron Curtain, BRIXMIS (the Military Mission to the Soviet forces in East Germany), and the large-scale interviewing of refugees in West Germany and Hong Kong. Some of these operations were 'owned' by overseas commanders or other non-intelligence authorities. Supervision, planning, guidance and feedback from London were variable.
3. That gave the Foreign Office responsibility for SIS and Sigint after the First World War, chairmanship of the JIC from 1939 onwards, and leadership of the Assessments Staff since its creation in 1968.
4. In the JIC sub-committees on scientific and technical subjects, at which the three services and the JIB slugged out their disagreements, in ways that in later years got papered over.
5. I had a whiff of this when looking for a job in 1952. After being put in touch with GCHQ by my Oxford tutor I was interviewed in the ambience of the college senior common room. The corresponding competition was run by the JIB jointly with the Inland Revenue and the (then) Post Office and Labour Exchanges, and produced an unexciting interview in uninspiring surroundings. More to the point, GCHQ's pay and prospects were far better. Has the imbalance on pay, careers and attraction yet been redressed?
6. Credit in getting the doctrine right in the post-war period is due among others to William Millward. His classic 'Life In and Out of Hut 3' (F.H. Hinsley and A. Stripp (eds), *Codebreakers: The Inside Story of Bletchley Park* (Oxford: Oxford University Press, 1993)) conveys the combination of modesty and clearheadedness that he subsequently brought from war to peace.
7. A simple illustration from the 1950s illustrates the issues. The scientific and technical part of JIB demanded our raw DF bearings on the newly discovered Soviet missile ranges, to plot them themselves, to validate our statistical methods. Was it simply our turf protection that led to a row over this demand, and other more complex ones that followed it on other data? Before you decide, remember that the Home Fleet's insistence on having raw DF bearings signalled to it in this way in the Bismarck chase in 1941 nearly caused the quarry to be lost; the flagship plotted them on the wrong kind of chart, and for a while moved the Fleet the wrong way (F.H. Hinsley *et al.*, *British Intelligence in the Second World War*, Vol 1 (London: HMSO, 1979), pp. 342–3, describes the Bismarck chase; for the use of the wrong chart see D. McLachlan, *Room 39* (London: Weidenfeld and Nicolson, 1968), p. 154). But producers are not always correct in using their right to select and interpret. In the Falklands War, on a quite different kind of target location, we should have been more forthcoming than we were. Fortunately it did not matter, as far as I know – but might have done. I still regret that I was not more insistent.
8. The maintenance of which was, of course, one of intelligence's highest priorities.
9. London: Hamish Hamilton, 1987. I recommend this and McLachlan's *Room 39* as the best introductions to the all-source role; together with N. Annan, *Changing Enemies: The Defeat and Regeneration of Germany* (London: Harper Collins, 1995)

for its description of wartime all-source intelligence, with its mixture of human virtues and frailties. For references to the informal discussion of interpretations between Bletchley and Whitehall in wartime see other articles in Hinsley and Stripp (eds), *Codebreakers*: R. Bennett, 'The Duty Officer, Hut 3', p. 35, and E. Thomas, 'A Naval Officer in Hut 3', p. 47.

10. For further discussion see Chapter 4.
11. Of course there should be community access to data bases. But that is yet another contentious subject...
12. Including naval ones. For a comment on naval intelligence in the 1960s and subsequently see K. Booth (ed.), *Statecraft and Security: The Cold War and Beyond* (Cambridge: Cambridge University Press, 1998), Chapter 4.
13. Security still inhibits discussion but one instance can be quoted. At the time of the INF debate in the early 1980s I asked why there seemed so little interest in detailed evidence on the SS-20 and Soviet nuclear strategy generally. A thoughtful RAF officer replied that Whitehall policy-makers did not really want to know more about the mobile SS-20. It was a symbol around which a whole set of Western policy debates had become focused.
14. I recall a young FCO desk officer who complained to me about the numerous (American) single-source bits and pieces he was receiving on fighting in Indo-China (in the 1980s); what he needed was an all-source weekly summary. It had never occurred to him to ask the DIS for it, but in any case the DIS when I approached them replied quite correctly that they were not staffed to provide it.
15. For example in the JIC report of 10 January 1945 on 'The Intelligence Machine' in which a postwar 'Central Intelligence Bureau' was proposed, to be formed from 'all existing intelligence sources' (Public Record Office CAB163/6).
16. Major-General Sir Kenneth Strong's reflections as head of the JIB and first DGI are relevant (K.W.D. Strong, *Intelligence at the Top* (London: Cassel, 1968)).
17. This was then *Central Intelligence Machinery* (London: HMSO, 1993). The description is better in the new version, *National Intelligence Machinery* (London: The Stationery Office, 2000), but the DIS still gets less attention than the covert agencies and the JIC.

Part IV

Intelligence and a Better World

13

Intelligence and International Ethics[1]

Intelligence services are integral parts of the modern state; as Sir Reginald Hibbert put it in the late 1980s, 'over the past half-century secret intelligence, from being a somewhat bohemian servant or associate of the great departments of state, gradually acquired a sort of parity with them'.[2] They have not withered away with the end of the Cold War. There has been some reduction in this decade, but not to the same extent as in the armed forces, and intelligence budgets have recently levelled off or begun to increase again.[3] American expenditure has been declared as $26 billion annually, around ten per cent of the cost of defence, perhaps with some recent increases in human source collection.[4] The equivalent British budget is probably more than £1 billion, rather more than the cost of diplomacy.[5]

Does this investment pose questions of international morality? Most Western governments recognize issues of democratic accountability and restrictions on domestic targeting, but like the rest of the world accept the need for 'foreign intelligence'.[6] On coming to power in 1997 the Labour Foreign Secretary, Robin Cook, emphasized the ethical dimension of his foreign policy, but soon spoke with unexpected warmth of the intelligence support he had received.[7] The Clinton Administration sponsored a study of CIA's ethics, but what emerged focused on intellectual integrity, not morality.[8] The media makes great play with any intelligence leaks, whistle-blowing and failures, but remains thrilled by secrecy. Its ethical concerns over intelligence tend to be inward–looking, concentrating on what it suspects to be part of the domestically repressive 'national security state', rather than on its foreign coverage. *The Times* pronounced in 1999 that 'Cold War or no Cold War, nations routinely spy on each other'.[9]

Nevertheless there is an underlying liberal distaste for what is felt to be 'stealing others' secrets'.[10] Peter Wright's autobiographical account of his 'bugging and burglary' of foreign embassies in London is routinely quoted.[11] John le Carré's novels denigratingly portrayed Soviet and Western intelligence as two halves of the same apple.[12] CIA-bashing remains a world industry, an element in the *bien pensant* view that the US is 'becoming the rogue superpower'.[13] At a more thoughtful level, two British academics have dismissed all espionage as 'positively immoral' apart 'from certain extreme cases' (undefined).[14]

This points to a genuine if muted question about intelligence and ethical foreign policy. Some years ago an Oxford student asked his college chaplain whether a Christian could apply in good conscience to work in intelligence. What was the right reply? Intelligence as an institution is an accepted part of the fabric of international society, but does it make for a better world or a worse one? Does it make any ethical difference at all? These are questions for intelligence practitioners as well as governments and publics. This chapter seeks to explore them.

STARTING POINTS

Intelligence has to be judged in the first instance by its manifest consequences. One test is whether it increases or decreases international tension and the risks of inter-state war.[15] Another, more topical test is whether it promotes or retards international cooperation in a world that now has elements of 'a true world community, with global responsibility for the preservation of a just order',[16] but has to cope with what seem increasing risks and disorder.

Yet judging it solely in this pragmatic, consequentialist way seems incomplete. The code of conduct that deters individuals from reading each others' mail does not rest only on the risks and results of being found out, and it is arguable that states are similarly bound by something more than reciprocal self-interest. The American authority on the history of code-breaking concluded (even during the Cold War) that it was 'surreptitious, snooping, sneaking... the very opposite of all that is best in mankind'.[17] Kant condemned wartime espionage not only for its consequences (that it 'would be carried over into peacetime'), but also since it was 'intrinsically despicable' and exploits only the dishonesty of others.[18] Ethics have a dimension of right conduct, not just of assessing consequences. The moral absolutist or intelligence pacifist cannot be kept entirely out of the discussion.

The 'foreign intelligence' to be judged here in these ways is basically the Western model: an institution with some commitment to telling truth to power, some separation from the power itself, and concerned much more with gathering information than with covert action. Contrary to Bacon's over-quoted dictum that knowledge is itself power, Western intelligence has on the whole not sought power or exercised it. Intelligence under communism and in other authoritarian states has a quite different tradition and would require a separate critique. But the Western ideal of objectivity is not a purely regional one, and has some wider currency. Military intelligence everywhere seeks to know its enemy properly, and Western intelligence applies the same aspiration more widely, as part of government by reason rather than ideology or caprice. It now has a place, albeit inconspicuously, in liberal democracy's worldwide baggage. However much intelligence is criticized for its failures, democratic rulers are in trouble with their electorates if they are known to have disregarded it.

Intelligence on this Western model needs to be considered in its two different aspects; the knowledge it produces, and the activities through which it produces it. Their effects differ. Thus the knowledge gained from Western overflights of the Soviet Union in the 1950s benefited international security through scaling down some exaggerated estimates of the Soviet threat; yet the flights themselves were threatening and provocative, culminating in the Soviet shoot-down of the U-2 on 1 May 1960 which wrecked the East–West Paris Summit a few days later.[19] Knowledge and activities can be examined separately but then integrated into an ethical balance sheet.

INTELLIGENCE KNOWLEDGE

General Effects

Intelligence knowledge is itself of two overlapping kinds: first, the product of special, largely secret collection and, second, assessments on those foreign subjects – mainly bearing on national security – on which intelligence is the national expert.[20] The common factor to both is some separation between intelligence and policy-making.

Some of this knowledge has no obvious ethical connotations. Intelligence on each side's negotiating positions may have figured in the 1999 US–European Union dispute over banana imports, but it is difficult to have moral feelings about the information itself – whatever may be thought of the means of obtaining it. Yet where intelligence knowledge bears on more obviously ethical issues of international security, justice and humanity it can be held to be a moral influence on its own account. If truth-seeking by the intelligence producers is linked with governments disposed to listen, the result should be an improvement in international perception; arguably this should reduce what have been termed 'war-conducive' acts reflecting national leaders' insensitivity, thoughtlessness and recklessness.[21]

Of course these conditions do not necessarily apply. Evil regimes are served by self-seeking or complaisant intelligence, and even in better states leaders use intelligence as selectively as domestic statistics. Intelligence cannot stop governments being wicked or misguided, and it provides no magic key to the future. But (like statistics) it can do something about governmental ignorance and misperception. John Gaddis argues that the Soviet documents from the Cold War show 'the dangers of making emotionally based decisions in isolation' when 'authoritarians do not consult experts'.[22] Writing about the Indo–Pakistan crisis in 1999 brought out leaders' mutual sense of siege, and the importance of 'methods of deployment, intelligence capabilities and command-and-control systems' in reducing the risks of the antagonists' nuclear momentum, with hopes that intelligence in both countries was up to the job.[23]

Even if this has some credence as a general proposition, good intelligence can still be accused of applying its own institutional 'spin', a *déformation professionelle* towards hawkish, 'worst case' assessments. Intelligence is partly a warning system; and as a former British Joint Intelligence Committee Chairman has put it, it specializes in 'the hard world of shocks and accidents, threats and crises... the dark side of the moon, history pre-eminently as the record of the crimes and follies of mankind'.[24] So it is not surprising if intelligence exaggerates threats and demonizes enemies. It is bound to be misleading sometimes (again like statistics),[25] but the charge is that it tends to be misleading always in the same direction, giving policy and decisions a systemic bias.

Yet historically this is a misrepresentation, not a measured judgement. There is indeed a danger of military intelligence reflecting the interest of the military-industrial lobby in increased defence expenditure, as was an element in the Cold War. Western assessments in connection with ballistic missile defence may now be under such pressure. Soldiers in any circumstances have to dwell on 'worst cases' since they pay the price of complacency. Intelligence's use of special sources does not make criticism of its hawkish assessments easy. But the overall intelligence record is far more varied than this image suggests. There are more instances of failing to detect surprise attacks than of ringing alarm bells for imaginary ones, and as many examples of underestimating opponents as exaggerating them. Moreover institutional checks and balances can be devised to provide some safeguards against bias. The British interdepartmental JIC system is caricatured as balancing military pessimism against diplomatic optimism, but the caricature has a grain of truth in it. International discussion of intelligence estimates is equally effective in improving national standards. Intelligence can err by striving too hard to be 'useful' to its customers, but this is balanced by the ethic of professional objectivity, the practitioner's self-image of telling truth to power, and the importance of organizations' international reputation. The effect over time has been that governments that have effective Western-style intelligence systems and listen to them behave as better international citizens than those that operate without them.[26]

Specific Applications

This generalization is supported by more specific connections with international morality, many of them springing from America's world role and its unmatched superpower intelligence. Intelligence is part of the American security umbrella over China's and North Korea's intentions towards their Pacific neighbours. It figures in America's role as international mediator, providing stabilization and reassurance. As part of the settlement after the 1973 Yom Kippur war Henry Kissinger undertook to provide Egypt and Israel with intelligence from regular airborne sorties.[27] The power of satellite surveillance has subsequently given a new dimension to this part of the American security tool-kit. The effect of intelligence briefings given to India and Pakistan in 1990 to prevent their drifting towards war illustrates intelligence satellites' place among the instruments of American power.[28] Similar intelligence support will presumably be offered to Israel in compensation for any eventual withdrawal from the Golan Heights.

But intelligence's direct contributions to international security are by no means limited to the American ones, and they extend beyond specific situations to a group of worldwide and long-term security issues. Terrorism is one such; the limitation of weapons of mass destruction and other arms proliferation is another, through the Missile Technology Control Regime, the Nuclear Suppliers Group and others of this kind; and international sanctions are a third category of wide-ranging, intelligence-driven cooperation. International arrangements between intelligence professionals underpin these political agreements. National intelligence tips off collaborating nations, or is used to keep them from backsliding.

It also supports the many agreements that now exist for arms control and other confidence-building measures. Historically it bore the main weight of arms control verification in the Cold War; the US–Soviet strategic arms control agreements of the 1970s depended entirely on intelligence for verification, since on-site inspection was still unacceptable to the Soviet Union. These agreements even had provisions for cooperative displays to each party's imagery satellites, and limitations on the encipherment of radio-telemetry from missiles. Astonishingly, the superpower antagonists undertook in this way to facilitate each other's secret intelligence collection.[29]

Arms control and confidence-building agreements now have large symbolic elements, but where there are real tensions, as between India and Pakistan, intelligence still operates in synergy with any agreements reached for transparency. Intelligence triggers treaty-based inspections; inspections plus declared confidence-building data provide leads for intelligence; each checks and steers the other. National Technical Means of collection (the Cold War euphemism for intelligence) are endorsed annually in the UN's re-endorsement of its 1988 Principles of Verification, and were recognized in 1996 in the Comprehensive Test Ban Treaty as legitimate triggers for international on-site inspection.[30] The power of modern intelligence is a prop, perhaps not sufficiently recognized, for the advocates of nuclear reduction or elimination.

Intelligence's most dramatic impact in recent years has however been in support for international intervention. Iraq since the Gulf War has been a classic intelligence target of almost Cold War difficulty, and UNSCOM–IAEA (United Nations Special Commission for Iraq and the International Atomic Energy Authority) inspections of Iraqi compliance with the Gulf War peace terms leaned heavily on national intelligence inputs, with as many as twenty nations contributing data.[31] Action over the no-fly zones and the Kurdish sanctuary has been similarly intelligence-steered.

Iraq may be *sui generis*, but Bosnia and Kosovo have pointed to a new pattern of intelligence support for international intervention of all kinds. All those responsible for such operations, from the UN Secretary-General downwards, have emphasized the importance of good intelligence.[32] A deluge of information is available from the many non-intelligence sources – the media, diplomatic reporting, deployed military units, NGOs, international officials – but all concerned echo T. S. Eliot's cry in *The Rock*:

Where is the wisdom we have lost in knowledge?
Where is the knowledge we have lost in information?

National intelligence is relied upon to fill gaps, validate other sources and, above all, assess. The concept of graduated force, surgical strikes, low casualties and minimum collateral damage is significantly intelligence-dependent. Military forces deployed in peace enforcement and peace building need virtually the full range of wartime intelligence support, and providing evidence on crimes against humanity for international legal use after the event now adds a whole new set of intelligence requirements.[33] International intervention is snowballing and – as put in one of the British agencies' recruitment literature – 'government cannot make the right decisions unless it has the full picture'.[34]

Meeting the need poses many problems. America's leading role cannot be guaranteed,[35] and in any case other participating nations have to be accommodated in the intelligence structure. Our intelligence dependence on America is a current issue for the European Union; coalitions of the willing need shared information, with some confidence that it is not being rigged by the US with British connivance. Small powers have the dilemmas posed by supporting international action while taking others' intelligence assessments on trust.

Yet the problems should not obscure modern intelligence's ability to deliver the goods. Satellites' scope is ever-increasing, as is the capability of high-flying aircraft and drones. So too are the opportunities provided by the electronic world in which every detachment commander, insurgent leader, terrorist director, hostage-taker or international drug-dealer seems to have his mobile phone or communicate via the internet. The cases of collateral damage during the Serbia–Kosovo campaign should not divert attention from what was demonstrated there of the striking power of sophisticated technical collection combined with precise weaponry.

Its support for international order may at last be making intelligence respectable; or at least some intelligence. In her aid programme for developing countries Ms Clare Short, as Britain's Secretary of State for International Development, has endorsed strengthening 'the capacity of [local] intelligence services to assess genuine outside threats'.[36] Considering her radical background, this could be taken as game, set and match for intelligence's ethical justification.

INTELLIGENCE ACTIVITIES

The Ethical Spectrum

But if this applies to intelligence's knowledge, there is still the problem of its activities. About 90 per cent of intelligence expenditure is on secret collection; is this a form of anti-social international behaviour? Absolutists hanker after a Woodrow Wilson-like world of open information openly acquired. Pragmatists may have no objection to covert methods *per se* but may worry about the effects. International law suggests some constraints; though actually not many. From any of these viewpoints it might be held that intelligence's activities undo the good done by the knowledge they produce.

Here a first approach is to consider the wide variety of intelligence's collection methods and their varied ethical implications. At one extreme no questions of propriety are posed by its use of public information and the results of military and diplomatic observations and contacts. Something of the same applies to some of its own collection, despite the secret intelligence label. Ships and aircraft collect intelligence in international waters and airspace without accusations of illegality, as do armies when deployed overseas (though the media always tags similar civilian observations as 'spying').[37] Satellite photography violates no international law and is now more or less accepted as a commercial as well as an intelligence activity.[38] *Pace* Kant, wartime intelligence-gathering is free from any legal or moral restraint, except on the torture of prisoners under interrogation. (There is also a legal concept of 'treachery',[39] but it has not yet been applied to intelligence.) Yet the wartime effort has to be practised and operational in peacetime, and cannot sit twiddling its thumbs.

Other types of intelligence collection and exploitation have less legitimacy, but are tolerated provided that they remain undeclared. Most electronic interception is at relatively long ranges and provides no indication of its precise targets; despite national privacy legislation, transmission via the ether is intrinsically a public means of communication. Routine anti-Americanism has not usually extended to condemning US technical collection, though the European Parliament has recently embarked on a crusade against the US–UK–Commonwealth 'Echelon' system for the interception of traffic on international communications satellites.[40] Russia now has a separate, large and probably effective Sigint organization but few in the West lose much sleep over it.[41] Armed forces assume that foreign intelligence services are targeted on them, and diplomats are not fussed by having their telegrams and phone calls intercepted. Intelligence collection in these categories does not seem particularly intrusive. Governments' attitudes to it have echoes of American policy under Clinton over homosexuality in the armed forces: 'don't ask, don't tell'.

But some other collection has bigger ethical question marks against it. The Western overflights of the USSR in the 1940s and 1950s, by balloons as well as aircraft, were clear breaches of territorial integrity, as was some of the US's muscle-flexing in provocative airborne sorties around the Soviet periphery in the early 1980s.[42] The same applied to the West's intensive intelligence collection in Soviet territorial waters, incompatible with maritime law on innocent passage.[43] There is also the position of embassies, as both intelligence targets and intelligence bases. Suborning foreign embassy staff to provide documents or ciphers has a long history, but the Cold War added the new dimension of bugging and electronic attacks against their premises. The new US embassy in Moscow has had to be abandoned, unused, hopelessly penetrated with microphones and bugs.[44] Gordievsky's autobiography recounts the claustrophobic precautions taken in the Soviet Embassy in London.[45] An American diplomat has written with honesty of the effects on his diplomatic judgement of being under intelligence siege in Moscow: 'it was hard not to let that situation impact on your own view of the former USSR'.[46]

The converse of this targeting of embassies has been the development in this century of 'diplomatic cover' for agent-runners and recruiters, after diplomats became too respectable to do this work themselves, and for other intelligence collection.[47] On most counts these various features of twentieth-century diplomatic life sit awkwardly with the 1961 Vienna Convention which governs it. On the one hand this provides for the inviolability of diplomatic missions and their premises. On the other it describes diplomacy's function as ascertaining conditions in the host country *by all lawful means*, with the stipulation that diplomatic premises are not to be used 'in any manner incompatible with the function of the mission as laid down in the present Convention or by other rules of general international law or by any special agreements in force between the receiving and sending state'.[48]

Most questioned of all is peacetime espionage, irrespective of any diplomatic involvement. In reality some human agents are just extensions of diplomatic sources; governments need some inconspicuous and unavowed contacts, as with the IRA before the 'peace process'. Others are like confidential press sources. But the dominant image is of the spy engaged in deeply concealed espionage. Even some of this deep espionage is defensive, part of the conflict between intelligence attack and defence; despite the

American shock-horror over Ames as a Moscow agent in CIA, his effect was to reveal US espionage in Russia.[49] Some spies have patriotic or ideological motives; one's view of them may depend on what side they are on. But avarice and other human weaknesses loom equally large, perhaps larger; in 1995 the CIA was restricted over recruiting 'unsavoury' agents.[50] Whatever the motives, espionage is feared for the damage it can do, and evokes the reaction associated with the betrayer, the Judas, the traitor, akin perhaps to the 'moral panic' over some domestic crime.[51] In England the betrayal of secrets to the Crown's enemies was identified with treason even before the 1351 Treason Act.

These feelings about espionage also attach themselves to foreign covert action, for which the Humint intelligence agencies are usually the executive agents. The intensity of Soviet espionage and covert action left a deep imprint on Western attitudes, reinforcing atavistic fears of the enemy within, and ambivalence about using such methods oneself.[52] Authoritarian regimes share the fears, though not the scruples.[53]

This survey suggests some inverse correlation between ethical acceptability and the degree of intrusion in intelligence's methods. Loch Johnson usefully postulates a 'ladder of escalation' for different degrees of intrusive collection, as well as different kinds of covert action.[54] But the picture remains cloudy, and international law does little to clarify it. The laws of war permit the execution of spies, but wartime espionage is not itself illegal; 'the spy remains in his curious legal limbo; whether his work is honourable or dishonourable, none can tell'.[55] No one knows what the Vienna Convention's 'lawful means' and 'rules of general international law' actually signify for diplomatic collection methods. Violations of national territory are illegal, but there is no code of conduct for information-gathering *per se*. Despite the liberal repugnance for covert means of information-gathering, there is no accepted international law of states' privacy in peacetime; legal opinions vary between a realist conclusion that 'espionage is nothing but the violation of someone else's laws' and the different view that it is a consistently practised illegal activity.[56] Moreover the state cannot defend its own secrets properly without being up to date on offensive techniques; the effective gamekeeper has to be a competent poacher.

Thus considering methods *in vacuo* does not get us very far. In reality the scale of intelligence operations may be as important as the precise methods used, particularly since all intelligence tends to be tarred with the brush of espionage (as in the way the media always refers to the British Sigint agency, quite inaccurately, as 'the Cheltenham spy centre'). Most

Western airborne and shipborne collection around the Soviet periphery did not infringe national airspace; yet the sheer weight of it probably reinforced Cold War tensions and threat perceptions. Some 40 American aircraft were shot down up to 1960, as well as the two innocent South Korean passenger aircraft much later, with grievous losses, reflecting a state of high East–West tension as well as exacerbating it.[57] Ethical judgements probably need to link methods with political circumstances, scale and cumulative effects, but the nature of the targets and reasons for targeting are also a factor.

Targeting of Non-States and International 'Baddies'

Here a shift over the last decade is important. Foreign intelligence is now directed more than previously towards two relatively new targets. One is the 'non-state' category, ranging from fragmented and dissolving states, through independence movements, terrorists, international criminals and illegal dealers in nuclear material, to others at the security-threatening end of the trading spectrum. The other, linked with the first group, is the small group of rogue states, exemplified by the Milosevic regime or states supporting terrorism. Many of these new targets, whether state or non-state, are either actors – sometimes victims or potential victims – in scenes of actual or incipient mayhem, or international 'baddies'. In targeting them most governments have altruistic motives overlaying narrow national interests, with intelligence manifesting ethical foreign policy in a direct way.

Arguably this combination of targets and policy objectives moves intelligence's ethical goalposts virtually to a wartime position; in a sufficiently good cause, against such targets, almost anything goes. Intelligence may be needed to provide protection or reduce suffering. Foreign non-state entities and failed states have no special claims for privacy, and rogue states have forfeited them by bad conduct, especially if they are gross violators of human rights. Unlike armed force, intelligence does not kill or cause suffering. Though he was speaking of military intelligence rather than covert collection, a thoughtful Victorian officer pointed out that 'the pursuit of intelligence has not, like swollen armaments, any tendency to bring about war'.[58]

Yet it can still be argued that some intelligence methods are ethically unacceptable in any circumstances. Using robust methods in compelling cases may be seductive; 'the exception would become part of the norm'.[59] Intelligence may be harmless in itself, but there is a danger of slipping into the American gun-lobby defence that 'guns don't kill people; people kill people'. Whatever the morality of the bombardment of Serbia, intelligence power was a prime element making it possible, not just an incidental supporter.

Ideally such problems of conscience might be solved by UN mandates. Thus at the end of the Gulf War the Security Council's request to all states to give UNSCOM 'maximum assistance, in cash and in kind', was interpreted to include intelligence.[60] IAEA has also benefited by services of national intelligence, on Iraq, Iran, South Africa and North Korea; and the new Organization for the Prohibition of Chemical Weapons has comparable requirements.[61] Yet it is difficult to see the UN leading with ethical criteria over intelligence methods. Its image is one of rectitude and transparency, and indeed has suffered from the allegations that UNSCOM cover was used for covert CIA operations.[62] It can be expected to favour the 'don't ask, don't tell' approach to the sources of the national intelligence it receives. In the long run the UN will need to control some intelligence collection and assessment on its own account, in the way UNSCOM had its own analysis unit plus American U-2 collection at its disposal; but that is a separate issue. For the time being the absolutist probably has to deal with intelligence's ethical problems without much UN guidance.

For the pragmatist, of course, reflecting *on these targets* – the limitation must be repeated – these absolutist concerns do not carry much weight. The greater the ethical emphasis in foreign policy, the less concern is needed over intelligence's methods and scale, always assuming that this collection is necessary. The scale of international suffering and crimes against humanity is a powerful warrant for intrusive collection, as is rogue states' sponsorship of terrorism and assassination of their political opponents overseas.

Targeting of 'Decent' States

But much intelligence is still directed against states whose standards of behaviour do not put them beyond the pale, and here other considerations apply.[63] International society is a society of states bound by cooperation, or at least toleration; they do not behave as if in a complete state of nature. The avoidance of inter-state aggression and war remains one of the world's highest priorities. Governments' reticence about intelligence collection is not related only to source protection, but also recognizes some conflict with a tacit code of behaviour between states over information-gathering – albeit a shadowy one. Some states with particularly close relationships refrain from regular covert collection against each other; much as they might like to know the other's bottom line in their many economic and other negotiations, the US and Canada probably do not tap each other's telephones to get it. Possibly the same applies between Norway and Sweden. Even without special relationships, responsible states think twice about using the more intrusive and risky intelligence methods against others; not all states are fair game for anything. Even against antagonists, issues of prudence arise over covert operations which if discovered will be taken as insults or confirmations of hostility. Cold War documents show British Ministers balancing the intelligence benefits from airborne collection, including U-2 flights based on Britain, against the effects on Anglo-Soviet relations.[64]

Of course states' behaviour depends on the facts of particular cases: the targets, the methods and the risks of being found out. But generally speaking the West has not assumed that intelligence had complete *carte blanche*, whether the targets were friendly states, unfriendly ones or something in between. Nineteenth-century European monarchies had ideas of national honour; so too had British radicals;[65] and perhaps the idea still lives on in some aspects of modern relationships, with vestiges of Victorian rectitude over covert methods and the pre-Second World War American maxim that 'gentlemen don't read each others' mail', even though neither has been observed with any consistency (and the American quotation was a post-1945 rationalization).[66]

These inhibitions exist; yet over the last decade they do not seem to have significantly limited intelligence's scale and methods. Press reports suggest the opposite; more espionage cases hit the media now than in the Cold War. Most of the permanent members of the Security Council have been accused of spying on each other, and membership of the European Union does not seem to convey immunity from being targeted by fellow-members. Russia seems to have sought an intelligence *détente* in the early 1990s. The last head of the KGB handed over the bugging plans for the new US Moscow embassy; there was some release of Soviet intelligence records; public statements claimed that its successor Foreign Intelligence Service was contracting its overseas collection and sought international cooperation[67] – but this period has now passed. The KGB's successor in collecting foreign intelligence through human sources is now flourishing, active and influential, still with 15,000 staff.[68] The domestic Russian Federal Security Service claimed to have caught 11 foreign agents and thwarted 39 attempts to send secret information abroad in the first half of 1997; there are regular official statements of this kind on agents detected and the foreign intelligence services involved; a Russian newspaper claimed in February 2000 that the number of Russians willing to sell secrets had grown to epidemic proportions.[69] Other countries are following these leads. Early in the 1990s a respected historian foresaw that claimants to regional dominance would seek superiority in intelligence collection, producing 'upward spirals and a new intelligence war'.[70] Reports that intelligence expenditure in the Far East had doubled from the end of the Cold War to 1997 may support his prognosis, as has the Chinese and North Korean concern reported over Japanese proposals to launch intelligence satellites within four or five years.[71] The media may exaggerate, but it seems that the global Information Age has in no way reduced states' interest in acquiring others' secrets.

Does Covert Targeting Matter?

Does this affect inter-state relationships? Much of it is accepted as part of the international system. Except in special relationships, intelligence collaboration between states has never been seen to rule out some discreet targeting of each other. It cannot be demonstrated that collection on either friends or enemies has affected the climate of the 1990s. The allegations of its economic espionage has not caused France to be blackballed in the European Union; neither have the claims of UK coverage of Europe via the Echelon system. The threats posed by acts of intelligence collection have not consistently increased military confrontation in Korea, South Asia or South Lebanon, and did not themselves provoke the war between Eritrea and Ethiopia. Conventional wisdom tolerates espionage on *The Times*'s grounds that everybody does it.

Yet it seems unrealistic to exclude intelligence from the unquantifiable grit of international friction. Collection is necessarily *against* someone; attack necessitates defence. It is difficult to believe that its more intrusive aspects do not have cumulative effects in reinforcing conflicts and impairing international cooperation. The Indian shoot-down of a Pakistani electronic collection aircraft in August 1999 contributed to the tension of the time; similarly the UN Secretary General is said to have pressed Israel to cease its collection flights over the Lebanon in an effort to prevent peacemaking in the area from foundering completely. The targeting of diplomats and diplomatic missions, and the facilities which diplomacy itself provides for intelligence, hardly promote the diplomatic function described by Alan James as 'the communications system of the international society'.[72] Ernest Bevin as Foreign Secretary said that a better world would involve being able to cross the Channel without a passport; his modern successors might say that it would involve being able to confer in their embassies abroad without worrying about foreign bugging. Being able to operate without reckoning with covert intelligence attacks may be a factor, if only a minor one, in the special quality of the English-speaking transatlantic and Old Commonwealth relationships, and perhaps of those of the Scandinavian countries. Intelligence-gathering within the EU hardly makes it easier for it to stagger towards its Common Defence and Security Policy. Allegations of espionage have been a damaging factor for some years in US–Chinese relations,[73] and the forcing down of the US electronic reconnaissance aircraft off the Chinese coast produced a crisis in them in April 2001.

Most important of all, the continuation of intelligence attack and defence surely has some influence on relationships between Russia on the one hand and the US plus NATO on the other.[74] The FSB, the successor of the KGB's internal security arm, announced at the end of 2000 that it had identified 400 foreign spies it would track in the following year; hunting foreign spies would be a top priority.[75] In the following March the United States expelled 50 Russian diplomats for intelligence activities; Russia announced a tit-for-tat expulsion of the same number; the British Prime Minister was said to have warned President Putin of the consequences of the increased Russian espionage effort in the UK and the rest of Europe. It was generally taken that the intelligence Cold War was again in full swing, with effects on both sides.

Perhaps the more open modern world helps to make covert intelligence more disturbing. In the age of worldwide investigative journalism intelligence is now far more exposed than formerly; no secrets remain secrets. Foreign policies are now more influenced by domestic politics, and it is difficult for politicians and opinion-formers to accept foreign intelligence attacks as natural parts of the international game. The modern humanitarian morality that 'something must be done' takes effective intelligence for granted, yet at the same time prizes international legality and clean hands. Even before the present British government's ethical foreign policy, its predecessor endorsed a 'moral base' for its defence doctrine; the 'concept of propriety, which seeks to ensure that the activities of the armed forces are viewed universally as being justifiable, fair, and apolitical'.[76] It can be argued that intelligence everywhere – an aspect of national power, like armed forces – needs a similar ethical foundation.

BALANCE SHEET AND DESIDERATA

Despite intelligence's modern status, states' policies and the actions that result from them are worth far more ethical scrutiny than the intelligence they use and the activities that produce it. Some intelligence knowledge does not affect the ethical standards of the foreign policies it influences, and many intelligence activities have no ethical significance in themselves. Nevertheless some of intelligence's knowledge and a smaller proportion of its activities probably have some general (and contradictory) effects on the morality of international society.

The ethical case for its knowledge is fairly clear. Despite intelligence's failures and distortions, its rationales of information-seeking and objectivity tend to make those leaders who draw on it behave 'better' internationally than those less concerned with an intelligence view of reality, or less exposed to it. (Of course it can be argued that the kind of governments that encourage objective intelligence inputs may well be disposed anyway to 'better' international behaviour than those that do not, but intelligence probably has some institutional influence; even the best of government intentions go wrong if not well informed.) The international community working *qua* community depends upon national intelligence inputs, particularly from American technical collection. It needs intelligence just as much as the population, health and environmental data that are its foundations for other international action.

Yet a minority of intelligence collection poses ethical problems. On some targets the ends justify the intelligence means, though perhaps not completely. (Should one torture terrorists to get intelligence to forestall planned murder?)[77] On the other hand, the more intrusive methods of peacetime collection – espionage, some bugging, and perhaps diplomatic targeting and the exploitation of diplomatic immunities – probably are disturbing factors when used against 'decent' states. The situation is not static. 'Since the end of the Cold War a universal international system has come into existence marked by the unprecedented situation in which almost all states are in diplomatic relations with other states.'[78] This aspect of globalization sits uncomfortably with the prospect that 185 states and statelets may all invest in covert intelligence collection to keep up with the international Joneses. If international arms limitation is a desirable objective, why not limit intrusive intelligence?

This balance sheet suggests three desiderata for strengthening the international attitudes and norms that already exist. The first is to recognize that the Western idea of objective, all-source intelligence assessment on foreign affairs, with some separation from policy-making, is a necessary part of good government in a world of intensified international contact. All states should be encouraged to develop the machinery, in the spirit of Ms Short's commendation of intelligence to the developing world.[79] A scaled-down version of the CIA's Directorate of Intelligence with its remit for analysis and assessment could be an international role-model. It is most regrettable that the way the US intelligence structure evolved has caused much of the world to identify this Directorate and its functions – and intelligence as a whole – with the very different covert collection and covert action of the Agency's separate Directorate of Operations.

The second is to emphasize the place of international exchanges between states at this all-source, 'finished intelligence' level. International action is no more cohesive than the intelligence exchanges that underlay it. The UN, EU, NATO and other regional institutions will eventually develop machinery for supra-national intelligence assessment, but it will be a long haul, and will have to build on inter-state exchanges. Two former American DCIs argued some years ago that American intelligence should become an international good,[80] and the US subsequently committed itself to intelligence support for international organizations.[81] To some extent this is already a *de facto* underpinning of international society, yet for its credibility the American input needs to be complemented by a community of national intelligence institutions capable of critically assessing it for their own governments. States cooperating internationally need exchanges and some kind of peer review of their own intelligence estimates. One wonders how far the impasses between NATO and Russia over Kosovo reflected different national intelligence inputs.

The third is to borrow the criteria of restraint, necessity and proportionality from 'Just War' doctrine to discourage gung-ho approaches to intrusive covert collection. Morality reinforces the requirements of cost-effectiveness that covert methods should only be used where overt material is inadequate. The more intrusive the methods the greater the justification needed; recruiting additional human sources to fill the gaps in technical collection runs its own ethical risks. Ethics should be recognized as a factor in intelligence decisions, just as in anything else. The Western notion of elected leaders' accountability for sensitive intelligence operations provides some check on the ethical dimension, though by no means a complete one. Similar considerations should be applied to covert action, though the essential difference should be recognized between the morality of information-gathering and action. Perhaps more should be done to separate the two.

This restraint implies some re-ordering of collection priorities. National security matters should remain central and legitimate requirements. These should include counterintelligence and counterespionage, which still comprise just over twenty per cent of the British Security Service's work.[82] But to these national security targets can now be added those bearing on international security, justice and humanitarian concerns. John Keegan has argued that democracy's professional soldiers are now international society's check upon violence; 'those honourable warriors who administer force in the cause of peace'.[83] *Mutatis mutandis*, national intelligence should now be seen partly in this light.

The counterpoint to this approach is some limitation over collection for national purposes unconnected with security or humanitarianism. Throughout the 1990s it has been fashionable outside the English-speaking countries to target covert collection on other countries' non-military secrets of economic, financial and technological kinds. Russia has seen this as a means of solving its economic problems *vis-à-vis* the West. French publicists have been rather proud of collection of this kind, though it is by no means a purely Gallic activity.[84] The issues over government activity of this kind are complex and would need separate discussion; but as a generalization the emphasis on covert collection by states for these reasons in a capitalist world is both provocative and overblown. The Soviet aircraft industry is said to have copied stolen plans of Concorde; much good it did them. Immediately after the Cold War some Americans argued that US intelligence should be redeployed to the 'trade war' with Japan and Western Europe, and Washington deserves credit for substantially rejecting the case.[85] Speaking of US Sigint, the DCI in 2000 affirmed over 'business intelligence' that 'if we are to maintain good relations with out allies, they have to know they can trust us not to become involved in missions not directly related to national security'.[86] Even for governments that want to get deeply into this field, using open and 'grey' sources and commercial information brokers is a better bet than tasking their intelligence agencies. The same applies even more to the international money market.

This restraint also implies extending the existing limitations on targeting other states for 'bargaining intelligence' on matters of purely national interest. Covert intelligence increases diplomatic effectiveness, but sometimes with the long-term costs already suggested. Firms in the private sector depend on knowing their competition, but those that care about their reputations are careful about how they do so. Perhaps governments should exercise similar care over the intelligence methods used against friendly powers, and rely instead on the investigative media's own intrusion.

This re-ordering of intrusive collection would need multilateral action of an inconspicuous kind, not unilateral intelligence disarmament. It would not come easily to the major intelligence powers, East or West; the US, Russia and Britain all have strong (and differing) reasons for keeping intelligence power unfettered. Yet two features of international norms may be helpful. First, some evolve gradually through informal international contacts and the influence of 'world opinion'. The international patchwork of multilateral and bilateral intelligence relationships already provides scope for confidential discussion of intelligence matters. In particular Western intelligence already has well-publicized links with Russia on international terrorism, drugs and other criminality, and evidence of war crimes, plus the military opportunities presented by the Partnership for Peace programme and other contacts. International understandings about methods and limitations may seem an unlikely outcome, but are not impossible. Before the SALT I and II and ABM agreements of the 1970s it would have seemed quite inconceivable that the superpowers would in effect legitimize aspects of each other's secret collection, yet they did.[87] Quite recently the OECD nations plus some others signed a 'bribery convention' in which 'the United States has got all the rich countries to play by roughly the same rules'.[88] This is still far removed from intelligence; but it is a reminder that unexpected things can happen when states are persuaded of common interests. Russia is reported to have pressed the UN Secretary-General in 1998 for an international treaty banning information warfare.[89] The possibility of mutual US and Russian reductions in espionage was raised, apparently from the American side, in July 1999 in Washington discussions between the US Vice-President and Russian Prime Minister, and remitted for further examination. The idea at least got to the conference table.[90]

Second, international law has a momentum of its own. An American naval officer writing on intelligence argued that there are limits of behaviour which 'create definable customary international norms.... To those who must work with these subjects, the norms are real, the boundaries tangible, and the consequences of exceeding them unacceptable – personally and professionally, nationally and internationally.'[91] Geoffrey Best takes us further by reminding us that 'much international law of the contemporary age... is "normative". Normative means standard-setting; adding to established State practice, the aspirational concept of State practice as it is expected, intended, or hoped to become at some future date.'[92] International law need not remain as silent on intelligence as it is now.

SUMMARY

Intelligence is now a permanent part of the nation state. Even lesser states need it and will soon have it. There is plenty for it to do. But the new millennium should seek to emphasize internationally

1. the value of accurate knowledge and policy-free intelligence assessment of international affairs, based on all sources of information and not necessarily the product of covert collection. This should be recognized as an aspect of good government in the globalized world;

2. the increased relevance of national intelligence, both covert collection and all-source analysis, to the working of international institutions, and to other international action in the interests of security, justice and humanitarianism. International exchanges are a necessity for international society. International action is no more cohesive than the intelligence assessments that underlie it. Structures for international assessment should be encouraged;

3. restraint in the use of the more intrusive methods of collection for purposes not geared to national security, good causes or other support for international society. Ethics should be a factor in national intelligence decisions, as in all others. The shadowy code of conduct that at present exists over intrusive intelligence methods should be extended, even if it cannot be made explicit.

In short, *The Times*'s dictum that 'Cold War or no Cold War, nations routinely spy on each other' provides a starting-point for considering intelligence ethics, but this realism is not the last word. Sir Michael Howard has reminded us that until the eighteenth-century Enlightenment it was assumed that war between states was equally routine. It 'remained an almost automatic activity, part of the natural order of things'.[93] 'If anyone could be said to have invented peace as more than a mere pious aspiration, it was Kant.'[94] Perhaps some limitation on espionage and other intrusive and provocative intelligence collection will in time be seen as a contribution to international peace, itself 'not an order natural to mankind: it is artificial, intricate and highly volatile'.[95] One of the challenges of the new century is to demystify intelligence's role and make it a fitter subject for international discourse. The role of armed forces already receives intensive treatment. The role and effects of intelligence now merit some comparable attention.

NOTES

1. Revised from 'Modern Intelligence Services: Have They a Place in Ethical Foreign Policies?' given at a conference at St Antony's College, Oxford in September 1999 on 'Intelligence Services in a Changing World', and published in H. Shukman (ed.), *Agents for Change: Intelligence Services in the Twenty-First Century* (London: St Ermin's Press, 2000). An earlier version was published as 'Intelligence Services and Ethics in the New Millennium', *Irish Studies in International Affairs*, 10 (1999).
2. R. Hibbert, 'Intelligence and Policy', *Intelligence and National Security*, 5, 1 (January 1990), p. 115.
3. Contrary to the peace dividend elsewhere, France planned a considerable expansion after the humiliation of depending on American intelligence in the Gulf War (P. Kemp, 'The Rise and Fall of France's Spymasters', *Intelligence and National Security*, 9, 1 (January 1994)).
4. 'Reborn CIA dusts off Cloak and Dagger', *Observer*, 14 March 1999. Expenditure for FY97 was $26.6 billion, and for FY98 $26.7 billion. Figures for FY99 have not been released; Congress is said to have approved an 'emergency' increase of $1.5–2.0 billion in the fall of 1998. (Press references summarized in Canadian Association for Security and Intelligence Studies Newsletter 34 (winter 1999), p. 20.) Subsequently there were reports of a substantial American increase, to around $30 billion for the year 2000.
5. The three intelligence agencies have a published budget of about three-quarters of a million pounds, but the cost of MoD and other strategic intelligence needs to be added. For costs of 'the national intelligence capability' see Chapter 4.
6. Within the European Union, the Republic of Ireland may be an interesting exception.
7. Speech, 23 March 1998.
8. Kent Pekel, 'Integrity, Ethics and the CIA', CIA's *Studies in Intelligence* (spring 1998), pp. 85–94.
9. Leader, 26 May 1999.
10. The phrase 'stealing others' secrets' comes from a radio interview with one of the British secret agencies' recent whistle-blowers.
11. P. Wright, *Spycatcher: The Candid Autobiography of a Senior Intelligence Officer* (New York: Viking, 1987), p. 54.
12. For a criticism of le Carré's moral stance see J. Burridge, 'Sigint in the Novels of John le Carré', CIA's *Studies in Intelligence*, 37, 5 (1994).
13. Attributed to Professor Huntingdon (as a comment on international opinion) by N. Chomsky, *Guardian*, 17 May 1999. Compare with Professor Watt's reflection on 'the current American politically correct doctrine according to which anything the

CIA turned its various hands to was morally wrong and legally contrary to the laws and ethos of the United States' (*Intelligence and National Security*, 15, 4 (winter 2000), p. 144).

14. L. Lustgarten and I. Leigh, *In from the Cold: National Security and Parliamentary Democracy* (Oxford: Clarendon Press, 1994), p. 225. This work concentrates on intelligence's domestic aspects, but incidentally provides some ethical criticism of foreign intelligence.

15. Previously discussed in Chapter 20 of M.E. Herman, *Intelligence Power in Peace and War* (Cambridge: Cambridge University Press, 1996) from the perspective of the early 1990s.

16. M. Howard, 'Introduction', in R. Williamson (ed.), *Some Corner in a Foreign Field: Intervention and World Order* (London: Macmillan, 1998), p. 9.

17. D. Kahn, *The Codebreakers* (London: Sphere edition, 1973), p. 456.

18. H. Reiss (tr. H.B. Nisbet), *Kant: Political Writings* (Cambridge: Cambridge University Press, 1991), pp. 96–7. But note that Grotius took a more robust view, that spies were 'beyond doubt permitted by the law of nations' and can be dealt with 'in accordance with the impunity which the law of war accords' (tr. F. Kelsey, *The Law of War and Peace* (Oxford: Oxford University Press, 1925), Book 3, Chapter 4, xviii, p. 655.

19. A US policy-maker of the time has claimed that the timing of the flight, on May Day before the conference, was taken by Khrushchev as a deliberately offensive US signal (Robert Bowie, BBC2 'Baiting the Bear', 8 October 1996).

20. Many other languages have a similar blurring between 'special collection' on the one hand and 'estimate' or 'assessment' on the other. Russian, for example, has 'shpionazh' for espionage, 'razvedka' as a more general term for intelligence-gathering and reconnaissance, and 'svedenie' as the estimate or assessment; but the distinctions are not systematic.

21. See H. Suganami, 'Stories of War Origins: A Narrativist Theory of the Causes of War', *Review of International Studies*, 1, 4 (October 1997) for a typology of 'war-conducive' acts comprising contributory negligence and insensitive, thoughtless and reckless acts.

22. J.L. Gaddis, 'History, Grand Strategy and NATO Enlargement', *Survival*, 40, 1 (spring 1998).

23. *The Economist*, 22 May 1999, p. 5.

24. Percy Cradock, *In Pursuit of British Interests: Reflections on Foreign Policy under Margaret Thatcher and John Major* (London: Murray, 1997), p. 37.

25. Compare intelligence with the many statistical failures such as over British earnings in 1997–98, set out for example in *The Economist*, 5 March 1999, p. 38.

26. For a discussion of American intelligence and policy in the Cold War see C. Andrew, *For the President's Eyes Only* (London: Harper Collins, 1995). For the CIA's record in estimating the Soviet Union see D.J. MacEachin, 'CIA Assessments of the Soviet Union', CIA's *Studies in Intelligence* (semi-annual unclassified edition no.1, 1997), and K. Lundberg, *CIA and the Fall of the Soviet Empire: The Politics of 'Getting It Right'* (Harvard Intelligence and Policy Project, 1994).

27. H. Kissinger, *Years of Upheaval* (London: Weidenfeld and Nicolson, Joseph, 1982), p. 828. Similar proposals were also made as part of the Israeli–Syrian settlement, p. 1254.

28. Statement by Robert Gates, BBC radio programme 'Open Secrets', 21 March 1995.
29. For discussion see Herman, *Intelligence Power*, Chapter 9.
30. The 1988 principles are in UN document A/45/372, 28 August 1988, Section II. Article 23 (Verification) of the CTBT permits NTMs to be used to back up a call for on-site inspection if the data has been collected 'in a manner consistent with generally recognized principles of international law'.
31. An early team leader from the UN Special Commission in Iraq wrote that 'In the face of the highly efficient Iraqi deception, the inspection could not have gone forward without accurate intelligence' (D. Kay, 'Arms Inspections in Iraq: Lessons for Arms Control', *Bulletin of Arms Control* (London: Council for Arms Control/Centre for Defence Studies), 7 (August 1992), pp. 6–7). For a more complete account see Tim Trevan, *Saddam's Secrets: The Hunt for Iraq's Hidden Weapons* (London: HarperCollins, 1999).
32. As early as 1971 the Secretary-General complained of the 'lack of authoritative information, without which the Secretary-General cannot speak' (U Thant letter of 30 March 1971, quoted by A.W. Dorn, 'Keeping Tabs on a Troubled World: UN Information-Gathering to Preserve Peace', *Security Dialogue*, 27, 3 (1996)). The theme was taken up again in the early days of intervention in the former Yugoslavia in statements such as 'intelligence is a vital element of any operation and the UN needs to develop a system for obtaining information without compromising its neutrality' (a British Admiral: *RUSI Journal*, 139, 1, p. 35 (February 1994)); and 'I have asked for numerous reforms in the structure of the UN in Yugoslavia, especially in the use of information, the capacity to analyse and reflect' (a French General, quoted in the *Independent*, 31 January 1994).
33. 'Aerial photographs and phone intercepts are giving instant evidence of atrocities' (A. Lloyd, *The Times*, 14 May 1999).
34. GCHQ graduate careers brochure, 1996.
35. As in its (reported) refusal to provide satellite results during the period of disunity before mounting IFOR.
36. DFID Policy Statement, *Poverty and the Security Sector*, the basis of an address at the Centre for Defence Studies, 9 March 1999, p. 6.
37. As in the TV programmes about British Cold War observations from trawlers in northern waters.
38. For this legal position see B. Jasani, 'Civil Radar Observation Satellites for IAEA Safeguards', *Journal of the Institute of Nuclear Weapons Management*, 27, 2 (winter 1999). UN resolutions such as A/RES53/76 have however stressed the need for transparency on the use of outer space and the avoidance of a space arms race.
39. For a brief description see *British Defence Doctrine JWP 0-01*, 1996, Annex B.6.
40. Probably owing something to the British protest group which for many years alleged that the American station at Menwith Hill in northern England was intercepting British communications.
41. In summer 2000 the Clinton Administration vetoed a Congressional Bill that provided for financial sanction against Russia if its intercept station on Cuba was not closed. The veto was on the grounds that it might provoke tit-for-tat Russian attempts to take action against US facilities (*Washington Post*, 20 July 2000). For a valuable account of Russian Sigint see G. Bennett, *The Federal Agency of*

Government Communications and Information (Camberley: Conflict Studies Research Centre, 2000).

42. The 1980 activity is described in B.B. Fischer, *A Cold War Conundrum: The 1983 Soviet War Scare* (CIA Center for the Study of Intelligence, 1997).

43. The relevant law on maritime collection is *United Nations Convention on the Law of the Sea 1982*, articles 19 and 29. 'Innocent passage' excludes 'collecting information to the prejudice of the defence or security of the coastal state' (19.2.(c)). For graphic accounts of special American submarine operations see S. Sontag and C. Drew, *Blind Man's Bluff: The Untold Story of American Submarine Espionage* (New York: Perennial paperback edition, 1999).

44. For a summary see Dick Nelson and J. Koenen-Grant, 'A Case of Bureaucracy in Action', *International Journal of Intelligence and Counterintelligence*, 6, 3 (fall 1993).

45. O. Gordievsky, *Next Stop Execution* (London: Macmillan, 1995), pp. 257–8.

46. D.R. Herspring, 'The Cold War: Perceptions from the American Embassy, Moscow', *Diplomacy and Statecraft*, 9, 2 (July 1998), p. 200.

47. Thus 62 Soviet listening posts of this kind were reported to be in action late in the Cold War (D. Ball, *Soviet Signals Intelligence (Sigint)*, Papers on Strategy and Defence No 47 (Canberra: Australian National University, 1989), pp. 38–70).

48. *Vienna Convention 1961*, Articles 3.1 and 41.3.

49. A Soviet defector, himself betrayed by Ames, claimed that up to 45 CIA agents had been identified (*The Times*, 18 February 1997). Other press reports quoted lower figures.

50. B.L. Gerber, *A Discussion of Intelligence Ethics* (paper at International Studies Association Convention, Toronto, March 1997), p. 6.

51. Compare with S. Cohen, *Folk Devils and Moral Panics: The Creation of the Mods and Rockers* (Oxford: Blackwell, 1987 edition).

52. The liberal view also includes the belief that the agent can be induced to 'betray obligations of loyalty which may be legitimately demanded of him' (Lustgarten and Leigh, *In from the Cold*, p. 225). This assumes, of course, that the regime (or the terrorist movement) spied upon deserves loyalty. Other elements are the risks to the agents and the (allegedly) corrupting effects on the officers running them; according to a former CIA General Counsel, 'the constant pressure of the clandestine life can try the moral ballast of the most honest man or woman' (quoted by Gerber, *Intelligence Ethics*, p. 30).

53. Thus China and Iran, in signing the Comprehensive Test Ban Treaty, made separate declarations that verification should not be interpreted as including the results of 'espionage or human intelligence'.

54. L.K. Johnson, 'On Drawing a Bright Line for Covert Operations', *American Journal of International Law*, 86 (April 1992), p. 284.

55. G. Best, *War and Law Since 1945* (Oxford: Oxford University Press, 1994), p. 291.

56. Summaries of the legal literature are given and discussed in J. Kish, *International Law and Espionage* (The Hague, London: Martinus Nijhoff, 1995); R.D. Scott, 'Territorially Intrusive Intelligence Collection and International Law', *Air Force Law Review*, 46 (1999), p. 217; and G.B. Demarest, 'Espionage in International Law', *Denver Journal of International Law and Policy*, 24, 2–3 (spring 1996). The realist quotation (by Demarest) is from Congressional testimony by the CIA Special Counsel in 1995.

57. This was particularly marked over the shooting-down of KAL-007 off the Soviet Far East in September 1983.
58. Major C.B. Brackenbury, 'The Intelligence Duties of the Staff Abroad and at Home', *RUSI Journal*, 19, 80 (1875), p. 265.
59. Lustgarten and Leigh, *In from the Cold*, p. 496.
60. Security Council resolution 699 (1991).
61. Tim McCarthy, 'Intelligence in Arms Control and Disarmament', T. Findlay (ed.), *Verification Yearbook 2000* (London: Vertic, 2000).
62. Accusations by Scott Ritter, reported for example in the *Guardian*, 30 March 1999.
63. The idea of 'decent' states – 'not liberal, but nor are they outlaws in any behavioral or moral sense of the term' – in international society is discussed by C.Brown, 'John Rawls, "The Law of Peoples," and International Political Theory', *Ethics and Foreign Affairs*, 1 (1989).
64. See R.J. Aldrich, *Espionage, Security and Intelligence in Britain 1945–70* (Manchester: Manchester University Press, 1998), pp. 33–4, 100–1, 103–4. For intelligence cases and diplomatic expulsions as an irritant in Anglo-Soviet relations see Anne Deighton, 'Ostpolitik or Westpolitik? British Foreign Policy, 1968–75', *International Affairs*, 74, 4 (October 1998), p. 896.
65. For example, in John Bright's advocacy of non-intervention overseas 'except in so far as it affects the honour and interest of England' (A.J.P. Taylor, *The Trouble-Makers: Dissent over Foreign Policy 1792–1939* (London: Panther edition, 1969), p. 66).
66. The official history of the Crimean War is said to have concluded that 'the gathering of knowledge by clandestine means were [*sic*] repulsive to the feelings of an English Gentleman' (quoted by B. Parritt, *The Intelligencers* (Ashford, Kent: Intelligence Corps Association, 2nd edition, 1983), p. 80). On the other hand, Lord Salisbury wrote in 1875 that 'we receive pretty constantly copies of the most important reports and references that reach the Foreign Office and War Office at St. Petersburg' (J. Ferris, 'Lord Salisbury, Secret Intelligence, and British Policy toward Russia and Central Asia, 1874–1878', in K. Neilson and B.J.C. McKercher (eds), *Go Spy the Land: Military Intelligence in History* (London: Praeger, 1992), p. 129). For 'reading each other's mail' see correspondence in *Intelligence and National Security*, 2, 4 (October 1987).
67. For Vadim Bakatin's handover of bugging details see J.M. Waller, 'Russia's Security Services: A Checklist for Reform', *Perspective*, 8, 1 (September–October 1997). Earlier reports of the handover were confirmed, with disapproval, by the Director of the Russian code-breaking organization in a Russian television interview of 25 October 1997. For statements by V.A. Kirpichenko, SVR Director, see *Krasnaya Zvezda*, 30 October 1993, p. 6.
68. Amy Knight, paper on Russian Intelligence at the Canadian Association for Security and Intelligence Studies conference, Ottawa, September 2000. The figure of 15,000 is said to represent a 30 per cent downsizing from the Cold War. The existence of the now separate Russian Sigint organization (FAPSI) must also be borne in mind in any comparison with Cold War numbers.
69. Reuters, quoted by *Jane's Intelligence Watch Report*, 1 July 1997. For the official statements and the newspaper comment see G. Bennett, *The Federal Security Service of the Russian Federation* (Camberley: Conflict Studies Research Centre, 2000), pp. 33–7.

70. J. Ferris, 'Intelligence After the Cold War: A Global Perspective', in A. Bergin and R. Hall (eds), *Intelligence and Australian National Security* (Canberra: Australian Defence Studies Centre, 1994), p. 8.

71. Quoted from D. Ball in *Far East Economic Review*, 9 June 1997. Chinese and North Korean reactions are referred to in VERTIC, *Trust and Verify*, 83 (November 1993), p. 6.

72. A. James, 'Diplomacy', *Review of International Studies*, 19, 1 (January 1993), p. 95.

73. Not limited to the alleged Chinese nuclear espionage. A Chinese academic had previously been arrested on his return from Stanford University and accused of betraying Chinese secrets (*Newsweek*, 29 March 1999).

74. The Russian *National Security Blueprint*, published 26 December 1997 (*Rossiskaya Gazeta*, Moscow), laid surprising emphasis on defence against 'leaks of important political, economic, scientific-technical and military information', 'the threat of foreign intelligence services' agents and operational-technical penetration of Russia', and the need for 'information security' – far more than in any comparable Western statement of national security policy.

75. *The Times*, 27 December 2000.

76. *British Defence Doctrine (JWP 0–01)* (London: HMSO, 1997), p. 3.10.

77. For some time Israeli courts approved the use of 'moderate physical pressure' in such circumstances (Gerber, *Discussion of Intelligence Ethics*, p. 7), but this was overtaken by a Supreme Court decision in 1999 (*Guardian*, 7 September 1999).

78. R.Cohen, *Diplomacy 2000 B.C.–2000 A.D.* (paper delivered to the British International Studies Association annual conference, 1995), p. 1.

79. The Russian national blueprint cited in Note 74 also highlights 'the objective and comprehensive analysis and forecasting of threats to national security'.

80. S. Turner, *Secrecy and Democracy* (New York: Harper and Row, 1986), pp. 280–5; W.E. Colby 'Reorganizing Western Intelligence', in C.P. Runde and G. Voss, *Intelligence and the New World Order* (Bustehude: International Freedom Foundation, 1992), pp. 126–7.

81. 'To the extent prudent, US intelligence today is... being used in dramatically new ways, such as assisting the international organizations like the United Nations... We will share information and assets that strengthen peaceful relationships and aid in building confidence' (*National Security Strategy of the United States* (Washington: White House, January 1993), p. 18).

82. *Intelligence and Security Committee Annual Report 1999–2000* (London: The Stationery Office, 2000), para.16. The targets included 'significant Russian activity in the UK'.

83. Concluding words in J. Keegan, *War and Our World* (London: Hutchinson, 1998) (Reith Lectures 1998), p. 74.

84. For examples of accusations and counter-accusations see N. Farrell, 'Hark Who's Talking (and Listening)', *Spectator*, 21 November 1998.

85. For a survey of the issues and of US thinking see L. Johnson, *Secret Agencies: US Intelligence in a Hostile World* (New Haven: Yale University Press, 1996), Chapter 6; also D. Clarke and R. Johnston, 'Economic Espionage and Interallied Strategic Cooperation', *Thunderbird International Business Review*, 40, 4 (July/August 1998).

86. George J. Tenet, 'Sigint in Context', *Defense Intelligence Journal*, 9, 2 (summer 2000), p. 10.

87. The US–USSR Incidents at Sea agreement of 1972 also had some implications for intelligence collection at close quarters.
88. *The Economist*, 16 January 1999, p. 28.
89. *Sunday Times*, 25 July 1999, p. 21.
90. Russian accounts of the press conference refer to 'total mutual understanding' having been reached on 'one sensitive topic', and existing agreements 'to work in a fairly correct sort of way' (FBIS and BBC translations of 28 and 29 July 1999 items).
91. M.E. Bowman, 'Intelligence and International Law', *International Journal of Intelligence and Counterintelligence*, 8, 3 (fall 1995), p. 330.
92. Best, *War and Law Since 1945*, p. 7.
93. M. Howard, *The Invention of Peace: Reflections on War and International Order* (London: Profile Books, 2000), p. 13.
94. Ibid., p. 31.
95. Ibid., p. 104.

14

Afterword: The World Trade Center Catastrophe of 11 September 2001

(Early Reactions, 15 September 2001)

Governments' and peoples' views of intelligence will be permanently affected by the events of 11 September 2001. There will be post-mortems on them as an 'intelligence failure'. One outcome may be to question the value of the investment in national intelligence – what use is it, if it failed on something as devastating as this? – but the more likely result will be enhanced status and a reorientation of priorities. International terrorism has been among the highest priority targets for some years, but this threat will now transcend all others. At one time, 'defence of the home base' was one criterion among British requirements and priorities in the quite different context of the Cold War, but it has now acquired a fresh and immediate significance. Intelligence will still be required to support government on a wide range of subjects, but 'national security' will be reaffirmed as the link between the core requirements. Intelligence will now have a special status among them as a principal defence against mass murder.

One result is that it will be even harder than ever to evaluate intelligence performance on any routine basis and assess what should be spent on it. Like the monitoring of Soviet military movements during the Cold War, some of the intelligence effort on terrorism is precautionary surveillance, with indirect rather than direct effects. It provides reassurance and discourages governments from action based on ignorance or exaggeration, but does not produce tangible results. Even where it produces positive evidence and leads to counter-terrorist action, much of this action takes the form of inconspicuous, tactical, pre-emptive moves rather than great coups. Counter-terrorist failures will continue to be more obvious than successes. Yet, just occasionally, intelligence will rise spectacularly to the occasion and save many lives.

Thus, in pointing to its crucial importance, the events of 11 September highlight intelligence's fundamental but often latent role: contributing to the defence of national integrity and the fabric of government itself, or at least of government whose values include protection from terror and violence. This is intrinsically part the nation state, but the New York catastrophe gives a new importance to the international dimension in which it is now played out. Intelligence of other kinds has become increasingly international; the UN, NATO and other international actions taken in the 1990s and beyond have demonstrated the need for intelligence support for the international use of military forces. But this is intelligence support for elective, discretionary action, for good humanitarian or other reasons but not at the heart of government's *raison d'être*. The threat posed by international terrorism now presents a more basic, non-elective requirement, and the shoulder-to-shoulder support promised to the United States underlines its international nature. Effective intelligence on terrorism depends on international cooperation, and civilized governments have now declared a common interest in developing it.

This means a change in focus. The security intelligence that has usually led on terrorism's 'threats to the home base' has traditionally operated in most countries as a specialized, essentially 'national', rather inward-looking activity closely linked with domestic policing. The move to the more globalized requirements of recent years has been at variable paces, often slowed by inter-agency differences both nationally and internationally. If the counter-terrorist action now proclaimed by the Security Council, NATO and national declarations is to have any real effect, it will depend on a new level of intelligence cooperation, in effect the creation of a new (or at least enhanced) international counter-terrorist intelligence community.

Principles for developing this can be suggested as follows:

- The immediate objective is frustrating or minimizing terrorism's successes. 'Winning the intelligence war' is cumulative. Individual intelligence victories on a large scale are a bonus.
- The most important element in frustrating terrorism is good defensive security – for example, the airline security now being revised. But defensive security depends on accurate intelligence assessment; not merely what the enemy *could* do, but a probability estimate of what he *will* do. Threat assessment is one of intelligence's major contributions.
- All powers have something to contribute; small ones can be players along with the great. The problems of counter-terrorist intelligence cannot be solved just by throwing money at them. On Humint there are severe limits to what big nations can do to expand their own collection, but they

can improve it by developing better liaisons with local intelligence services. Similar considerations apply to some technical sources.

- Apart from source protection and other technical issues, cooperation requires the right kind of political support. Those able to provide intelligence on terrorism may be unsavoury services serving unsavoury governments. Ethical foreign policies have to face up to the dilemma of means and ends.

- Governments and publics also need to decide what sacrifices should be made for intelligence effectiveness. The present layers of accountability, oversight and legal regulation and process have their operational penalties. So too has the resistance to international agreement over access to electronic communications and control of commercially available encipherment systems. Liberal writers criticized Anglo-Saxon intelligence some years ago on the grounds that, 'above all, security officials are bureaucrats. They live by rules and paper, and function by committee.' The CIA is now said to have 60 lawyers; the British Security Service has moved from one to six. This is what democracies have chosen for intelligence. They should now consider what space should be left in it for entrepreneurial qualities.

- Terrorism should be distinguished from the other 'non-state' targets that also lack clear governmental affiliations. Thus, British intelligence is committed to support for law enforcement in general, and is targeted on the drugs trade and a variety of other organized crimes. There is an overlap between terrorism and this 'normal', non-political criminality, and interplay between the two. Nevertheless, terrorism should be recognized as intelligence's special and distinctive target, distinguished from its more generalized back-up to law enforcement, and not confused by it. In principle, over time, law enforcement should develop its own intelligence capabilities to meet its own requirements.

- The development of an international 'coalition of the willing' for counter-terrorist intelligence cooperation cannot be without some consequences for intelligence's normal coverage of other states. Those states which support or tolerate terrorism will, of course, continue to be principal targets. Some mutual targeting of each other by 'decent', legitimate states will also continue to be tacitly accepted as part of the international game. But the counterpoint to more effective counter-intelligence exchanges between governments is some scaling-down of their intrusive intelligence collection on each other, particularly on economic and other intelligence not bound up with national security. In the long term, there is some incompatibility between seeking closer cooperation with foreign states and continuing to spy on them.

* Intelligence on terrorism is like intelligence on other 'hard' targets: the reliability of its product is determined more by matters of organizational culture and individual quality than by the scale of resources available. At a national level the counter–intelligence task spans the traditionally separate areas of domestic and foreign intelligence. Whatever organizational solutions states adopt, effectiveness will depend on inter-agency cooperation and practical measures to develop it, and on individual talent and expertise. The quality of individual contributions depends on practical matters of management: recruitment, conditions, career planning and training, with particular reference to the position of the specialists, including those with particular area and linguistic knowledge. These are profoundly unexciting matters, yet often the practical determinants of intelligence success and failure.

I have argued earlier in this book that intelligence's future in this new century lies partly in becoming more internationalized. This conclusion sprang from the recent record of coalition interventions and other similar operations, and the requirements they have posed to provide participants with relevant politico–military intelligence. The horrors of 11 September reinforce this conclusion in the different context of counter-terrorism. The United States cannot generate the intelligence to protect its home base entirely from its own resources. A worldwide body of states profess to see the threat as a common one and have offered to cooperate. In counter-terrorism, as in other things, collective action depends on shared intelligence and common assessments. There is now more reason than before to regard intelligence, in some of its aspects, as an international good, and to organize and plan accordingly.

Index

academia 88
accountability, democratic 136, 217
Acoustint (acoustic intelligence) 5, 142
action on intelligence 56, 57, 124
activities, intelligence 3, 4–6; *see also*
    ethics; individual activities
Aden 117
Admiralty 89, 114, 192
advantage, comparative 7
Afghanistan 116, 163n, 185
African intelligence systems 20
aid, overseas 71, 76
Aids 6–7
airborne collection 69–70, 90–1, 207;
    Cold War 137, 159, 160, 162, 211;
    ethics 208, 211, 213, 214, 215;
    Norwegian 142, 143; UK 69, 137,
    197n, 213; US 162, 203, 212, 213,
    215; *see also* overflights of USSR
aircraft: shooting down of civil 162,
    211, 225n; Soviet copying of plans
    of Concorde 218
air power 14, 49, 73, 207, 212
air-sea rescue 103
alliances *see* international intelligence
    cooperation
allies, targeting of 7, 8, 212–14, 215,
    218
all-source analysis xi, 4, 32–3, 79; in
    CIA 132, 217; development of
    institutions 32–3; by DIS 82,
    84–90, 104–5, 191–8; holistic
    approach 31, 86–90; international

exchanges of 23, 217; open source
    material 4, 19, 68, 79, 81–2, 120,
    152; processing prior to 10–11,
    197n; and single-source intelligence
    xi, 4, 32–3, 68–9, 119–20, 191–4,
    222n, (balance) x, 79–82, 104–5,
    120, 130; subject expertise 68, 192;
    in UK intelligence process 79; UK
    need for better 79–82, 85, 86–90,
    99, 105, 120, 191–8
all-source assessment, top-level 4, 16,
    79, 90; consensual nature of UK 36,
    85, 118–19, 123, 127, 132–3, 133–4,
    167; diplomats' role 41–2; and
    single-source intelligence 32–3,
    120, 130, 203, 222n; and policy
    making 16, 37, 74; *see also*
    Assessments Staff; Joint
    Intelligence Committee, UK
    (production and assessment)
Ames, Aldrich 210
amphibious operations 144, 147n
analysis *see* all-source analysis; single-
    source intelligence; traffic analysis
Andropov, Yuri 163n
Annan, Noel 197–8n
Antarctica 152
ANZAM conference 116, 117, 122,
    124
ANZUS alliance 149
Arab intelligence systems 19, 21
Arctic 143, 144–5
area specialization 86–90